NARRATIVE AND PROFESSIONAL COMMUNICATION

ATTW Contemporary Studies in Technical Communication

M. Jimmie Killingsworth, Series Editor

Published in cooperation with
the Association of Teachers of Technical Writing

NARRATIVE AND PROFESSIONAL COMMUNICATION

edited by
Jane M. Perkins
A.T. Kearney, Inc., Chicago

and

Nancy Blyler
Iowa State University

Ablex Publishing Corporation
Stamford, Connecticut

Printed in the United States of America

Library of Congress Cataloguing-in-Publication Data

Narrative and professional communication / edited by Jane Perkins & Nancy Blyler.
    p. cm.— (ATTW contemporary studies in technical communication ; v. 10)
Includes bibliographical references and index.
ISBN 1-56750-448-5 (cloth) — ISBN 1-56750-449-3 (pbk.)
    1. Communication of technical information. 2. Technical writing. I. Perkins, Jane (Jane M.). II. Blyler, Nancy Roundy. III. Series.
T10.5.N37   1999
601'.4—dc21   99–19561
                                                    CIP

Ablex Publishing Corporation
100 Prospect Street
P.O. Box 811
Stamford, Connecticut 06904-0811

For Bruce, Mark, and our families

*For Merlin and for our canine companions,
present and past—Digger, Mop, Dusty, Hildie, Pandy, and Dolcie*

Contents

Preface

When M. Jimmie Killingsworth, the editor of the ATTW series Contemporary Studies in Technical Communication, suggested that we might want to edit a collection related to narrative, we didn't hesitate. Nancy had been researching and publishing on narrative, as well as teaching graduate and undergraduate seminars, and Jane had been presenting conference papers and exploring workplace narrative practices in her research and writing. Such a collection seemed to fit naturally with our ongoing research and pedagogic interests.

As a preliminary step to issuing a call for papers, we brainstormed about focus and scope. Should we define narrative for potential contributors, we wondered, and describe for them the types of submissions we might be interested in, or should we cast a wide and generous net, so that our colleagues could make the connections between narrative and professional communication that they found meaningful?

As a compromise, we decided to include in the call a list of possible areas of interest—for example, narrative histories about business, technical, and scientific communication; narratives of professional communication contexts; analyses of narrative forms in professional communication documents; and discussions of narrative pedagogies. With this list, however, we had an inclusive intent: to suggest a broad range of scholarly inquiry, in order to legitimize narrative—which we felt had been devalued in professional communication—and help shape future work.

Now, from a different vantage point—at the end of our work on this collection—we continue to embrace our original inclusive intent. Indeed, we believe that the contributions to this collection do suggest a broad range of scholarly inquiry, and that, by doing so, these contributions both legitimize narrative in professional communication as a vibrant focus of research, pedagogic, and practical interest and offer many possible directions for future work. (As a side note, we further believe that these contributions reinforce the formative nature of scholarship in this area, where so many stories remain to be told.)

In linking narrative to this broad, inclusive range of scholarly inquiry, we solved one problem—how to write our call for papers in a way that would encourage but not limit submissions. Throughout our work, however, we've been aware that the question "What is narrative in the context of professional communication?" has never fully gone away. It has, furthermore, been overshadowed by a follow-up question—"Why is narrative important to our field?" The contributors to this collection provide many and varied takes on these persistent questions, and as they do so they extend the core of professional communication studies.

In this preface, therefore, we want to begin the task of defining what narrative in professional communication is and why narrative is important by introducing the chapters in this collection. Following our own overview of the scholarship on narrative in professional communication, our contributors write about more specific narrative issues. Singly and together, these contributors suggest powerful answers to our persistent questions—answers that we preview for you here.

In the Introduction, Jane Perkins and Nancy Blyler posit that in addition to its importance as a form of discourse, narrative is also a means of being and acting in the world and therefore a complex perspective that can be adopted when considering topics of importance to professional communication. As a perspective, say Perkins and Blyler, narrative encourages researchers, teachers and trainers, and practitioners to bring context and connection to the fore, to view human experience as essentially storied, and to consider knowledge-making as a narrative endeavor. Perkins and Blyler's discussion of the benefits of narrative then suggest the value to our field of taking a narrative turn.

Following the introduction, the two chapters in Part I, Narrative and Research Methodologies, illustrate on a more local level Perkins and Blyler's claims that experience is storied and knowledge-making is a narrative endeavor. Specifically, these chapters argue for the central role narrative plays in case study and ethnographic research, which have become increasingly important in professional communication as methodologies for studying particular organizational contexts. In Chapter 1, "What Can We Learn from a Sample of One? The Role of Narrative in Case Study Research," Kathy Rentz claims that narrative is the natural form for examining complex phenomena taking place over time. The virtue of narrative, says Rentz, is its high level of detail—its particularity, not generality—where readers are encouraged to add their own experiences to the story a case tells. She further explains that because of this particularity narrative is crucial to the making of everyday, experiential knowledge and thus to the verisimilitude and validity of case study research.

Jane Perkins, in Chapter 2, "Narrative, Rhetoric, and Lives: Doing Ethnography," tells a story of professional communication's appropriation of ethnography against a backdrop of anthropological experience, theorizing, and cautions. Set amidst ongoing discussions of research and knowledge-making, her story focuses on changing dimensions of narrative in ethnographic writing and research, and especially on characterization. She traces ethnographers' and theorists' moves toward narrative awareness and the accompanying tensions that surround textualization, ethical responsibility, and received assumptions. Finally, she suggests that narrative and characterization can put lives into our research—the lives of researchers, readers, and cultural others.

Part II begins a series of three parts that look at narrative within the scope of particular disciplines or professions. Thus, Part II, Narrative and Science Writing, examines the role of narrative in the writing of scientists, whose communication has often been viewed as quintessentially nonnarrative in nature. In Chapter 3, "Getting the Story, Telling the Story: The Science of Narrative, the Narrative of Science," Cheryl Forbes presents a compelling case for narrative in the writing that scientists and science journalists do for a "general, liberally educated audience." In particular, Forbes examines essays by Angier and Gould, indicating that the impact of their writing depends on "the conventions of narrative—place, time, characters, dialogue, dramatic tension, humorous incongruity, suspense, mystery, intrigue, plot, a believable, reliable narrator." Although Forbes focuses on science writing for a general audience, she also "press[es] the claim" that narrative elements can be important parts of all good science writing.

In Chapter 4, "The Limits of Narrative in the Construction of Scientific Knowledge: George Gaylord Simpson's *The Dechronization of Sam Magruder*," Debra Journet examines a novella in which Simpson, a highly respected paleontologist, explored "the nature of historical narrative"—that is, how scientists know about the past and what the limitations on that knowledge are. Historical narratives, says Journet in her discussion of Simpson, both present a chronological sequence and suggest why events happened as they did. All historical narratives, then, are interpretive, but the paleontologist's interpretive act is made all the more difficult because the distant past cannot be observed, and fossil evidence of this past is necessarily incomplete. In his novella, Simpson uses his main character to dramatize his recognition that knowledge of evolutionary sequences—and hence narratives about those sequences—are never definitive but remain always contingent, uncertain, and hermeneutic in nature.

The chapters included in Part III, Narrative and Managerial Communication, suggest that scholars will gain from taking a narrative perspective on issues pertaining to management. Mark Zachry, in Chapter 5, "Management Discourse and Popular Narratives: The Myriad Plots of Total Quality Management," analyzes Total Quality Management (TQM), which has become endemic in industry and indeed in other institutional settings such as those in education and government. Zachry suggests that TQM can profitably be examined as a shifting "assemblage of narratives" that serves to "create shared cultural values." Zachry's analysis provides insights into ways these stories of TQM—as stock stories with "easily recognized scenarios and popular appeals"—communicate the kinds of workplace behaviors management endorses, thus establishing control, forming workers' identities, and structuring workplace practices.

In Chapter 6, "Strategic Communication As Persuasive and Constitutive Storytelling," Janis Forman discusses the value of narrative to executive MBA students, revealing her discovery of the importance of story as the "most basic discourse that underlies the students' communication." Based on her experiences as the communications expert for a capstone MBA project—a 20-week, executive-level study for an international company—Forman creates a framework for viewing strategic communications as storytelling. She claims that seeing communication as storytelling—despite students' resistance to such a view—can help them connect disparate pieces of data into coherent and persuasive accounts, while also enabling them to prepare multiple versions of a given story line for different audiences and purposes.

Part IV, Narrative and Health Care Professions, focuses on the importance of narrative discourse to the work of two types of health care professionals—traditional midwives and Emergency Medical Care (EMS) providers. In Chapter 7, "Midwives' Birth Stories: Narratives That Expand the Boundaries of Professional Discourse," Mary M. Lay argues that the birth stories she examined from the listserv MIDWIFE enable practicing midwives to create knowledge about the birth process, exchange advice, and release emotions common for those who must handle life and death situations. Perhaps most crucially, however, the stories also function as a means of resistance. Lay believes that these birth stories—and narratives in general—may be a particularly appropriate way to express resistance because the dramatic detail available in narrative and its ability to engage readers build a "concrete knowledge base" and an audience response that supports storytellers in their engagements with a dominant culture.

Roger Munger, in Chapter 8, "Prehospital Care Narratives: A Time For Reflection and Personal Growth," finds that narrative, in the form of prehospital care or "run" reports, is central to the work of the EMS providers he studied. These reports, Munger asserts, allow providers to "document" the "interpretive thinking" they do on a run, where emergencies are common and where complicated situations that must be described often arise without warning. Although "discrete facts," says Munger, might be recorded by checking boxes on a form rather than by providing a narrative, the run report allows EMS providers to show relationships among the events that occurred on a particular run. Run reports also enable these providers to connect "signs, symptoms, treatments, and outcomes" and thus to recognize "standard narratives" for life-threatening conditions and give appropriate treatment. And finally, run reports provide EMS providers with the opportunity for the professional growth that occurs when they can reflect on what they and other emergency providers have done on their runs, thus improving patient care.

Part V, Narrative and Electronic Sites, broadens the discussion of narrative to include major discourse forms—computer-mediated communication, and especially Web design—that cut across particular disciplines or professions. Though Part V includes only one chapter—Chapter 9, "The Rhetorical Construction of Environmental Risk Narratives in Government and Activist Websites: A Critique," by M. Jimmie Killingsworth and Martin Jacobsen—we believe this chapter's extension of narrative study to the burgeoning area of electronic communication indicates a rich direction for future work. In their chapter, Killingsworth and Jacobsen advocate narrative modeling, or narrative imagination, as a means for designing computer-mediated communication that results in citizen participation. Specifically, in their analyses of the websites of the Environmental Protection Agency and Greenpeace International, Killingsworth and Jacobsen raise questions about the ability of the Web to accommodate user agency for environmental action, suggesting that, as currently constituted, websites only support passive information exchange and promote the sponsoring organizations. Killingsworth and Jacobsen argue, however, that through narrative analysis and design, professional communication teachers can help shift social responsibility for action to website users.

The chapters in Part VI, Narrative and Society, broaden the discussion of narrative still further to address the larger cultural narratives shaping social life. Taken together, these chapters suggest that—though these cultural narratives have profound effects on our individual and collective lives, the narratives are still open to revision. In Chapter 10, "The Business of Living: Letters from a Nineteenth-Century Landlady," Margaret Baker Graham uses narrative study to explore the connections between the private sphere—the activities of domestic life—and the public sphere—the "traditionally male-dominated activities that occur in sites such as government, military, and business." Specifically, Graham examines the letters of Margaret Bruin Machette, a widow who ran a boardinghouse during the Civil War. By means of her narrative analysis, Graham argues that although the private and public spheres are in fact permeable, the "fiction" of their separateness and the tension resulting from this fiction have had real consequences for social life. In particular, this fiction has "produced gendered differences in peoples' perceptions of reality and the discourses they use"—differences that have circumscribed the ability of women to become "heroes of their own stories." Graham further argues that women can assume narrative agency when their labor is legitimized and that, by telling the stories of the "lives of women and other groups of people who have been ignored in our field," scholars in professional communication can create "a more egalitarian narrative."

In the final chapter, "Story Telling, Story Living: Sustainability, Habermas, and Narrative Models in the Rot Belt," Nancy Blyler claims that the stories we tell—which are drawn from and reflect our culture's stories or narrative models—give form to the lives we live. Blyler uses Habermas's theory of purposive rational and communicative action to analyze the narrative models of the family and the factory farm. She concludes that the narrative model of the family farm is sustainable because, as with Habermas's concept of communicative action, the goal is to create and maintain interdependent, mutually beneficial relationships. The narrative model of the factory farm, on the other hand, is not sustainable because, as in Habermas's concept of purposive-rational action, the goal is domination and control. Blyler suggests that, as a society, we ought to care about these narrative models because they represent common possibilities, among which we must choose wisely if we are to live in sustainable ways.

Taken as a whole, these chapters range widely concerning the narrative issues they address and the answers they provide to our persistent questions: What is narrative and why is it important to professional communication? Despite this breadth, however, we believe that common threads do exist, pointing to topics of more general interest and suggesting fruitful directions for future work.

One common thread, for example, concerns the contention we make in our opening chapter that, more than simply a discourse form, narrative is a complex perspective affecting the way research and pedagogical issues in professional communication are viewed. Forman's concept of strategic management communication as persuasive and constitutive storytelling and Killingsworth and Jacobsen's concept of narrative modeling in relation to websites both suggest the power of narrative when viewed as this complex perspective. For Forman and Killingsworth and Jacobsen, narrative provides a framework for critiquing strategic communication and websites respectively, as well as a means for suggesting more viable strategic discourse or website construction.

A second common thread concerns an examination of the political or ideological implications of narrative in professional communication. A number of chapters, for example, discuss ways in which dominant narratives marginalize alternate stories, thus linking narrative and social control on the one hand or narrative and resistance on the other. Concerning narrative and social control, Zachry discusses ways in which the dominant narratives of Total Quality Management are used to shape organizational culture and therefore workplace participation. Graham also touches on narrative and social control in her discussion of the public and private spheres, suggesting that the fiction of these spheres' separation has greatly shaped social life. When, however, work in the private sphere or what has traditionally been women's labor is legitimized, women's lives can be made into stories rather than nonstories.

Concerning narrative and resistance, Lay is explicit that the birth stories she studied enable traditional midwives to resist the dominant medical discourse about birth. Blyler, in addition, discusses Habermas's concept of a conflict zone, where a dominant narrative model such as that of the factory farm loses its allure, and alternate, more sustainable models for story living are preferred.

Given this focus of a number of our contributors on the political and ideological implications of narrative, we believe that studying narrative in relation to issues such as social control and resistance may represent a valuable direction for future work. A second valuable direction concerns the conflictual nature of narrative and its potential for incompleteness and lack of closure, rather than its tendency to produce, as White (1987) suggested, seamless wholes with neat beginnings, middles, and ends. With her concept of evolutionary narratives as contingent, uncertain, and hermeneutic, Journet suggests that lack of closure may be more central to narrative knowledge-making in historical sciences than we have perhaps imagined. In addition, Graham explicitly addresses lack of closure as a feminist approach to history, illustrating this lack with her story of Andrew, but a focus on lack of closure is of course common to other poststructuralist theoretical frameworks (for example, cultural studies) as well.

Given the cutting-edge nature of these directions for future work on narrative, it is perhaps not surprising that a third common thread in this collection is the tendency of contributors to push at the borders of professional communication as a discipline, expanding notions of what constitutes effective or acceptable professional discourse and urging scholars to view that discourse in new ways. Forbes and Journet, for example, show us that narrative is central both to good science writing and to the way scientists in certain disciplines make knowledge and envision their work, while Lay and Munger point to the value of narrative in the healthcare field. Narrative, claim Rentz and Perkins, is central to two of our most useful research methodologies. The stories told by marginalized groups and individuals—traditional midwives, a 19th century landlady—are brought to the center, and stories that might not be viewed as important to professional communication—agricultural narratives in the Rot Belt, environmental risk narratives—are legitimized. If a function of scholarship is to enable us to view our field and our discourse in new ways, we believe this collection succeeds in doing just that.

We want to close our preface by acknowledging the many people whose assistance helped make this collection a reality. First and foremost, we want to thank M. Jimmie Killingsworth, the editor of the ATTW series in technical communication, for suggesting that we put the collection together and for his unwavering support and guidance throughout the project. We also want to thank our undergraduate and graduate students—Nancy's at Iowa State University, for contributing to many hours of lively discussion on narrative and professional communication and Jane's at Clemson University for supporting the inclusion of a narrative perspective in all her classes. The ideas we present in our opening chapter and in our individual chapters in part originated in our work with these students, and we acknowledge their help with sincere gratitude.

We are also grateful to Charlotte Thralls of Iowa State University and Carl Lovitt of Clemson University for their thoughtful reading and insightful suggestions for our work-in-progress. Though busy themselves, both of these colleagues gave unstintingly of their time in reading our overview chapter, and we deeply appreciate their kindness. Our work is stronger for their contributions.

Jane also thanks her professors and colleagues in anthropology and rhetoric and professional communication at Iowa State University for sharing their learning about ethnographic methods and theories. She is grateful to her colleagues, friends, and "co-researchers" at VisionCorp for their voices and stories, and for sharing the ethnographic experience. In addition, she feels fortunate to have colleagues in the consulting field who are helping to promote a narrative approach. She thanks Nancy for her constant support and patience, for the "waves" of turn-taking in writing, and for the understanding she gained about narrative, editing, and collaborating. Finally, she is grateful to her family for their story-making and the memories.

Nancy acknowledges Iowa State University for its generous support of this project in the form of a portion of a faculty improvement leave. She is grateful to Jane for asking her to collaborate and for helping to make that collaboration a rich one. Jane's insights on drafts, her questions that spurred further thinking, and above all her sensitivity to the collaborative process and warmth as a friend are deeply appreciated. Nancy is also grateful to her husband, Merlin Pfannkuch, for his support throughout the work on this collection and for the many hours of conversation about agriculture that lie behind Nancy's stories of the family and factory farms in her individual chapter. Finally, Nancy acknowledges the contributions of her father-in-law, Melvin Pfannkuch, an Iowa farmer for 65 years who tells wonderful stories about the past; her mother, Betty Blyler, and her father, Lee Blyler, who raised her to be a reader and a lover of stories; and the many dogs who have shared her life and enriched her storyliving—Dolcie, Pandy, Hildie, Dusty, Mop, and Digger.

Last but far from least, we want to thank those who helped us prepare this collection for publication. In particular, we acknowledge the invaluable assistance of the collection's anonymous reviewers and the work of the editors at Ablex, who saw us through the production process.

—Jane Perkins and Nancy Blyler

REFERENCE

White, H. (1987). The value of narrativity in the representation of reality. In *The content of the form: Narrative discourse and historical representation* (pp. 1–25). Baltimore, MD: Johns Hopkins University Press.

Introduction

Taking a Narrative Turn in Professional Communication

Jane Perkins
A.T. Kearney, Inc., Chicago

Nancy Blyler
Iowa State University

We begin this chapter with a confession: Worried about how to define narrative and convey its importance, we had been brainstorming, outlining, and writing for many weeks before we realized that although we were developing a thesis and areas of support, we had not discussed how we would present our story. We had not talked, that is, about a narrative voice or voices we might use; about characters we might create, actual or metaphorical; or about events we might describe. Moreover, we had not considered the intellectual and emotional responses we hoped to elicit from our readers nor gauged their patience for narrative details. In short, because we had assumed the form of a traditional academic argument, with its characteristic voice and presentation style, we had not considered questions of our own storytelling. And thus we had neglected rhetorical opportunities—those, in fact, that we hope to convince you to consider.

Let us start, then, not with a definition of narrative and not with thesis and support, but rather with our own stories. We want to speak to you about some of the meaningful events that have shaped our thinking about narrative and some of the characters who have influenced us, in order to suggest why we consider narrative to be so important and why, jointly and individually, we are committed to taking a narrative turn. We believe that by reading these stories, you will better understand our use of the word *narrative* and appreciate the scope of our examination. We further believe that you will be better prepared for the scholarly argument we are creating about the devaluing of narrative in professional communication and the benefits we see of a narrative turn.

Briefly, these benefits include connecting with an interdisciplinary community, considering previously excluded research topics, encouraging less objectivist ways of writing, refocusing pedagogy on professional communication as knowledge making, understanding professional communication as change, better managing information for databases and Web environments, and building human relationships in the workplace. But before we get ahead of ourselves, let's tell you our stories.

NANCY'S STORY: NARRATIVE AND THE CONSTRUCTION OF SELF

A few years ago, when I was engaged in some soul-searching about academic life in general and mine in particular, I found myself reflecting on alternate careers I might have pursued. "If I had it to do over," I thought, "I'd take up wildlife biology and become a park ranger. None of this being chained to a desk, writing scholarly papers for me!"

By that time in my life, I thought I knew who I was: a person who felt that a good investment was a 185-acre parcel of Iowa fields and timber no one else wanted—perfect for discovering spring's shy trilliums or the purple and gold of big bluestem in the fall. A career that would allow me to be out in the natural world seemed like a heaven-sent blessing.

Even in the midst of those thoughts, however, I was aware that being a park ranger was not a likely possibility. My choices had already been shaped by a mother who was an elementary school teacher, a set of parents who believed in the social and monetary value of a Ph.D., and a previous marriage spent almost entirely in academe. My past had, in other words, been constructed in relation to a number of possible stories, from and against which, for various reasons that at times even I don't fully understand, I had pieced together the narrative I would tell of my life.

This preamble is a roundabout way of explaining to you what the word *narrative* means for me and why I have—personally, in my understanding of my life, and professionally, in the direction of my research—chosen to take a narrative turn. To me, narrative is more than a discourse form, to be included in manuals, proposals, and reports. Rather, narrative is also integral to the way we understand our existences and construct ourselves as human beings: We live the stories we tell of our lives.

Because I believe we do live narratively, taking a narrative turn in my research enabled me to join a compelling personal insight with the work I do day after day. Furthermore, taking a narrative turn allowed me to address issues that were, for me, of increasing urgency: my need, for example, to connect my scholarly endeavors with my public life outside of academe; and my desire to write about what I believe are pressing social and political issues in a narrative way. I hoped that my work would reach and make a difference for audiences of various kinds—those who are not academics as well as those who are.

This fall will find me, therefore, not behind a desk but instead—tape recorder in hand—out in the field audiotaping narratives of rural midwesterners who are telling and living what I believe are more vital and viable stories than those of our mainstream, consumer-driven, and technologically "advanced" culture: the stories, for example, of members and producers of the Magic Beanstalk in Ames, Iowa—a grassroots, sustainable-agriculture organization committed to community-supported agriculture as a way of linking small family farmers and buyers, thereby rebuilding connections among food, people, and the land. This fall will find me, in other words, documenting, preserving, reflecting on, and retelling possible stories that I believe matter in terms of the lives we as humans may narratively construct.

JANE'S STORY:
NARRATIVE AND THE CONSTRUCTION OF KNOWLEDGE

I believe in stories all the way down the line. Stories are integral to theorizing about "interpretation all the way down" and "rhetoric all the way down." We interpret stories as we make knowledge from others and for others—configuring connections and layering contexts. Stories are also rhetorical, listener-fashioned to appeal and persuade. Too often, however, we don't acknowledge that rhetoric is storied; we separate the two and deny ourselves a full range of influence and knowing.

As you, no doubt, can tell, my story grows from ethnographers' "interpretive," "rhetorical," "narrative" turns. Like them, many of whose ideas we take up soon, my beliefs of narrative and knowing are implicit in doing. Anthropologists speak in reverent tones of going into the field and afterward understanding in a way that could not be described beforehand; similarly, my beliefs "were made" by doing ethnographic research. My research has taught me that I am at all times analyzing and narrating—creating meaning and crafting it for (and with) others. But I need to start closer to a beginning.

My narrative turn in professional communication stems from a goal to blend workplace practitioners' knowledge with that of teachers and researchers in the academy. Based on my background as a freelance writer before and during my return to university teaching and research, and now with experience as a communication specialist for a global management consulting firm, I am convinced of the importance of this blend. Ethnographic research offers the potential for meaningful mergings. Further, as a graduate of a newly created Ph.D. program in rhetoric and professional communication, I have, perhaps, less to turn away from; I largely bypassed disciplinary endeavors to objectify, to structure acontextually, and to universalize professional communication knowledge—goals that, we will argue, diminish narrative awareness and value. Thus, as I draft in currents of postmodern theories and experimental qualitative methodologies, it is, perhaps, easier for me to connect narrative and professional communication theoretically and methodologically. My steeper challenges involve the specifics of writing and discussing ethnographies as narratives, and of teaching students and professionals that their stories define and empower their professional communication.

As a professional communicator and ethnographer, I promote stories of workplace communication. I observe professionals communicating within their organizational contexts, analyzing their communication processes and artifacts (hard copy, electronic, and film documents); more significantly, I engage these professionals in sharing stories, challenge them to consider and explain communicative actions, and fashion knowledge with them. For an interpretive ethnographer, it's storytelling all the way down. I engage, select, arrange, argue, and stylistically fashion words and visuals for readers. This telling, however, doesn't reflect my initial struggle with knowledge making; it isn't the story of my first ethnography. Back then, I scribbled self-reflexive questions in draft margins about my narrator's voice, my limited knowledge of all the participants in the ad hoc culture I was researching, and my concerns about the acceptance of my academic readers—those who were, I believed, conditioned to value "harder" professional communication knowledge. Since that first professional turning toward narrative, my ethnographic struggle hasn't dissipated. It continues with other variations.

This brief recounting, however, isn't even close to a beginning of my relationship with narrative. That relationship must go back to stories as my preferred way of learning and my need for contextual details to help me know *my way*. Recently, my young-adult children gathered for a weekend and included me in their reminiscing. My daughter's analysis taught me about the depth of my narrative dependence: "Mom, you raised us with stories." She was not referring to the endless readings of *The Saggy, Baggy Elephant* or the Richard Scarry collections but to the countless, storied examples from which they learned. Eyes shining, their laughter spilling over each others' words, they chided me: "It wasn't easy, you know, figuring out so much for ourselves."

* * * * *

As these stories we have told suggest, we believe narrative is central to our lives. In addition to its importance as a form of discourse, narrative is a means of being and of acting in the world and therefore an extraordinarily complex perspective to take when considering issues such as the construction of self and knowledge—issues that we, along with scholars in many other disciplines, find both personally and intellectually compelling.

In the next section, we review some of the interdisciplinary discussion on these two issues we have identified, in order to suggest the power of narrative when viewed as a perspective, and the range and richness of scholars' explorations.

NARRATIVE AS A PERSPECTIVE: INTERDISCIPLINARY DISCUSSION ON THE CONSTRUCTION OF SELF AND KNOWLEDGE

As scholars in many fields have taken an "interpretive turn" (Rabinow & Sullivan, 1987), focusing on representation rather than on truth, narrative has also come to the fore as a topic for scholarly inquiry (Mumby, 1993, p. 1). Scholars, for example, view narrative as important to meaning-making, particularly in relation to human experience (Bruner, 1987, 1991; Gergen & Gergen, 1983; Kerby, 1991; White, 1987). As Bruner (1987) says, "We seem to have no other way of describing 'lived time' save in the form of a narrative" (p. 12); in this way, we give experience meaning (Bruner, 1986, p. 12). Other scholars' interpretive turns have grown from methodological concerns about ways of knowing—how it is that they can, in fact, make knowledge claims and how their research affects the cultures and individuals they study. For these scholars, a revision in methodological ways of knowing means writing "ethnographies of intimacy, not distance; of stories, not models; of possibilities, not stabilities; and of contingent understandings, not detachable conclusions" (Van Maanen, Manning, & Miller, 1990, p. 5).

This recognition of the importance of narrative in the context of interpretation and meaning-making has led scholars to explore a variety of issues, including the construction of self and knowledge.

The Construction of Self

Scholars interested in narrative and the construction of self focus on the relation between the stories we tell of our lives and the selves we fashion. Kerby (1991), for example, claims that narratives are not only "descriptive of the self," but also "fundamental to [the self's] emergence and reality" (p. 4): "The self, as implied subject, appears to be inseparable from the narrative or life story it constructs for itself or otherwise inherits" (p. 6).

Saying that narrative is "a form not only of representing but of constituting reality" (1991, p. 5), Bruner also claims that the self is a construction resulting from narrative: "In the end, we *become* the autobiographical narratives by which we 'tell about' our lives" (original emphasis, 1986, p. 15). To Bruner, then, "a life as led is inseparable from a life as told—or more bluntly, a life is not 'how it was' but how it is interpreted and reinterpreted, told and retold" (p. 31) in the context of one's daily activities. Our life, Bruner asserts, is a "narrative achievement" (p. 13).

This narrative achievement, however, is not solely an individual feat. Rather, Mumby (1993) claims, there is "an integral link between narrative and the social" (p. 5). Our life stories are influenced by our culture—by the way "other people narrate us" and by "our language and the genres of storytelling inherited from our traditions" (Kerby, 1991, p. 6). Indeed, Kerby asserts, "much of our self-narrating is a matter of becoming conscious of the narratives that we already live in and with" (p. 6).

Bruner (1987) makes a similar point, positing that we become "variants of the culture's canonical forms" (p. 15). "Stories," says Bruner (1986), "define the range of characters, the settings in which they operate, the actions that are permissible and comprehensible." By providing these permissible canonical forms, our culture's narratives constitute "a map of possible roles and of possible worlds" (p. 66) from which we construct the stories we will tell of our own existences.

In providing these canonical forms—this map of possible roles and worlds—our culture's narratives also function as a means of social control (Bruner, 1991; Ehrenhaus, 1993; Kerby, 1991; Mumby, 1993). More specifically, narratives form what White (1987) calls "a particularly effective system of discursive meaning production by which individuals can be taught to live... an unreal but meaningful relation to the social formations in which they are indentured to live out their lives and realize their destinies as social subjects" (p. x). In doing so, narratives "organize and coordinate social and institutional arrangements and imbue them with meaning" (Ehrenhaus, 1993, p. 85), thus providing the "canonical past" (Bruner, 1991, p. 20) that limits and constrains our individual storytelling.

Narratives, then, cannot be viewed as innocent constructions. Rather, they are implicated in a "struggle over the ways in which meaning gets 'fixed'" (Mumby, 1993, p. 7), helping to "construct the subjectivity of those who accept them" (Bennett & Edelman, 1985, p. 161) and helping to construct a shared social world as well (see also Bormann, 1985). Narrative is thus implicated in politics and power, "part of the complex and shifting terrain of meaning that makes up the social world," (Mumby, 1993, p. 3)—and part of the "transformative possibilities" that come with "a contingent view of society" (p. 8).

As representations, then, that serve to map possible lives and construct subjectivity, narratives are far more important to our individual and collective existences than we in professional communication may have acknowledged. Narratives are also important in the construction of knowledge, especially as a way of knowing cultures.

The Construction of Knowledge

For anthropologists, the originators of ethnographic writing, the interpretive turn has resulted in communal and individual questioning about the very nature of research activities, the relationships of researchers to cultures and with individual informants, and the ethics of representation. While Van Maanen (1995) sees "the breakdown of standard ethnographic topics, borders, and styles as something to celebrate, not mourn" (p. 13), the "crisis" is for others an erosion of scientific credibility. For many anthropologists, narrative is not just a mode of discourse; nor is it a complement to scientific knowledge. When, as Van Maanen explains, ethnographers no longer believe "there is something like culture or, for that matter, atoms and quarks thought to come first while our understandings, modes, or representations of culture, atoms, or quarks come second," then interpretation and the narratives told are, in fact, all that we can know. "Language," therefore, "is now auditioning for an *a priori* role in the social and material world, a role that carries constitutional force—bringing facts into consciousness and therefore being" (p. 14). Issues of representation, of language, of tropes—the specifics of narrative writing—are significant to ethnographers as they have never been before.

Geertz (1988), in particular, discusses the need for a "narratological" rather than an "epistemological" perspective on ethnographic knowledge, claiming that the central question is not one of "subjectivity"—that is, "how to prevent subjective views from coloring objective facts"—but instead one of "signature" or authorship—that is, "how best to get an honest story honestly told" (p. 9). Decrying ethnographers' preoccupation with "author-evacuated" texts, the "mechanics of knowledge," and the "problematics of fieldwork," rather than with questions of authorship and discourse (pp. 9–10), Geertz claims that "the writing of ethnography," and hence, ethnographic knowledge, involve "telling stories, making pictures, concocting symbolisms, and deploying tropes" (p. 140). Making ethnographic knowledge, then, is not simply "a matter of sorting strange and irregular facts into familiar and orderly categories." Rather, ethnographic knowledge is at heart "a kind of writing" (p. 1) and, as such, is intimately connected to narrative.

In addition to claiming that narrative is central to the construction of ethnographic knowledge, Geertz (1988) also raises issues attendant on telling the story of the other—especially issues of politics and power. He reminds us that "anthropologists now writing find themselves in a profession that was largely formed in an historical context—the Colonial Encounter—of which they have no experience and want none" (p. 134). However, the motivation to "distance themselves from the power asymmetries upon which that encounter rested...is generally quite strong" (p. 134), providing a vivid reminder that politics and power are implicit in ethnographers' fieldwork and writing.

Other scholars have also theorized about politics and power—that is, about non-homogeneous cultures of study and underrepresentation of nondominant members, about obligations to include others' voices and to question the researcher's position as narrator, and about the justification for cultural critique and action. Rosaldo (1989), for example, contrasts "the classic view, which posits culture as a self-contained whole made up of coherent patterns"—and which typically uses male members of high cultural standing as representative of the entire culture—with interpretive views of culture "as a more porous array of intersections where distinct processes crisscross from within and beyond its borders" (p. 20). Thus, although "differences of age, gender, class, race, and sexual orientation" (p. 20) were not acknowledged in classic ethnographic writings, they now come to the fore.

Power issues such as Rosaldo identifies are directly related to narrative, since classic ethnographic goals of generalizing and filling universal categories result in writing that differs significantly from narratives of unique, local, heterogeneous cultures. Furthermore, Marcus and Fischer (1986) remind us of the need for "rhetorical self-consciousness about the selection and bounding of ethnographic subjects....One is obliged to be self-consciously justifying (or strategic) in the placement of ethnography precisely because of the sensitivity to the broader system representation which is at stake" (p. 93). In other words, Marcus and Fischer believe ethnographers need to be aware of the power they have to determine a culture—who and what is included within the knowledge-making and who and what is not—because that content or focus determines the story that is told. Cultures do not exist intact; they are constructed.

Related to cultural heterogeneity are issues of voice and narrators. Marcus and Fischer (1986) explain that, while "realist texts continue the convention of allowing the ethnographer to remain in unchallenged control of his narrative" (p. 67), "experimental ethnographies" challenge this univocal representation: The "experience represented in the ethnography must be that of the dialogue between ethnographer and informants, where textual space is arranged for the informants to have their own voices" (p. 67). Marcus and Fischer not only endorse experimenting with alternate ways of writing that include informants' voices, but they also suggest that innovations in textuality are ethnographers' ethical responsibility.

In keeping with this responsibility, when ethnographers no longer strive to maintain scientific objectivity, they can openly rethink their capacity to interact with cultures and therefore write participatory narratives—those that include the ethnographer, perhaps in a more autobiographical role, and those that consciously use ethnographic writing to promote cultural change. As Goodall (1994) explains, "I have learned that my position in the narrative arena is inherently a *political* one, and that every act I undertake as a teacher, writer, speaker, or researcher is either complicit with the *status quo* or engaged in the struggle to change it" (p. 185). Clifford (1986) summarizes the issues attendant in constructing ethnographic knowledge: "These contingencies—of language, rhetoric, power, and history—must now be openly confronted in the process of writing.... But is there not a liberation, too, in recognizing that no one can write about others any longer as if they were discrete objects or texts?" (p. 25).

* * * * *

Though scholars interested in the narrative construction of self and of ethnographic knowledge underscore the value—indeed, the interpretive and ethical necessity—of taking a narrative turn, in our work for this chapter we noted the same curious discrepancy that other scholars (e.g., Barton & Barton, 1988; DiPardo, 1990; Rentz, 1992) discuss: Despite the burgeoning interest in narrative common to many other fields, in professional communication narrative has, until recently, largely been devalued.

In the sections to follow, we further explore this issue of a narrative turn that, to date, many scholars in professional communication have been reluctant to take. We first support our claim that narrative has been devalued in professional communication, then speculate about why narrative has been held in such low regard. Finally, we suggest benefits of taking this narrative turn—benefits that also represent a few of the possible directions for professional communication research, pedagogy, and practice.

NARRATIVE DEVALUED IN PROFESSIONAL COMMUNICATION

Both pedagogy—which, early on, served to constitute professional communication as a field (see Connors, 1982, and Hagge, 1995, for discussions of the origin of such instruction in America)—and research indicate our discipline's low regard for narrative.

Professional Communication Pedagogy

Because textbooks codify and shape both pedagogical practices and disciplinary beliefs, we examined a sampling of early and more recently published texts for their treatment of narrative. Although this sampling cannot be considered definitive, in it we did find striking evidence of our field's low regard for narrative.

The early texts we examined, for example, make little mention of narrative, discussing it only briefly as a familiar "thought pattern"—"the normal interest in a time sequence, in following any series of events one after another in chronological order" (Harbarger, Whitmer, & Price, 1943, p. 53)—and as an organizational strategy (Park, 1932). As such a strategy, "factual narration" might be used to structure a section of a report—for example, one describing an apparatus and discussing how it works (Harbarger, Dumble, Hildreth, & Emsley, 1938). In these early texts, however, narrative is not seen as central to technical students' understanding of themselves and the world or to the professional discourse they might write.

As with these early texts, the more recent texts we examined also make little mention of narrative. For example, our search of tables of contents, indexes, and headings of 40 business and technical communication texts, all published within the last 10 years, turned up only 11 references to narrative—most occupying from a paragraph to a page or two, although a few textbooks include 3 to 6 pages of explanation and examples. With an average of 600 pages per text, even 6 pages of discussion hardly argues for narrative as an important area of pedagogical concern.

Furthermore, as with references in the early texts, many references to narrative in these more recent texts involve chronological arrangement or elements of time (Andrews & Andrews, 1992; Brusaw, Alfred & Oliu, 1997; Galle, Nelson, Luse, & Villere, 1996; Houp, Pearsall, & Tebeaux, 1995; Killingsworth, 1996; F. White, 1996). About an equal number of references recommend narrative for its ability to catch readers' interest (Bovee & Thill, 1995; Timm & DeTienne, 1995; Houp et al., 1995; Killingsworth, 1996; Pauley & Riordan, 1990; F. White, 1996). Finally, some references are about organizational methods—those for describing procedures (Eisenberg, 1992; F. White, 1996) and for arranging sections in specific types of documents, such as reports or proposals (Boone, Kurtz, & Black, 1994; Killingsworth, 1996). (In one text, however, narrative is given a broader scope by being viewed as stories encoding cultural values [Killingsworth, 1996].)

Although we cannot say, therefore, that narrative is entirely absent from more recent professional communication texts, we do claim that its inclusion appears to have changed little since its discussion in the early texts we examined—save perhaps for a recognition of the ability of narrative to attract readers' attention. Furthermore, we claim that, because narrative is frequently used in contrast to more highly valued ways of writing, even its inclusion indicates a subtle devaluing. For example, since Andrews and Andrews (1992) restrict narrative to denoting an objective sequencing of events, they assume that narrative has limited use and therefore less value than hierarchical patterns of organization: "When you write to record, you're likely to use a narrative. But when you write to inform or to persuade, don't let the clock or the calendar serve as your only organizing device. Instead, arrange information to support a main point" (p. 61). Similarly, Bovee and Thill (1995) find that, although "good for attracting attention and explaining ideas," narrative is inferior because it "lacks statistical validity" (p. 135).

Comments such as these demonstrate that narrative tends to be granted little status in professional communication pedagogy. The same is true in professional communication research.

Professional Communication Research

In their seminal article "Narration in Technical Communication" (1988), Barton and Barton assert that "a literature review finds us almost mute on the subject of narrative in technical communication" (p. 38). Although, nearly a decade after the Bartons' important work, we cannot claim that professional communication research is as mute as it once was concerning narrative, we do assert that existing research on narrative is still limited, not necessarily in quality but rather in terms of the amount of scholarship produced and its scope.

To support this claim, we surveyed 11 major journals that publish articles on professional communication for the period from 1990 to 1997, examining tables of contents and abstracts of relevant articles.[1] Although we included only articles in this informal survey and not, for example, books or book chapters, we nonetheless believe that, because journals represent an important outlet for scholarship in any field, their contents are one useful indicator of the state of research on narrative.

We found that narrative manifests itself in these journals in three ways, only one of which, we claim, constitutes a narrative focus for research. First, the authors of some articles use narrative, as recent professional communication pedagogy recommends, to contextualize and arouse interest in their analyses, but these authors do not directly address narrative as an issue. Wells's (1996) "Rogue Cops and Health Care: What Do We Want from Public Writing," for example, begins with a story that serves to situate the scholarly discussion of public writing. Second, the authors of other articles also do not address the issue of narrative directly; however, narrative is implicit because of the methodology these authors select. Examples here include the many case studies, ethnographies, and historical studies that appeared in professional communication scholarship over the time period we selected (e.g., Dulye, 1993; Tebeaux, 1993; Winsor, 1993).

Because in both of these categories narrative itself remains unexamined, we argue that the authors cannot be said to focus on narrative as a research topic. Third, however, the authors of at least 12 articles do examine narrative explicitly in a variety of ways—theoretically, functionally, methodologically, and stylistically. Of these 12 articles, three discuss the status or role of narrative within professional communication (Blyler, 1995, 1996; Rentz, 1992); four theorize about narrative methodologies (Cintron, 1993; Cross, 1994; Henry & "G.," 1995; Ledwell-Brown & Dias, 1994); three are cultural examinations of narrative, in nature writing and in the rhetoric of science (Galindo & Brown, 1995; Journet, 1990, 1991); and two discuss narrative and theory in relation to specific forms of professional discourse (Blyler, 1992; Gregson & Selzer, 1990).

While these categories of concerns and the 12 articles represented are undeniably important, as a group they cannot hope to reflect in either range, inclusiveness, or depth the rich scholarly discussion occurring in other disciplines, where bodies of work on narrative have emerged. Thus, although we believe that the explicit examination of narrative found in these articles represents an important advance over the muteness the Bartons note, we still contend that narrative is not highly enough regarded in professional communication to spur broad scholarly inquiry. As a result, in our discipline, narrative appears to be merely an occasional topic for research, rather than an important perspective.

In the next section, we speculate about why our field has persisted in devaluing narrative.

SPECULATION ABOUT DEVALUING

The treatment of narrative in our texts and the paucity of journal articles focusing on narrative indicate strength and persistence in our field's disciplinary view: Narrative continues to be relegated to an inferior position—a situation that we assert has contributed to scholars' reluctance to take a narrative turn.

Although our reasoning must be speculative, we believe that this disciplinary climate is the result of at least six complex and interrelated factors:

- the Western tradition of privileging logic and science;
- the linking of professional communication to an objectivist view of rhetoric and to the concept of skills-oriented writing;
- the ties of narrative to the feminine, the subjective, and the emotional;
- the influence of cognitive theories of development;
- the classification of narrative as one of the modes of discourse; and
- the positioning of professional communication within English departments.

We are aware that these six factors may not fully account for narrative's low status. We are also aware that, because of space limitations, we must content ourselves with tracing only the barest outline of a scholarly story concerning each of the factors. Nonetheless, we want to begin the work of identifying influences in our professional communication culture that we speculate have contributed and continue to contribute to the devaluing of narrative.

Western Tradition of Privileging Logic and Science

Scholars in numerous fields discuss a tradition in Western thought that, since classical times, has privileged logic and science, seeing these as the way to reach a foundational truth that exists independent of human subjectivity (e.g., Bruner, 1986, 1991; DiPardo, 1990; Fish, 1989; Fisher, 1984; Geertz, 1983; Halloran, 1978; Kent, 1993; Maines, 1993; Richardson,; Rorty, 1987).

Tracing to Aristotle the origins of systematic rhetoric—the idea that language is foundational or codifiable—Kent (1993), for example, asserts that the Greek philosopher "generates a logico-scientific superstructure for rhetoric" (p. 20). Bizzell and Herzberg (1990) further explain that Aristotle believed "only scientific demonstration and the analysis of formal logic" allowed one to "arrive at transcendent truth" (p. 144)—a view that Fish (1989) asserts persisted through the Enlightenment "rediscovery of reason and science" and continues to the present (pp. 484–485). Indeed, paralleling Fisher's (1984) claim for two "paradigms" of human communication, the "rational world" and the "narrative" (pp. 1–3), and Bruner's (1986) assertion of "two modes of thought," the "logico-scientific" and the "narrative" (p. 11), Fish (1989) states that "the history of Western thought could be written as the history" of a "quarrel" between two differing views of truth (p. 484)—a quarrel that Bruner (1986) claims has been tilted heavily in the direction of logic and science (p. 13).

This privileging of logic and science has influenced professional communication, despite changing views that now suggest the rhetorical nature of the scientific enterprise (e.g., Halloran, 1978; Selzer, 1993) and the contingent and "local" status of knowledge (e.g., Geertz, 1983). For example, an early professional communication textbook (Harbarger, Whitmer, & Price, 1943) privileges logic, establishing the importance of "common patterns of logical thought" as the primary "tool" for shaping "the raw material of expression" (p. 12). Using this tool, the authors claim, enables the "technical man" to tame the "rich variety" of "impressions, associations, and relationships" that he has "stored up out of daily experience," so that he can "report this material of everyday living" to others in technical documents (pp. 11–12).

Similarly, in another early attempt to conceptualize professional communication, Britton (1975) discusses "the type of thought processes involved" in technical writing (p. 10). Focusing on the "sequential thought" that "belongs to mathematics and science" rather than on the "chronological, spatial, or emotional relationships" of "associative thought," Britton draws on Kirkman, who finds the associative pattern of thought incompatible with scientific subjects (pp. 10–11). Clearly, Britton's remarks suggest that the "chronological" relationships inherent in narrative—as opposed to the logical relationships thought to be inherent in science—are unsuited to professional communication.

And finally, Harris, in his 1978 definition of technical writing, calls it "the rhetoric of the scientific method" because of technical writing's deductive nature, its focus on objectivity, and its concern with "demonstrable truth" (p. 137). Though in this definition "truth" is demonstrable rather than transcendent—as it was for Aristotle—nonetheless, the desire to seek truth and the prestige accorded to logic and science as the means for seeking it remain.

We believe, therefore, that, because professional communication has been influenced by the Western tradition privileging logic and science, like this tradition (Bruner, 1986; Fisher, 1984) professional communication has also failed to consider adequately the importance of narrative. This privileging of logic and science has usually resulted in a view of language as a medium that, as Fish (1989) notes, "faithfully reflects or reports on matters of fact," adhering to which "makes one a seeker after truth and an objective observer of the way things are" (p. 474). Dasenbrock (1987) asserts that this view, which gives priority to "disinterested clarity," has been extraordinarily durable in Western thought (p. 293).

In the past, professional communication has tried to approach this ideal of disinterested clarity (Dasenbrock, 1987; Dobrin, 1983) through its links to an objectivist view of rhetoric and a concept of skills-oriented writing.

Links to an Objectivist View of Rhetoric and to Skills-Oriented Writing

A number of scholars link professional communication to an objectivist view of rhetoric (e.g., Lay, 1991, 1993; Limaye, 1983; Miller, 1979; Miller, 1991; Rutter, 1991; Sullivan, 1990). Miller (1979), for example, connects technical writing to a "positivist view," where "objectivity on the part of the observer minimizes personal and social interference, reducing observation to the accurate recording of the self-evident" (p. 612). Miller (1991) underscores this point, noting the "belief" that "teachers of technical and business writing" have in "scientific objectivity" (p. 64). Though, as Lay (1991) suggests, this belief may now be a "deceptive ethos" rather than a firmly held conviction about the objective nature of truth (p. 356), still, Lay claims, the rhetorical stance of objectivity persists in professional communication as a means of "enhanc[ing] legitimacy" for the field (p. 358).

Scientific objectivity and the removal of the personal from professional communication may in part be the legacy of Taylor's scientific management, which originated around 1885 and is still practiced in disciplines such as engineering and professional management—and in professional communication. (See Ritzer, 1993, on the pervasive influence of Taylorism on many aspects of business and industry, as well as on society in general.) Drucker (1954) describes this scientific approach as "the organized study of work, the analysis of work into its simplest elements and the systematic improvement of the worker's performance of each of these elements" (p. 280). In a scientific approach such as this, says Ritzer, control, is an important goal (p. 24). Yates (1989) then traces the rise of professional communication to management's need for control and to the necessary means by which that management system was created. For example, prescribed and objectivist discourse forms became necessary for tracking and measuring work (p. 100).

The persistence of this objectivist rhetorical stance can be demonstrated by examining textbooks in the field. Miller (1979), for example, notes the presence of this stance in the texts of the 1970s, where adjectives such as "objective," "scientific," "impartial," "clear," and "unemotional" were used to describe technical writing (p. 611). Indeed, looking further back, a 1938 text for students in applied sciences uses language similar to that identified by Miller, positing, for example, that "the object of any factual description in words is to make the reader or listener see material things...clearly, vividly, accurately" (Harbarger, Dumble, Hildreth, & Emsley, 1938, p. 159)—untouched, that is, by the writer's subjectivity.

This objectivist view of rhetoric is connected as well to the concept of skills-oriented writing. Miller (1979), for example, illustrates this connection when discussing technical writing as the "skill of subduing language" so that it can "accurately" convey reality (p. 610). With such a concept, claims Halloran (1978), writing is simply "a set of technical skills practiced by specialists" (p. 221) and, says Sullivan (1990), technical genres are "reduced to the notion of form" (p. 377) in a way that makes them easy to teach and learn.

Given this linking of professional communication to an objectivist view of rhetoric and to the concept of skills-oriented writing, we should not be surprised to find narrative placed within an objectivist, skills-oriented framework. One early text (Harbarger, Dumble, Hildreth, & Emsley, 1938), for example, describes "factual narration" solely as a genre "always present in report writing," whereby the "effects of the work" the writer has done are accurately recorded. Factual narration is, then, a "slow-motion picture" in which "the reader sees the equipment and the material not at rest but moving, working, and producing results" (p. 158). As the visual metaphor in this text suggests, the purpose of narrative is to transmit directly an image of the world untainted by the writer's subjectivity. (See Belenky, Clinchy, Goldberger, & Tarule, 1986, for a discussion of the visual metaphor as a means of "promot[ing] the illusion" of "disengagement and objectification" where "subject and object" do not interact [p. 18].) The skill of writing factual narration is, moreover, easily acquired: "The simplest way is to tell what happens step by step, from start to finish" (Harbarger et al., 1938, p. 158).

As the treatment of narrative in this early text suggests, within an objectivist, skills-oriented framework narrative's role is greatly circumscribed. Specifically, narrative is reduced to a form for objectively recording events in chronological order. Because this chronological mirroring of events is not given priority within an objectivist view of rhetoric and because acquiring the skill needed to write such narrative forms is seen as an easy task, we theorize that narrative has been held in low regard.

This devaluing of narrative within an objectivist, skills-oriented view of writing is then connected in complex ways to the low status accorded to narrative because of the perception that it has close ties to the feminine, the subjective, and the emotional.

Ties to the Feminine, the Subjective, and the Emotional

In feminist scholarship within professional communication, Lay (1991) contrasts the high value given to objectivist rhetoric found in science with the lower status accorded to "subjective types of writing," linking the first to the masculine and the second to the feminine (p. 358; see also 1993, pp. 221–222). "Science," says Lay (1993), "has a long history of rejecting the feminine," valuing the objective over the subjective and "rational thinking" over the "emotions" (p. 222). This rejection on the part of science has of course been noted by feminist scholars outside of professional communication (e.g., Flynn, 1995; Harding, 1987), who view the rejection as part of a larger pattern of devaluation for women's ways of knowing (Belenky, Clinchy, Goldberger, & Tarule, 1986).

This devaluing of the feminine, the subjective, and the emotional, in favor of the masculine, the objective, and the rational, has, feminist scholars assert, greatly affected professional communication. Lay (1991) claims, for example, that professional communication "ranks" objectivist writing "higher than other supposedly *subjective* types of writing," in order to remain connected to "patriarchal institutions of power" (original emphasis; p. 358). Carrell's (1991) analysis of "gender scripts" in professional communication texts published from the 1930s through the 1950s supports Lay's claim about the relative ranking of objective and subjective writing and the presence of gender stereotyping in these rankings. Carrell finds women portrayed in these texts as emotional, nonlogical thinkers, to be persuaded by arguments from pathos, while men are seen as rational thinkers. Hence, says Carrell, these texts recommend that "logos is to be reserved for men only" (p. 464).

In addition to affecting our discipline as a whole and the way past textbooks have been written, this devaluing of the feminine, the subjective, and the emotional has, we believe, shaped the way narrative is viewed. More specifically, because the subjective or personal experience—which Lay (1993) finds essential to the feminist perspective (p. 224)—is often understood and expressed in narrative terms, we theorize that narrative has been similarly devalued. Belenky, Clinchy, Goldberger, and Tarule (1986) note, for example, that "the stories of the women drew us back into a kind of knowing that had too often been silenced by the institutions in which we grew up and of which we were a part" (p. 20). Narrative, the feminine, the subjective, and the emotional are inextricably linked, and all are held in low regard.

Dragga's (1993) claim that as a profession becomes feminized, its status decreases (p. 313) offers a related explanation for the devaluing of narrative in connection with the feminine. Dragga's work suggests that disciplines may resist a trend toward feminization because such a trend might reduce their status. Regarding narrative, therefore, we speculate that our discipline also fails to accord it more

worth since doing so might be viewed as furthering any movement toward feminization that is perceived to exist.

Along with links to the feminine, the subjective, and the emotional, theories of
cognitive development have also influenced the devaluing of narrative.

The Influence of Cognitive Theories of Development

The application of cognitive psychology and developmental processes of learning
to professional communication has been shaped most prominently by the research
of Flower and Hayes. Their contribution to the collection *New Essays in Technical
and Scientific Communication: Research, Theory, Practice*—described as "the best
current scholarly work" (Anderson, Brockmann, & Miller, 1983, p. 13) in an area
that has been "repetitious, unmethodical, and trivial" (p. 7)—added the concept of
the scenario principle to professional communication. This key concept evolved
from Flower and Hayes's theories of developmental writing, where writers must
transform their own simple narrative information to meet readers' needs for hierarchically ordered information. Hence, "the narrative or descriptive structure of
writer-based prose" is viewed as inferior to "reader-based prose" (Flower, Hayes,
& Swarts, 1983, p. 49).

We agree with the value of ordering information so that readers more easily
understand a document's significance; however, Flower and Hayes's concept of
writer-based prose is problematic because their developmental theories separate
narrative from supposedly more complex cognitive processes. The psychological
research upon which Flower and Hayes based their concept further explains their
restrictive use of narrative.

In "Writer-Based Prose: A Cognitive Basis for Problems in Writing," Flower
(1979) adapts the research of Piaget and Vygotsky in the psychology of language
and cognitive processes, in particular using their explanations of the development
toward complex, higher-order thinking that optimally culminates in abstract mathematical symbolism. Flower equates writer-based prose with Piaget's egocentric
speech and Vygotsky's inner speech—the kinds of speech children move through
on their way to developing more complex thinking and forms of communication. In
this equation as well, Flower connects narrative to writer-based prose, which she
claims "reflects the associative, narrative path of the writer's own confrontation
with her subject" (p. 269). In this narrative path, Flower further asserts, underde-
veloped writers do not form causal or logical relationships but instead use what
Piaget calls "juxtaposition" to link one thought with another, speaking or writing in
"complexes" that group concrete objects rather than employing "concepts" that
"express abstract, logical relationships" (pp. 270–271).

When Flower (1979) applies aspects of writer-based thought specifically to an
analysis of a document, she opposes narrative, which "simply copies the structure
of the perceived information," to more valued analytic discourse: "By burying ideas
within the events that precipitated them, a narrative obscures the more important

logical and hierarchical relationships between ideas" (p. 276). Furthermore, in the validation of the logical and the hierarchical, "facts, scenarios, and details" are abandoned in favor of "concepts" (p. 292).

Since the 1980s, Flower and Hayes's cognitive-process research has influenced professional-communication textbooks, in which narrative is viewed as distinct from more complex types of thinking and writing—such as arguing or analyzing—and narrative continues to be situated as the developmental starting point. Exceptions do exist (for example, Anderson, 1991; Killingsworth, 1996; Lay et. al., 1995). However, a developmental influence appears to pervade topic organization in professional communication texts.[2]

In an academic culture in which narrative is devalued by the ascendancy of logic and science; efforts toward objectivism and skills-oriented writing; and an association with the feminine, the subjective, and the emotional; we contend that narrative's worth becomes further suspect when it is seen as requiring lesser cognitive abilities and is correspondingly identified as the developmental prelude to more valued types of thinking and writing. Additionally, theories of modes of discourse also contribute to the devaluing of narrative.

The Influence of Theories of Modes of Discourse

Rigid classification systems, in terms of both written products and function, typically add to the devaluing of narrative in professional communication. The most pervasive classification system in professional communication as in composition studies in general—the modes of discourse—typically classifies types of writing as narrative, expository, descriptive, and persuasive.

When these modes are used as the theoretical basis for professional communication texts, as in Brusaw, Alfred, and Oliu's (1997), the scope and meaning of narrative are restricted to the "presentation of a series of events in chronological order." As chronological representation, therefore, narrative is separated from the "presentation of facts and ideas with the purpose of informing the readers" (exposition), "attempt[s] to re-create an object or situation with words so that the reader can visualize it mentally" (description), and "attempts to convince the reader that the writer's point of view is the correct or desirable one" (persuasion) (p. 233).

Rhetoric and composition scholars (for example, Faigley, Cherry, Jolliffe, & Skinner, 1985; Kent, 1993; Kinneavy, Cope & Campbell, 1976) trace the long and pervasive history of the modes to Greek and Latin antiquity. During this long history, a point of high interest and application is attributed to Bain, who stirred in composition scholars a "fascination with categories which was to become one of the hallmarks of the rigidly formalized rhetoric of the late nineteenth century" (Connors, 1988, p. 25). The influence of the modes is still strong in professional communication scholarship and pedagogy and continues to result in a devaluing of narrative.

Kinneavy, Cope, and Campbell's (1976) theory of the modes of discourse, for example, has been pervasive in professional communication during approximately the last 20 years. This strong influence might be explained, at least in part, by the scientific approach the modes promise: "The isolation of each mode in a study of composition is only made in order to focus attention on one feature of the universe of discourse. This is a necessity imposed on us by the nature of the human mind and the nature of scientific analysis" (p. 10). Although Kinneavy, Cope, and Campbell blur the edges of the modes, insisting that the categories blend into one another[3] and add sophisticated theory to the basic classification system, they still suggest that if students just understand the modes (or forms or genres), they will be able to organize their writing accordingly. In that static ordering, however, narrative is fundamentally restricted to chronological telling.

Because the modes became so widely accepted, Connors (1988) explains, single-mode texts began to appear (p. 30). As a result, exposition became the focus of composition courses, persuasion (as argument) slipped into speech communication courses, and narration and description became the subject matter of creative writing courses. In the midst of turf-defining such as this, professional communication has continually worked to explain its positioning within English departments—usually with no claims to narrative.

Positioning of Professional Communication within English Departments

Although scholars in professional communication lament its presumed lack of focus (e.g., Meese & Wahlstrom, 1988; Rentz, 1993), one commonality is the positioning of professional communication within English departments as distinct from literature and consequently separated from narrative. This distinction has been imposed by both sides. For example, in many English departments where professional communication courses are considered "service courses" (Forman, 1993, p. 338), staffed by teachers with little to no training in or inclination toward the area, professors distinguish between the courses that are available for staffing, such as the many service courses in professional communication, and the professors' real research and pedagogical interests in literature.

Scholes (1985) articulates this separation as "the binary oppositions which organize the flow of value and power in our institution" (p. 4). He sees the two main binaries as the distinctions between literature and nonliterature and between the consumption and production of texts—with literature and consumption being privileged: "This is, of course, an invidious distinction, for we mark those texts labeled literature as good or important and dismiss those non-literary texts as beneath our notice" (p. 5). When the literary is isolated from the nonliterary, the narrative connection is often claimed for such literary genres as novels, short stories, and epics.

Correspondingly, in early efforts to explain and shore up professional communication, those who taught it often distinguished it from the literary or poetic. Kelley and Masse (1977), for example, describe teaching their students the definition of technical writing by contrasting this writing with literary selections. In doing so,

Kelley and Masse claim that the writer's attitude in technical writing is "not subjective, but objective," and they circumscribe the domain of technical writing around facts: "These facts are pieces of information that can be verified objectively. In other words, they are pieces of information that can be proved accurate by simple experience or by scientific observation and experimentation" (p. 95). Objectively presented "pieces of information," obviously, lack characteristics of narrative, which makes experience meaningful by forming connections.

Similarly, as we discussed, Britton (1975) uses his summary of Kirkman's work to distinguish between thinking and writing about literary and scientific subjects, locating narrative only with the literary: "Associative thought," says Britton using Kirkman—with its "mode of expression" where "statements are linked together by connnectives like *then* and *rather,* indicating chronological, spatial, or emotional relationships—belongs to history, literature, and the arts." Meanwhile, "sequential thought," with its mode of expression where "statements are connected by words like because and therefore"—"belongs to mathematics and science" (pp. 10–11). While this explanation would probably not be credible today, nonetheless it is part of the differentiating that lingers in English departments as distinctions between professional communication and the study of literature continue to be reinforced because of programmatic and political motivations.

* * *

We believe that, taken together, these six factors have served to define our discipline as one remarkably inhospitable to a narrative turn. As we note, however, research on narrative in professional communication appears to be on the rise. In part, we base this claim on the valuable work of the contributors in this collection, who, by viewing narrative as a complex and important perspective, are expanding narrative research in useful directions. In our concluding section, therefore, we argue for the benefits to professional communication of continuing this narrative turn.

BENEFITS OF A NARRATIVE TURN

Ten years ago, Barton and Barton (1988) concluded their seminal article by envisioning the advantages of narration for professional communication; in the intervening years, those advantages have barely been explored. We build here on Barton and Barton's vision by again emphasizing some benefits of narrative—especially narrative viewed as a complex and important perspective—for academic and workplace researchers, as well as for teachers, trainers, and professional communicators in the workplace. Our hope is that these benefits, the possibilities they suggest, and the thought-provoking chapters in this collection will act as an impetus for professional communication's narrative turn.

Academic and Workplace Researchers

We believe that expanding research on narrative will position academic and workplace researchers to connect with a vital interdisciplinary community. We further believe that these researchers will be freed to consider topics previously excluded from attention and empowered to write in less objectivist ways.

Connecting with an Interdisciplinary Community

In her Outstanding Researcher Award lecture for the Association for Business Communication, Locker (1994) argues for the desirability of interdisciplinary research, claiming that it is "perhaps essential if we wish to advance knowledge" (p. 141). By encouraging academic and workplace researchers to access important work in other fields, a narrative turn will, we claim, advance Locker's goal of including more interdisciplinary research, thus enabling us to "[connect] our own findings with larger conversations" (p. 142).

As we have discussed, these larger conversations concerning narrative grow out of the interpretive turn, with its focus on meaning-making rather than on truth. Scholars in a range of fields are examining narrative in connection with making-meaning—for example, in cultural anthropology (e.g., Clifford, 1986; Geertz, 1983, 1988; Rosaldo, 1989; Van Maanen, 1995), education (e.g., McLaren, 1991), graphics and visual communication (e.g., Tufte, 1997), historiography (e.g., H. White, 1987); management (e.g., Czarniawska-Joerges, 1992), organizational communication (e.g., Brown, 1986; Mumby, 1987, 1993), political science (e.g., Bennett & Edelman, 1985), psychology (e.g., Bruner, 1986, 1987; Gergen & Gergen, 1983), sociology (e.g., Maines, 1993; Maines & Bridger, 1992; Richardson, 1988, 1995), and communication studies (e.g., Bormann, 1985; Fisher, 1984; Hymes, 1996; Kerby, 1991).

Despite differences in subject and in disciplinary perspective, these scholars agree with Lyotard's (1979/1993) postmodernist rejection of metanarratives (p. xxiv). In doing so, they prefer to examine stories—or as Geertz (1983) terms them, "shapes of knowledge"—that are "always ineluctably local, indivisible from their instruments and their encasements" (p. 4), and that, as Mumby (1993) says, "continuously challenge the stability" of what we believe we know (p. 3). Additionally, these scholars also agree that narrative is important as a way of thinking and communicating and as a means of conceptualizing, lending meaning to, and constructing experience—whether that experience results from ethnographic fieldwork, from analyses of culture or texts, from workplace or pedagogical practice, or from other venues.

By connecting with this vital interdisciplinary community, academic and workplace researchers will, we claim, be freed to consider topics that have previously been excluded from attention.

Considering Excluded Topics

The failure to grant narrative serious scholarly attention has, we believe, been accompanied by the exclusion of a range of topics from our consideration. Most obviously, feminist scholars assert that, as narrative ways of knowing have been marginalized, women's experiences and some types of discourse often produced by women (e.g., diaries, journals, and letters) have suffered scholarly neglect as well. Bringing narrative from the margins to the center will, we believe, open up possibilities for feminist research while also, as Graham and Lay argue in this collection, expanding the borders of professional discourse to include texts that women have traditionally authored and giving a voice to those whom—in our privileging of logic and science and our inclination toward an objectivist view of rhetoric—we have tended to ignore.

Perhaps not quite so obviously, however, failing to grant narrative serious scholarly attention has denied academic and workplace researchers access to important work on the topic of the political nature of reality construction. As we discussed earlier, the identities of social groups and the subjectivities of those who belong to these groups are produced and reproduced in part by narrative, which is found in all cultures throughout time (Barthes, 1966, p. 79) and as such is integral to the construction of human life. Rather than being politically innocent, then, narrative is implicated in complex and contradictory ways in "an ongoing 'struggle over meaning'" (Mumby, 1987, p. 5) and in issues of power. "The social construction of reality," says Mumby, is "the product of the complex relations among narrative, power, and culture" (pp. 6–7)—relations that "are always open to," and indeed always subject to "contestation and change" (p. 6).

By viewing narrative from this more complex perspective involving reality construction, power, and the struggle over meaning, academic and workplace researchers will, we believe, be able to shed additional light on the settings and discourses they examine, thus enriching our knowledge base concerning professional communication and expanding our field's understanding of the world. In addition, because these issues of reality construction, power, and struggle are germane to the writing researchers do, a focus on narrative will, we claim, empower them to write in less objectivist ways.

Writing in Less Objectivist Ways

As we have also discussed previously, ethnographic theorists (e.g., Clifford, 1986; McLaren, 1991; Rosaldo, 1989) point to researchers' propensity for objectivizing when telling the story of the other. When objectivizing, says McLaren, researchers "ignore the partiality of their own perspectives that assign cultural otherness to certain groups in order to render invisible how such a practice is often a form of ideological violence and an exercise of the power to dominate" (p. 161). Researchers thus make themselves "the privileged reference point for judging not only the cultural and social practices under [their] gaze but also those who engage in them" (p. 161), while ignoring the reference points and the voices of the participants in the research.

This tendency to privilege the researcher—rather than viewing the researcher as positioned (Rosaldo, 1989, p. 8) and the researcher's perspective as partial (Clifford, 1986, p. 7)—may result in some of the objectivist rhetoric that we claim can be found in professional communication. As McLaren (1991) says, "discourses...derive their meaning from the power relations of which they are a part" (p. 151). Power relations that involve dominating and marginalizing participants rather than viewing them as coconstructors of knowledge and of the research narrative are consistent with objectivist writing.

By considering narrative, however, as implicated in a struggle over meaning, academic and workplace researchers may be sensitized to the potential for domination and objectivism inherent in the research process. They may then follow the lead of scholars in other fields who are considering less objectivist ways of writing.

In sociology, for example, Richardson (1988) focuses on telling a "collective story"—telling, that is, "the experience of a socially constructed category of people in the context of larger sociocultural and historical forces"—for the purposes of "break[ing] down isolation between people, empower[ing] them, and lead[ing] to collective action" (p. 201). Similarly, in cultural anthropology, Rosaldo (1989) uses "personal experience as an analytic category" in order to narrate the story of Ilongot head-hunting. Positioned by his own experience with grief to better understand the Ilongots' rage and their subsequent desire to hunt heads, Rosaldo views his story as "an act of mourning" and "a personal report," as well as an ethnographic narrative (p. 11). Says Rosaldo: "Such terms as *objectivity, neutrality,* and *partiality* refer to subject positions once endowed with great institutional authority, but they are arguably neither more nor less valid than those of more engaged, yet equally perceptive, knowledgeable social actors" (p. 21).

Focusing on narrative may, we believe, lead academic and workplace researchers to similar insights and thus to less objectivist forms of writing that may be more suitable to the kinds of knowledge some scholars wish to convey and to the politics of their research situations.

In addition to these benefits that may accrue to researchers, however, a narrative turn may also be advantageous for teachers, trainers, and workplace professionals.

Teachers, Trainers, and Workplace Professionals

Teachers, trainers, and workplace professionals will, we claim, benefit from a narrative turn in a number of ways. For example, by encouraging teachers and trainers to refocus their pedagogy on professional communication as knowledge-making, a narrative turn will, we believe, revitalize classroom and workplace teaching. We further believe that a narrative turn will enable teachers, trainers, and workplace professionals to understand the importance and implications for communication of change in workplace settings, and that narrative will greatly assist with managing information for databases and Web environments. Finally, we claim that narrative can help build relationships in workplace settings, especially those where innovation and creative problem solving are valued.

Refocusing Pedagogy: Professional Communication as Knowledge-Making

Professional communication courses, both as service courses for other majors and as courses for English majors, have typically been skills-oriented, teaching practical, applicable workplace techniques; promoting correctness; endorsing template filling; and subordinating writing to the work that it supports, describes, and promotes (Johnson-Eilola, 1996; Selber, 1995). As we discussed earlier, this teaching approach aligns with the devaluing of narrative in a skills-oriented view of writing. We suggest, however, that a narrative perspective can help teachers and trainers refocus this pedagogy.

We join with Johnson-Eilola (1996) in his argument that too often, professional-communication pedagogy reinforces an outdated "self-deprecating, industrial approach" (p. 245) rather than preparing students and professionals for a postindustrial workplace where employees are valued as "symbolic-analytical" (p. 245) or knowledge workers (for example, Drucker, 1993; Stewart, 1997; Toffler, 1990). The challenge is, then, to help professional communication students and workplace professionals acquire "the abilities to identify, rearrange, circulate, abstract, and broker information...[to] deal with situations not easily addressed by routine solutions" (Johnson-Eilola, 1996, p. 255). In other words, students and workplace professionals must understand that their communications and processes make knowledge and that a narrative perspective can help them with that knowledge-making.

To be knowledge makers, student and professional writers need to think of their communication situation as a narrative opportunity. Rather than defaulting to standard forms, styles, and approaches, they can consider narrative issues usually absent from professional communication: How do I engage my reader in my story , fashioning it appropriately for this communication situation? What effect does the storytelling have on this information? Who is the narrator, and am I in this story? How should I portray the characters in my story? How do I best design this story line—where does the story begin and end, to what extent can I rearrange time sequence, and where do I expand, compress, and connect? Can I include visuals and graphs as part of my story?

In guiding students and workplace professionals to consider issues such as these, teachers and trainers can help them think about knowledge-making as narrative, with different kinds and degrees of descriptive details, voices, tones, characterizations, plot lines, and narrator presences. (See Forman, in this collection, for more indepth discussion of the issues a narrative perspective raises for professional communication pedagogy.)

When teachers and trainers help students and workplace professionals realize that the knowledge they are making is a narrative—whether they are explaining a new software application or making recommendations based on sales forecasts—they can better understand that, as Barton and Barton (1988) explain, communication problems do not occur because of conflicts "between modes of discourse, one narrational and the other nonnarrational, for both discourses are ultimately narrational" (p. 44). The old binary of narrative and nonnarrative/analytical is inadequate for today's knowledge makers; they need to consider more communication issues and make more rhetorical decisions. As teachers and trainers, our starting point is to help students and workplace professionals learn "how best to get an honest story honestly told" (Geertz, 1988, p. 9).

When we understand professional communication as knowledge-making and a narrative perspective as a catalyst for this rethinking, change is inevitable. Therefore, a narrative turn will, we claim, help teachers, trainers, and workplace professionals understand communication as change.

Understanding Professional Communication as Change

We have speculated about causes for the devaluing of narrative in professional communication; many of these causes also support a static view of communication. Classification systems such as the modes of discourse reinforce the concept of communications as codifiable in unchanging categories. This static view has also been reinforced in business and industry by scientific approaches or systems of management. The aim of Taylor's scientific management, for example, is to break work down into discrete units of production, increase these units' efficiency, and thereby optimize the overall mechanism; the analogy for work is a machine—solid and unchanging. This lack of change, and therefore the static nature of communication, depend on implications of timelessness and decontextualization—and thus on the absence of narrative.

Today's professional environment, however, is not one of static classifications, efficiencies, or preservation. Professional communication happens within and, concurrently, creates change. Research in our field is just beginning to reflect the effects of change (for example, Capps, 1993; Dulye, 1993; Freed, 1993; Gatien, 1990; Hansen, 1992; Redish, 1995; Rogers & Allbritton, 1995; Sopensky & Modrey, 1995). As with most of the other researchers writing about change in the professional environment, Tebeaux (1989) contemplates the impact of innovations on communication technologies, organizational restructurings, and the very way that work is accomplished in an Information Age.

Although researchers in professional communication are just beginning to be influenced by the concept of change in professional environments and to contemplate the effects on our field—that is, on how we communicate in the workplace and on what we teach—popular business publications are motivated by, focused on, and fueling change. Many publications are written by acknowledged change agents—business leaders, consultants, and academics who are engaging readers and firing their imaginations and workplace actions (for example, Bergquist, 1993; Davidow & Malone, 1992; Drucker, 1993; Hammer & Champy, 1993; Kanter, 1989; Peters, 1992; Savage, 1990; Taylor & Wacker, 1997; Toffler, 1990). Of these change agents, Taylor and Wacker (1997) tell one of the strongest stories of change.

Although they are writing primarily for a business audience, their descriptions of change and its implications are inclusive: "It is the work of the tributaries that we take up here—the convergence of changes in values, motives, perspectives, communications, information, lifestyles, and empathy that are both driving and being merged into the meta-changes in logic, organization, and economics" (p. 63).

We believe that narrative and change of the kind Taylor and Wacker (1997) describe are interdependent. Indeed, we claim that narrative is requisite for change. For both, context (place and space) and movement (time) are key aspects. Today's workplace offers countless examples of this relationship between narrative and change. An obvious one is the importance placed on company vision statements. Although strategic and incremental planning are not new to businesses, vision statements and their development are now recognized as important for engendering organizational change. A vision statement is a company's narrative of where it is going, and, often, how it will get there. Creating a viable vision statement means recognizing needs and telling a good story of change. While vision statements don't guarantee improvement for employees or their communities, change offers potential.

Narrative can also help us manage one of the most pervasive causes of change: technological innovations, especially those in computing technologies, which now mandate the managing of information for databases and Web environments.

Managing Information for Databases and Web Environments

Although as teachers, trainers, and workplace professionals, we may be unsure of our exact roles in technological change, we are without doubt connected to these changes through expertise with language and communication. We help build, manipulate, and access databases and design the new Web-style logics and communications that are redefining personal lives, education, and business. A narrative perspective is valuable for conceptualizing and working with databases, Internet sites, intranets, and extranets, for knowledge management.

Data or chunks of data might represent an interpretable narrative; however, data more usually appears as static, discrete, and decontextualized information. A narrative perspective is needed to add context, significance, elements of sequence or of time, plot lines, characters, and narrators—all essential aspects of creating relations and thereby making meaning. As Mok (1996) writes about the convergence of business designs, technologies, and information structuring, he makes a case for the importance of narrative:

> Computing technology moves information around in enormous volumes and at high speeds; if information is directed at everyone and no one in particular, it can easily be severed from origin and meaning. Without context and purpose, information is mere data. Information has become a product that requires designers who can give the narrative structure and context with social purpose and intellectual economy. (p. 16)

A number of other researchers have made narrative connections to computing technologies. For example, Laurel (1993) introduces the idea of computers as theater to enhance and guide the design of computer interfaces, adding a storied approach that has beginnings, middles, and ends as a way to help humans engage with the interfaces they see on their computer screens. Hawkes (1994) suggests that the concept of scenario is helpful in developing hypertext documents, especially as a way to include Burkean rhetorical theory that takes into account the variable possibilities of language due to the interaction of individuals, objects, and courses of events (p. 240). Lopuck (1996) identifies eight models for structuring multimedia. One of these models is interactive stories, which entails giving the audience control over the presentation through decision points and designing story lines that are both linear and branching. All of these examples indicate how narrative elements help designers and their audiences make sense of, navigate, and interact with computer capabilities.

Professional communicators will increasingly require a narrative perspective for making databases and websites meaningful, accessible, and navigable for users. These professional communicators can meet the challenge of data management, turning pieces of data into knowledge or meaning, by creating narrative connections, flow, and story lines. Too often the databases in which organizations attempt to store their organizational knowledge and history fail to provide the really significant learnings that could guide future work. For example, a database might include all of the details about a past project: dates, places, names of people involved, even documents that were written for the project. The organizational learnings, however, are meager from this kind of information. When a similar project comes up again, the people involved will want to know the answers to questions such as these: What worked? What didn't? What can we do better this time? They need narrative details to better understand and apply past experiences.

Electronic Web communication also benefits from a narrative perspective. While the medium forces designers to think about narrative structures and options as they create links for users to move linearly, hierarchically, or in iterative Web fashion, aware and reflective designers will consider the most appropriate and creative options rather than relying only on what others have done. Place/space and time/movement are inherent in Web design, and narrative is foregrounded rather than assumed.

Perhaps even more challenging than creating and managing databases and Web environments through narrative is building human relationships.

Building Human Relationships

In a time of radical change and fragmentation of assumed business and industry standards, procedures, and structures, narrative offers advantages for enhancing human relationships. Ten years ago, Barton and Barton (1988) noted the fragmentation of modern business structures and the need for alternative forms of communication:

The old view of organizations as monoliths, with commonality and convergence of goals, is now largely discredited.... One finds, rather, an increasing recognition of pluralism in organizations, of politically-based coalitions with competing goals, and a recognition as well of the need for new communication models to foster negotiation and compromise. (p. 45)

In conjunction with this call for new models of communication, Barton and Barton recognize narrative as a "promising candidate," noting that narrative can help organizations function, enable them to resolve internal conflicts and solve problems, promote tolerance for others' views, and assist with "acculturating employees" (p. 45).

In addition to benefits for an organization's internal communications and relationships, Taylor and Wacker (1997) write about the need for businesses to create "dimensionality" (p. 112), or relationships of trust, with their customers. They contend that "dimensionality is established in three ways: through physical illustrations and objects...through statistics...and most intriguingly and centrally, through myth, through storytelling" (p. 113). Of these, they claim that the most effective and believable way to establish trust is through narrative.

With accelerated moves toward, for example, outsourcing, bundling of businesses and services, globalization, and innovative business designs, the need for a narrative perspective is as relevant today for professional communication as it was 10 years ago. These business and industry changes mean that human relationships and communications are also changing. Businesses need new relationships with outsource providers who may be less involved in the core business. Employees of different business cultures are frequently thrust together as a result of mergers and alliances and need skills in forming overarching relationships. Communicators need increasingly to forge relationships with coworkers and customers in a diversity of locations around the world, and most businesses today are motivated to form innovative relationships with customers to build loyalty.

These examples all call for communication that "foster(s) negotiation and compromise" (Barton & Barton, 1988, p. 45) and therefore a narrative perspective. For narrative to be integral in developing and advancing relationships, the aspects we have been forwarding all along come into play: narrative and the construction of self, narrative and the construction of knowledge. Relationships are built on actively making knowledge for and of ourselves and others—on building shared understanding as best we can.

CONCLUSION

We believe that these benefits to academic and workplace researchers, as well as to teachers, trainers, and workplace professionals, argue strongly for the value of narrative and for the wisdom of continuing a narrative turn in professional communication. Indeed, we predict that, 10 years in the future, our field will no longer be marked by the muteness Barton and Barton (1988) noted. Rather, we foresee a burgeoning of interest in narrative, as the factors contributing to its devaluing increasingly lose their influence and researchers, teachers and trainers, and workplace professionals are freed to recognize narrative's considerable strengths.

But that, as Barton and Barton (1988) say, is another story—one that the contributors to this collection have taken up in their efforts to understand narrative and its relationship to professional communication.

NOTES

[1] The 11 journals we examined are *College Composition and Communication, College English, IEEE Transactions on Professional Communication, Journal of Advanced Composition, Journal of Business Communication, Journal of Business and Technical Communication, Journal of Technical Writing and Communication, Rhetoric Review, Technical Communication, Technical Communication Quarterly,* and *Written Communication.*

[2] For example, Houp, Pearsall, and Tebeaux (1995) move through techniques of informing from chronological arrangement to arguing; Pattow and Wresch (1993) order writing techniques as follows: technical definition, description, process description, summary, analysis, argumentation; White (1996) organized separate chapters on "Basic Rhetorical Techniques I: Presenting Information Clearly and Accurately" with subsections on defining and categorizing terms, describing the characteristics, and narrating events and "Basic Rhetorical Techniques II: Argument in Technical Writing."

[3] In Kinneavy, Cope, and Campbell's (1976) well-known diagram of this system, each of the modes is arranged along a side of a rectangle representing reality. They explain that "any one mode gives only a partial account of reality, that each mode needs to be supplemented by the other modes to make any pretense to a full account" (p. 9).

REFERENCES

Anderson, P. V. (1991). *Technical writing: A reader-centered approach* (3rd ed.). Fort Worth, TX: Harcourt Brace Jovanovich.

Anderson, P. V., Brockmann, R. J., & Miller, C. R. (1983). Introduction. In P. Anderson, R. J. Brockmann, & C. R. Miller (Eds.), *New essays in technical and scientific communication: Research, theory, practice* (pp. 7–14). Farmingdale, NY: Baywood.

Andrews, D., & Andrews, W. (1992). *Business communication* (2nd ed.). New York: Macmillan.

Barthes, R. (1966). Introduction to the structural analysis of narrative. In *Images—music—text* (pp. 79–124). New York: Hill and Wang.

Barton, B. F., & Barton, M. S. (1988). Narration in technical communication. *Journal of Business and Technical Communication, 2*(1), 36–48.

Belenky, M. F., Clinchy, B. M., Goldberger, N. R., & Tarule, J. M. (1986). Introduction: To the other side of silence. In M. F. Belenky, B. M. Clinchy, N. R. Goldberger, & J. M. Tarule

(Eds.), *Women's ways of knowing: The development of self, voice, and mind* (pp. 3–20). New York: Basic Books.

Bennett, W. L., & Edelman, M. (1985). Toward a new political narrative. *Journal of Communication, 35*(4), 156–171.

Bergquist, W. (1993). *The postmodern organization: Mastering the art of irreversible change.* San Francisco: Jossey-Bass.

Bizzell, P., & Herzberg, B. (Eds.). (1990). *The rhetorical tradition: Readings from classical times to the present.* Boston: Bedford Books.

Blyler, N. R. (1992). Narration and knowledge in direct solicitations. *Technical Communication Quarterly, 1*, 59–72.

Blyler, N. R. (1995). Pedagogy and social action: A role for narrative in professional communication. *Journal of Business and Technical Communication, 9*, 289–320.

Blyler, N. R. (1996). Narrative and research in professional communication. *Journal of Business and Technical Communication, 10*, 330–351.

Boone, L., Kurtz, D., & Black, J. (1994). *Contemporary business communication.* Englewood Cliffs, NJ: Prentice Hall.

Bormann, E. G. (1985). The critical analysis of seminal American fantasies. In *The force of fantasy: Restoring the American dream* (pp. 1–25). Carbondale, IL: Southern Illinois University Press.

Bovee, C., & Thill, J. (1995). *Business communication today* (4th ed.). New York: McGraw-Hill.

Britton, W. E. (1975). What is technical writing? A redefinition. In D. H. Cunningham & H. A. Estrin (Eds.), *The teaching of technical writing* (pp. 9–14). Urbana, IL: National Council of Teachers of English.

Brown, M. H. (1986). Sense making and narrative forms: Reality construction in organizations. In L. Thayer (Ed.), *Organization—communication: Emerging perspectives I* (pp. 71–84). Norwood, NJ: Ablex.

Bruner, J. (1986). *Actual minds, possible worlds.* Cambridge, MA: Harvard University Press.

Bruner, J. (1987). Life as narrative. *Social Research, 54*, 11–32.

Bruner, J. (1991). The narrative construction of reality. *Critical Inquiry, 18*, 1–21.

Brusaw, C., Alfred, G., & Oliu, W. (1997). *Handbook of technical writing* (5th ed.). New York: St. Martin's Press.

Capps, R. (1993). Communicating sudden change in tasks and culture: The Inglis Montmagny story. *IEEE Transactions on Professional Communication, 36*(1), 30–34.

Carrell, D. (1991). Gender scripts in professional writing textbooks. *Journal of Business and Technical Communication, 5*, 463–468.

Cintron, R. (1993). Wearing a pith helmet at a sly angle, or, can writing researchers do ethnography in a postmodern era? *Written Communication, 10*, 371–412.

Clifford, J. (1986). Introduction—partial truths. In J. Clifford & G. E. Marcus (Eds.), *Writing and culture: The poetics and politics of ethnography* (pp. 1–26). Berkeley, CA: University of California Press.

Connors, R. J. (1982). The rise of technical writing instruction in America. *Journal of Technical Writing and Communication, 12*, 329–352.

Connors, R. J. (1988). The rise and fall of the modes of discourse. In G. Tate & E. Corbett (Eds.), *The writing teacher's sourcebook* (pp. 24–34). New York: Oxford University Press. (Reprinted from *College Composition and Communication, 32,* 444–455)

Cross, G. A. (1994). Ethnographic research in business and technical writing: Between extremes and margins. *Journal of Business and Technical Communication, 8,* 118–134.

Czarniawska-Joerges, B. (1992). *Exploring complex organizations: A cultural perspective.* Newbury Park, CA: Sage.

Dasenbrock, R. W. (1987). J. L. Austin and the articulation of a new rhetoric. *College Composition and Communication, 38,* 291–305.

Davidow, W., & Malone, M. (1992). *The virtual corporation: Structuring and revitalizing the corporation for the 21st century.* New York: HarperCollins.

DiPardo, A. (1990). Narrative knowers, expository knowledge: Discourse as dialectic. *Written Communication, 7,* 59–94.

Dobrin, D. N. (1983). What's technical about technical writing? In P. Anderson, R. J. Brockmann, & C. R. Miller (Eds.), *New essays in technical and scientific communication: Research, theory, practice* (pp. 227–250). Farmingdale, NY: Baywood.

Dragga, S. (1993). Women and the profession of technical writing: Social and economic influences and implications. *Journal of Business and Technical Communication, 7,* 312–322.

Drucker, P. (1954). *The practice of management.* New York: HarperBusiness.

Drucker, P. (1993). *Post-capitalist society.* New York: HarperCollins.

Dulye, L. (1993). Toward better two-way: Why communications process improvement represents the right response during uncertain times. *IEEE Transactions on Professional Communication, 36*(1), 24–29.

Ehrenhaus, P. (1993). Cultural narratives and the therapeutic motif: The political containment of Vietnam veterans. In D. K. Mumby (Ed.), *Narrative and social control: Critical perspectives* (pp. 77–96). Newbury Park, CA: Sage.

Eisenberg, A. (1992). *Effective technical communication* (2nd ed.). New York: McGraw-Hill.

Faigley, L., Cherry, R., Jolliffe, D., & Skinner, A. (1985). *Assessing writers' knowledge and processes of composing.* Norwood, NJ: Ablex.

Fish, S. (1989). *Doing what comes naturally.* Durham, NC: Duke University Press.

Fisher, W. R. (1984). Narration as a human communication paradigm: The case of public moral argument. *Communication Monographs, 51,* 1–22.

Flower, L. (1979). Writer-based prose: A cognitive basis for problems in writing. *College English, 41,* 19–37.

Flower, L., Hayes, J. R., & Swarts, H. (1983). Revising functional documents: The scenario principle. In P. Anderson, R. J. Brockmann, & C. R. Miller (Eds.), *New essays in technical and scientific communication: Research, theory, practice* (pp. 41–58). Farmingdale, NY: Baywood.

Flynn, E. A. (1995). Feminism and science. *College Composition and Communication, 46,* 353–368.

Forman, J. (1993). Business communication and composition: The writing connection and beyond. *Journal of Business Communication, 30,* 333–352.

Freed, R. (1993). Postmodern practice: Prospectives and prospects. In N. Blyler & C. Thralls (Eds.), *Professional communication: The social perspective* (pp. 196–214). Newbury Park, CA: Sage.

Galindo, R., & Brown, C. (1995). Person, place, and narrative in an Amish farmer's appropriation of nature writing. *Written Communication, 12*, 147–185.

Galle, W., Nelson, B., Luse, D., & Villere, M. (1996). *Business communication: A technology-based approach.* Chicago: Irwin.

Gatien, G. (1990). Managing in the new corporate environment. *Technical Communication, 37*, 415–419.

Geertz, C. (1983). *Local knowledge.* New York: Basic Books.

Geertz, C. (1988). *Works and lives: The anthropologist as author.* Stanford, CA: Stanford University Press.

Gergen, K. J., & Gergen, M. M. (1983). Narratives of the self. In T. R. Sarbin & K. E. Scheibe (Eds.), *Studies of social identity* (pp. 254–273). New York: Praeger.

Goodall, H. L. *Casing a promised land.* Carbondale, IL: Southern Illinois University Press, 1994.

Gregson, G., & Selzer, J. (1990). Fictionalizing the readers of scholarly articles in biology. *Written Communication, 7*, 25–58.

Hagge, J. (1995). Early engineering writing textbooks and the anthropological complexity of disciplinary discourse. *Written Communication, 12*, 439–491.

Halloran, S. M. (1978). Technical writing and the rhetoric of science. *Journal of Technical Writing and Communication, 8*, 77–88.

Hammer, M., & Champy, J. (1993). *Reengineering the corporation: A manifesto for business revolution.* New York: HarperBusiness.

Hansen, C. (1992). Communication technologies in corporate settings. *The Bulletin of the Association of Business Communication, 55*(4), 3–9.

Harbarger, S. A., Dumble, W. R., Hildreth, W. H., & Emsley, B. (1938). *English for students in applied sciences.* New York: McGraw-Hill.

Harbarger, S. A., Whitmer, A. B., & Price, R. (1943). *English for engineers.* New York: McGraw-Hill.

Harding, S. (1987). Introduction: Is there a feminist method? In S. Harding (Ed.), *Feminism and methodology: Social science issues* (pp. 1–14). Bloomington, IN: Indiana University Press.

Harris, J. S. (1978). Expanding the definition of technical writing. *Journal of Technical Writing and Communication, 8*, 133–138.

Hawkes, L. (1994). Nested dialogues. *IEEE Transactions on Professional Communication, 37*, 240–244.

Henry, J., & "G." (1995). Workplace ghostwriting. *Journal of Business and Technical Communication, 9*, 425–445.

Houp, K., Pearsall, T., & Tebeaux, E. (1995). *Reporting technical information* (8th ed.). Boston: Allyn and Bacon.

Hymes, D. (1996). *Ethnography, linguistics, narrative inequality: Toward an understanding of voice.* London: Taylor & Francis.

Johnson-Eilola, J. (1996). Relocating the value of work: Technical communication in a post-industrial age. *Technical Communication Quarterly, 5*, 245–270.

Journet, D. (1990). Forms of discourse and the sources of the mind: Luria, Sacks, and the role of narrative in neurological case histories. *Written Communication, 7*, 171–199.

Journet, D. (1991). Ecological theories as cultural narratives. *Written Communication, 8*, 446–472.

Kanter, R. M. (1989). The new managerial work. *Harvard Business Review, 67*(6), 85–92.

Kelley, P. M., & Masse, R. E. (1977). A definition of technical writing. *Technical Writing Teacher, 4*, 94–97.

Kent, T. (1993). *Paralogic rhetoric: A theory of communicative interaction.* Lewisburg, PA: Bucknell University Press.

Kerby, A. P. (1991). *Narrative and the self.* Bloomington, IN: Indiana University Press.

Killingsworth, M. J. (1996). *Information in action: A guide to technical communication.* Boston: Allyn and Bacon.

Kinneavy, J., Cope, J., & Campbell, J. W. (1976). *Writing—Basic modes of discourse.* Dubuque, IA: Kendall Hunt.

Laurel, B. (1993). *Computers as theatre.* Reading, MA: Addison-Wesley.

Lay, M. M. (1991). Feminist theory and the redefinition of technical communication. *Journal of Business and Technical Communication, 5*, 348–370.

Lay, M. M. (1993). Gender studies: Implications for the professional communication classroom. In N. R. Blyler & C. Thralls (Eds.), *Professional communcation: The social perspective* (pp. 215–229). Newbury Park, CA: Sage.

Lay, M., Wahlstrom, B., Duin, A., Little, S., Selfe, C., Selzer, J., Rude, C., & Doheny-Farina, S. (1995). *Technical communication.* Chicago: Irwin.

Ledwell-Brown, J., & Dias, P. X. (1994). The way we do things: The significance of narrative in research interviews. *Journal of Business and Technical Communication, 8*, 165–185.

Limaye, M. R. (1983). Redefining business and technical writing by means of a six-factored communication model. *Journal of Technical Writing and Communication, 13*, 331–338.

Locker, K. O. (1994). The challenge of interdisciplinary research. *Journal of Business Communication, 31*, 137–151.

Lopuck, L. (1996). *Designing multimedia.* Berkeley, CA: Peachpit Press.

Lyotard, J.-F. (1993). *The postmodern condition: A report on knowledge* (G. Bennington & B. Massumi, Trans.). Minneapolis, MN: University of Minnesota Press. (Original work published 1979)

Maines, D. R. (1993). Narrative's moment and sociology's phenomena: Toward a narrative sociology. *Sociological Quarterly, 34*, 17–38.

Maines, D. R., & Bridger, J. C. (1992). Narratives, community and land use decisions. *Social Science Journal, 29*, 363–380.

Marcus, G., & Fischer, M. (1986). *Anthropology as cultural critique: An experimental moment in the human sciences.* Chicago: University of Chicago Press.

McLaren, P. (1991). Field relations and the discourse of the other: Collaboration in our own ruin. In W. B. Shaffir & R. A. Stebbins (Eds.), *Experiencing fieldwork: An inside view of qualitative research* (pp. 149–163). Newbury Park, CA: Sage.

Meese, G., & Wahlstrom, B. (1988). Designing graduate programs to prepare the communication leaders of 2000+. *Journal of Business and Technical Communication, 2*(1), 21–35.

Miller, C. R. (1979). A humanistic rationale for technical writing. *College English, 40*, 610–617.

Miller, T. P. (1991). Treating professional writing as social praxis. *Journal of Advanced Composition, 11*, 57–72.

Mok, C. (1996). *Designing business: Multiple media, multiple disciplines.* San Jose, CA: Adobe Press.

Mumby, D. K. (1987). The political function of narratives in organizations. *Communication Monographs, 54*, 113–127.

Mumby, D. K. (1993). Introduction: Narrative and social control. In D. K. Mumby (Ed.), *Narrative and social control: Critical perspectives* (pp. 1–12). Newbury Park, CA: Sage.

Park, C. W. (1932). *English applied in technical writing.* New York: F. S. Crofts.

Pattow, D., & Wresch, W. (1993). *Communicating technical information: A guide for the electronic age.* Englewood Cliffs, NJ: Prentice Hall.

Pauley, S., & Riordan, D. (1990). *Technical report writing today* (4th ed.). Boston: Houghton Mifflin.

Peters, T. (1992). *Liberation management: Necessary disorganization for the nanosecond nineties.* New York: Alfred A. Knopf.

Rabinow, P., & Sullivan, W. (1987). The interpretive turn: Emergence of an approach. In P. Rabinow & W. Sullivan (Eds.), *Interpretive social science: A second look* (pp. 1–30). Berkeley: University of California Press.

Redish, J. (1995). Adding value as a professional technical communicator. *Technical Communication, 42*, 26–39.

Rentz, K. C. (1992). The value of narrative in business writing. *Journal of Business and Technical Communication, 6*, 293–315.

Rentz, K. C. (1993). Editorial: Negotiating the field of business communication. *Journal of Business Communication, 30*, 233–240.

Richardson, L. (1988). The collective story: Postmodernism and the writing of sociology. *Sociological Focus, 21*, 199–208.

Richardson, L. (1995). Narrative and sociology. In J. Van Maanen (Ed.), *Representation in Ethnography* (pp. 198–221). London: Sage.

Ritzer, G. (1993). *The McDonaldization of society.* Thousand Oaks, CA: Pine Forge Press.

Rogers, E., & Allbritton, M. (1995). Interactive communication technologies in business organizations. *Journal of Business Communication, 32*, 177–195.

Rorty, R. (1987). Science as solidarity. In J. S. Nelson, A. Megill, & D. N. McCloskey (Eds.), *The rhetoric of the human sciences* (pp. 38–52). Madison, WI: University of Wisconsin Press.

Rosaldo, R. (1989). *Culture and truth: The remaking of social analysis.* Boston: Beacon Press.

Rutter, R. (1991). History, rhetoric, and humanism: Toward a more comprehensive definition of technical communication. *Journal of Technical Writing and Communication, 21*, 133–153.

Savage, C. (1990). *Fifth generation management: Integrating enterprises through human networking.* Maynard, MA: Digital Press.

Selber, S. (1995). Beyond skill building: Challenges facing technical communication teachers in the computer age. *Technical Communication Quarterly, 3*, 365–390.

Scholes, R. (1985). *Textual power: Literary theory and the teaching of English.* New Haven, CT: Yale University Press.

Selzer, J. (1993). Introduction. In J. Selzer (Ed.), *Understanding scientific prose* (pp. 3–19). Madison, WI: University of Wisconsin Press.

Sopensky, E., & Modrey, L. (1995). Survival skills for communicators within organizations. *Journal of Business and Technical Communication, 9*, 103–115.

Stewart, T. (1997). *Intellectual capital: The new wealth of organizations.* New York: Doubleday/Currency.

Sullivan, D. L. (1990). Political-ethical implications of defining technical communication as a practice. *Journal of Advanced Composition, 10*, 375–386.

Taylor, J., & Wacker, W. (1997). *The 500-year delta: What happens after what comes next.* New York: HarperCollins.

Tebeaux, E. (1989). The high-tech workplace: Implications for technical communication instruction. In B. Fearing & W. K. Sparrow (Eds.), *Technical writing: Theory and practice* (pp. 136–144). New York: Modern Language Association.

Tebeaux, E. (1993). Technical writing for women of the English Renaissance: Technology, literacy, and the emergence of a genre. *Written Communication, 10*, 164–199.

Timm, P., & DeTienne, K. (1995). *Managerial communication: A finger on the pulse* (3rd ed.). Englewood Cliffs, NJ: Prentice Hall.

Toffler, A. (1990). *Powershift: Knowledge, wealth, and violence at the end of the 21st century.* New York: Bantam.

Tufte, E. (1997) *Visual explanations: Images and quantities, evidence and narrative.* Cheshire, CT: Graphics Press.

Van Maanen, J. (1995). An end to innocence: The ethnography of ethnography. In J. Van Maanen (Ed.), *Representation in ethnography* (pp. 1–35). London: Sage.

Van Maanen, J., Manning, P., & Miller, M. (1990). Introduction. In D. Rose (Ed.), *Living the ethnographic life* (pp. 5–6). Newbury Park, CA: Sage.

Wells, S. (1996). Rogue cops and health care: What do we want from public writing? *College Composition and Communication, 47*, 325–341.

White, F. (1996). *Communicating technology: Dynamic processes and models for writers.* New York: HarperCollins.

White, H. (1987). The value of narrativity in the representation of reality. In *The content of the form: Narrative discourse and historical representation* (pp. 1–25). Baltimore, MD: Johns Hopkins University Press.

Winsor, D. (1993). Owning corporate texts. *Journal of Business and Technical Communication, 7*, 179–195.

Yates, J. (1989). *Control through communication: The rise of system in American management.* Baltimore, MD: Johns Hopkins University Press.

part I
Narrative and Research Methodologies

1

What Can We Learn from a Sample of One?—The Role of Narrative in Case Study Research

Kathryn C. Rentz
University of Cincinnati

A popular kind of research in professional communication has been the in-depth study of the single case. In contrast to experimental research or correlation studies, which draw conclusions from numerous subjects, treat them as comparable rather than unique entities, and pare away extraneous contextual influences, studies of the single case typically have examined a unique individual or constellation of events within its specific, detail-rich, and nonreplicable social setting.

Several factors help explain the attraction of this kind of research for professional communication researchers. In the early 1980s, when serious efforts were being made to inject theory and research into this area of professional practice, the idea that writing was, at least to some extent, an observable process, not just a product, was revolutionizing the field of composition studies. Such researchers as Sondra Perl, Janet Emig, and Linda Flower had begun to popularize the careful study of individuals, and that approach was picked up by researchers in professional writing, many of whom had strong ties to composition. As a field, we have always had an interest in how writing gets made in the workplace, and that interest in process has led us to focus on single writers or acts of writing.

But by the mid- to late-1980s, we also had begun to develop an interest in the social nature of writing, mostly because of the developing theories—in composition, literature, and organizational communication—about the existence of interpretive communities. The publication of Odell and Goswami's *Writing in Nonacademic Settings* (1985) and Matalene's *Worlds of Writing: Teaching and Learning in Discourse Communities of Work* (1989) helped generate a widespread curiosity about the relation between writing and social context. This curiosity has been intensified by our interest in philosophers of language (Bakhtin, Derrida, Foucault); analysts and philosophers of social knowledge (Toulmin, Berger and Luckman), especially in science (Kuhn, Latour and Woolgar); and modern and postmodern ethnographers (Clifford and Marcus, Geertz, Van Maanen). The result has been many observations of writing—as both event and document—in single settings.

Given the importance of this kind of research in our discipline, it benefits us to ask, as education researcher Robert Stake (1994) does, "What can be learned from the single case?" (p. 236). What kind of knowledge can we say that these sorts of studies contribute to the field? Is it possible to generalize from a sample of one? And given the particular focus of this collection, we may further inquire, to what extent is narrative used in these cases, and does the use of narrative influence what kind of knowledge is made or how well it is made?

In order to pursue these lines of inquiry, I decided to examine case studies because this kind of research is well known for focusing on single entities—or on a few entities treated singly, which then are said to constitute a "collective case study" (Stake, 1994, pp. 236–237). The 34 case studies that I analyzed demonstrate that the single case is, in fact, capable of generating five kinds of knowledge, and that the use of narrative is often critical to these efforts.

After explaining how I chose the 34 studies, I will establish what the salient traits of case studies in professional communication seem to be. I will then discuss the role of narrative in the studies' making of knowledge in professional communication.

COLLECTING THE CASE STUDIES

To gather the samples upon which I would base my observations, I first looked for studies in professional communication that are explicitly labeled as case studies. I skimmed selected issues of the main journals that publish professional communication research: *IEEE Transactions on Professional Communication, Journal of Business and Technical Communication, The Journal of Business Communication, Journal of Technical Writing and Communication, Management Communication Quarterly, Technical Communication, Technical Communication Quarterly,* and *Written Communication.* I also read the essays in eight professional communication research anthologies: Anderson, Brockmann, and Miller (1983), Odell and Goswami (1985), Matalene (1989), Bazerman and Paradis (1991), Forman (1992), Blyler and Thralls (1993), Spilka (1993c), and Duin and Hansen (1996). Finally, I included two labeled case studies from other journals—Selzer's "The Composing Processes of an Engineer" in *College Composition and Communication* (1983) and

Miles's 1989 study of the Three-Mile Island crisis in *Issues in Writing*—and two book-length studies identified by their authors as case studies: Doheny-Farina's *Rhetoric, Innovation, Technology: Case Studies of Technical Communication in Technology Transfers* (1992) and Winsor's *Writing Like an Engineer: A Rhetorical Education* (1996). This search yielded 31 studies that were labeled—either by their authors or by their editors—as case studies.

To extend my sample, I read these 31 cases and, on the basis of what I deemed their primary trait—a focus on an entity in its natural setting—added 13 more, for a total of 44 studies that would likely be regarded as case studies in our field. To see if, in fact, my concept of the case study was shared by others in the field, I set up an expert panel consisting of 12 members. Eight of these were present or past editors of professional communication journals: Rebecca Burnett, editor, *Journal of Business and Technical Communication*; Patrice Buzzanell, editor, *Management Communication Quarterly*; Kim Sydow Campbell, editor, *IEEE Transactions in Professional Communication*; Mary Lay, coeditor, *Technical Communication Quarterly*; Kitty Locker, editor, *The Journal of Business Communication*; John Sherblom, past editor, *The Journal of Business Communication*; Charles Sides, editor, *Journal of Technical Writing and Communication*; Charlotte Thralls, past editor, *Journal of Business and Technical Communication*. The remaining four were prolific, award-winning researchers in professional communication: Stephen Doheny-Farina, Janis Forman, Rachel Spilka, and Dorothy Winsor.

After procuring their agreement to serve on the panel, I requested their opinions on whether or not the cases on my list of 44 were case studies. I faxed them the list and asked them to mark any studies that they thought did not belong with a "no"; to mark any that they weren't sure about with a "?" and, if possible, give a brief reason; and to add at the end any case studies that they felt needed to be included. Since I wanted some sense of which studies were well known in the field, I asked the panelists to respond on the basis of their memories, instructing them not to do any additional reading to formulate their responses. I also did not define the terms "case study" or "professional communication" for them, preferring to see what definitions their responses would imply.

Table 1.1 shows the number of affirmative responses that each case received from the 12 panelists. In general, if panelists recognized a study, they affirmed that it was a case study, and two respondents (Forman and Thralls) called all the studies case studies. The studies receiving only a few positive votes were those with which the panel was largely unfamiliar—in particular, the studies from *Journal of Technical Writing and Communication* and *IEEE Transactions in Professional Communication*. Only three "no's" were registered, and they were all on different works. Two panelists (Burnett and Sides) did not complete the survey but did comment on a few of the studies. Burnett felt that there was a distinction between "case studies" and "studies with case-study elements," and was not able, without reviewing the 44 studies, to say which were which—though she did say that Cross (1990) and Locker (1992) were case studies. Sides marked only five studies, all with a "?";

TABLE 1.1.
Number of Affirmative Votes Received by the 44 Studies

Number of "Yes" Votes	Studies in the Survey
9	Cross (1990)*, Ice (1991)
8	Berkenkotter and Huckin (1993)*, Burnett (1996)*, Cross (1993)*, Cross (1994)*, Dautermann (1993)*, Doheny-Farina (1986), Kleimann (1993)*, Locker (1992), Selzer (1983), Spilka (1993b), Winsor (1996)
7	Clark and Doheny-Farina (1990), Doheny-Farina (1989), Doheny-Farina (1992), Huettman (1996), Killingsworth and Steffens (1989), McCarthy (1991)*, Moore (1992), Myers (1985), Paré (1993)*, Segal (1993), Winsor (1990)*, Yates (1985)
6	Alford (1989), Hansen (1996)
5	Broadhead and Freed (1986)*, McCarthy and Gerring (1994)*, Patterson and Lee (1997), Shenk (1994), Thralls (1992), Winsor (1994)*, Zimmerman and Marsh (1989)
4	Lindeborg (1993); Louhiala-Salminen (1997); Ostroff, Donelly, and Fried (1992)
3	Amsden and Amsden (1993), Brown (1994), Brown (1996), Lindeborg (1990), Trimbur and Braun (1992)
2	Eiler (1989), Miles (1989)

Note: All other votes from the 12 panelists were question marks that meant "do not know the study," except for 3 "no" votes (for Broadhead and Freed, 1986; Segal, 1993; and Winsor, 1990) and for 5 question marks from Sides (for Cross, 1990; Doheny-Farina, 1986; Miles, 1989; Myers, 1985; and Winsor, 1996), who thought these 5 studies might be extended examples instead of case studies. Sides marked only these 5 studies, and another panelist, Burnett, marked only 2. An asterisk (*) marks the 13 cases that were not labeled as case studies by their authors and/or editors.

he commented, "The entries I questioned strike me as something other than what I understand a case study to be. In other words, what are the key differences between case studies and extended examples?" With their write-ins, the panelists suggested adding another 19 studies to the list,[1] but none of these was written in by more than one panelist.

I will use the 34 studies that got five or more positive votes as the basis for the analysis that follows (see Table A.1 in the Appendix). But we can observe here that, while there is some dispute about how narrowly to define "case study," the general inclination of the panelists is toward inclusiveness. We can also note that whether or not the case study in question called itself a "case study" appears to have made no difference in the panelists' responses; in fact, of the 13 studies that got the most affirmative votes, 7 had not been labeled by their authors as case studies. Perhaps most noteworthy is the sheer number of studies that are regarded as case studies by the panelists. While 34 studies received five or more positive votes, and in that sense could be seen as the main corpus of case-study research in professional communication, the total number of studies considered to be case studies by at least one panelist was 63 (the 44 case studies on my list plus the 19 that the panelists added). The case study is certainly an important strand of research in professional communication.

THE CASE STUDY IN PROFESSIONAL COMMUNICATION

What constitutes a case study in our field? Since several methodological authorities cited in our case studies are social scientists (for example, Miles & Huberman, 1984; Glaser & Strauss, 1967) or professional communication researchers who cite social scientists (for example, Doheny-Farina & Odell, 1985), I looked to the fields of sociology, anthropology, and education for a definition to test our studies against. While there is some dispute in the social sciences about the nature of case studies (see Ragin & Becker, 1992), Yin's (1984) definition is widely shared: the case study is a study that "investigates a contemporary phenomenon within its real-life context, when the boundaries between phenomenon and context are not clearly evident, and in which multiple sources of evidence are used" (p. 23).

Does this definition accurately describe the case study in professional communication? Judging from the 34 studies in my sample, our cases match the social science profile in most ways, but there are some notable departures. By and large, these exceptions draw on a different research tradition than that of social science: the humanities tradition of close textual and/or rhetorical analysis.

The following sections take up the social scientists' criteria one by one.

Contemporaneity

Only one of the 34 case studies in my sample was clearly an historical study: Yates's (1985) account of the use of graphics at DuPont between 1904 and 1949. One panelist (Locker) commented that she did regard historical case studies as case studies and added two such studies to my questionnaire (Hildebrandt, 1985; Locker, 1985), but, while no panelists gave Yates's study a "no," neither did any other panelists add a case that could be regarded as historical. It is interesting, however, that 7 studies out of the 34, while not exactly historical, were completely retrospective in nature (Ice, 1991; Killingsworth & Steffens, 1989; Patterson & Lee, 1997; Segal, 1993; Shenk,1994; Thralls, 1992; Winsor, 1990)—that is, the phenomena were studied through texts and, sometimes, the researcher's own memory, rather than being observed in real time. Four more researchers reconstituted the past with the help of retrospective interviews with participants (Burnett, 1996; Doheny-Farina, 1992.3.1, 1992.3.2; Locker, 1992; Moore, 1992). Thus, while we can conclude that, as with social science research, the purpose of case study research in professional writing is largely to understand a contemporary phenomenon, we must also note that in 10 of the studies of these phenomena, the event being analyzed had already ended before the researcher's study began.

Focus on a "Phenomenon"

What do case studies in professional communication study? We mostly use case studies to look at processes—for example, why a collaborative writing project failed, or how context influenced composing choices. Out of the 34 case studies, 29 examine processes, and of these, 22-1/3 (the one-third being Doheny-Farina, 1992.1), which essentially replicates his 1986 study) can be said to focus on composing processes—whether those were used by primary authors (see, for example, Huettman, 1996; Myers, 1985; Selzer, 1983), by a collaborative writing group (see, for example, Dautermann, 1993; Doheny-Farina,1986; Locker, 1992), or by an organization (see, for example, Kleimann, 1993; Cross, 1990). The process-focused studies that can't be said to focus primarily on the composing of documents (Burnett, 1996; Clark & Doheny-Farina, 1990; Doheny-Farina, 1992.2, 1992.3.1, 1992.3.2; Moore, 1992; Winsor, 1990; Winsor, 1994; Yates, 1985) nevertheless look at interesting processes related to the production or effects of discourse—for example, the process of transferring a technology from the developers to the users, the rise of graphics in an organization, or the decision-making process behind the *Challenger* accident.

The heavy emphasis on processes accords with the kind of phenomena explored in case studies in the social sciences. In those disciplines and ours, the case study method is typically chosen when the goal is to understand a complex phenomenon as it exists in its natural setting over real time. But we differ strikingly from the social scientists in having a significant body of case studies that focus almost exclusively on what texts reveal. While social science case studies, according to Creswell (1998), require the boundaries of place and time (p. 61), the boundaries of our case studies are sometimes created largely by the boundaries of a document or series of documents. Six of the 34 studies in our study focus on static entities, and 5 of these consist almost exclusively of textual analysis (Ice, 1991; Killingsworth & Steffens, 1989; Patterson & Lee, 1997; Segal, 1993; Shenk, 1994). How can we account for the panelists' affirmation of these five studies as case studies?

A likely answer is that, as professional communication researchers, we are naturally more focused on texts than the social scientists are. The five studies in question cite authorities on rhetorical/discourse analysis (for example, Aristotle, Lanham, Burke, Habermas, Toulmin, Bazerman), not authorities in social science—and in fact, even our case studies that do employ empirical research methods cite textual as well as social science authorities. To a certain extent, then, it makes sense for us to appropriate the term "case study" for our field by having it embrace textual as well as empirical research. But our willingness to call textual analyses case studies makes even more sense when we note that in these textual studies, the texts are being used to suggest larger social processes; for example, a medical text is shown to demonstrate the influence of disciplinary norms (Segal, 1993) or an environmental impact statement is shown to squelch subversive viewpoints through a rhetoric that privileges "balanced" opinions (Patterson & Lee, 1997). Given the prevailing belief in our field that discourse is, besides other things, a form of social action, it is not surprising that we would think of textual analysis as a form of social analysis; one can find "implications of process" (Eiler, 1989, p. 57) in the artifact.

Real-Life Context/Boundaries Between Phenomenon and Context

Case study researchers in professional communication have wholeheartedly embraced the precept that the case study should examine a phenomenon "within its real-life context" when "the boundaries between phenomenon and context are not clearly evident" (Yin, 1984, p. 23). All 34 case studies in our sample demonstrate a strong interest in perceiving the central phenomenon, whether process or static entity, in its natural context, and in showing that the central phenomenon is heavily shaped by, and often shapes, that context.

Yet, context has been construed in different ways in our case studies. Some treat context as a structured environment that generates the exigencies and resources for an individual or group's writing task. The focus of these studies is largely on how the composing gets done in this environment (for example, Broadhead & Freed, 1986; Selzer, 1983). Other articles identify organizational culture—the organization's "pattern of basic assumptions" about "the correct way to perceive, think, and feel" in response to company problems (Schein, 1985, qtd. in Locker, 1992, p. 54)—as a significant determinant of communication processes (see, for example, Hansen, 1996; Locker, 1992). Yet others, taking a broader, social constructionist view, dwell extensively on how "acts of communication define, organize, and maintain social groups." They "view written texts not as detached objects possessing meaning on their own, but as links in communicative chains, with their meaning emerging from their relationships to previous texts and the present context" (Faigley, 1985, p. 235). Context, for this group, is not an external factor that influences communicative process, but the very stuff of any given person or group's reality.

Despite these variations, the studies examine phenomena in multifaceted contexts rather than isolating variables from those contexts and testing them. While social scientists point out that case studies are not necessarily qualitative and naturalistic (Ragin & Becker, 1992; Stake, 1994, 1995), they certainly take that form in our field—that is, if the textual analyses can be said to explore "natural" realms of discourse.

Multiple Sources of Evidence

Our case studies follow a somewhat predictable pattern in their use of sources. The studies focusing on texts as entities as opposed to processes are among the least methodologically various; 6 out of 7 of these (all but Hansen, 1996) depend either on reading of texts, and of earlier comments on similar texts, or on reading coupled with limited interviewing. Three studies of processes use reading almost exclusively

(Moore, 1992; Winsor, 1990; Yates, 1985), and these are about events of such historic remove or national scope that other kinds of methods were probably not feasible.

Five other studies of processes (Burnett, 1996; Locker, 1992; Myers, 1985; Thralls, 1992; Winsor, 1996) rely almost exclusively on written texts and personal interchanges with authors (and sometimes with their supervisors). Most of these researchers are studying the case retroactively rather than observing processes as they are taking place. One study (Clark & Doheny-Farina, 1990) uses feedback on an earlier version of the study and additional theoretical readings as its main sources. Parts of one study (Doheny-Farina, 1992.3.1, 1992.3.2) rely on interviewing alone.

The remaining 17 cases and 2/3 of another one (Doheny-Farina, 1992.1, 1992.2)—with all of them except Hansen (1996) focusing on processes—use mutiple methods and sources, such as formal and informal interviews, discourse-based interviews, direct observation on site, tapes of meetings, drafts of texts, and notes taken by the subjects. Like the qualitative *bricoleur* described by Denzin and Lincoln (1994, p. 2), the researchers use whatever combination of methods and sources seems appropriate, given their research goals and their access to the phenomena under study.

Having tested our case studies against a social-science definition, we can, on the one hand, see why 2 of our 12 expert panelists questioned the principles of selection behind my list of 44 possible case studies. Even the 34 studies that were endorsed by 5 or more panelists include studies whose empiricism is questionable; some of these studies, as we have noted, are entirely retrospective, and some look at texts almost exclusively. Yin (1994) claims that one can "do a valid and high-quality case study without leaving the library and the telephone" (p. 22), but, as he says, he is in the minority in distinguishing the case study from field research.

On the other hand, our studies indicate a powerful interest in naturally occurring phenomena, whether events or texts. In her thoughtful response to my survey, Burnett remarks that one element of case studies is the "underlying assumption" that "complex rhetorical situations cannot be fully or satisfactorily explained/understood by quantitative displays of information," with the related assumption "that some information simply cannot be explained other than through…a discussion of context, actors, agency, and so on" (personal communication, February 4, 1998). I would say that virtually all of the 34 studies in our sample exhibit these assumptions—and it is largely for this reason, as well shall see, that narrative elements are central to most of these studies.

KNOWLEDGE AND NARRATIVE IN PROFESSIONAL
COMMUNICATION CASE STUDIES

Narrative is often linked to the case study. Yin (1984) calls narrative the "traditional" written form of the "classic single-case study" (pp. 127–128). Stake (1994) remarks that "it is not uncommon for qualitative case researchers to call for letting the case 'tell its own story,'" though he points out that "it is the researcher who decides … what of the case's own story he or she will report" (pp. 239–240). Newkirk (1992) claims that "to write a case study that works, the writer needs to see the data in terms of one of a variety of culturally grounded narratives" that "signal to the reader the types of judgments to be made" (p. 137). Van Maanen (1988) believes that all "fieldwork accounts" have an "inherent story-like character" (p. 8). What is the relation between case studies and narrative? Do we learn more from case studies in narrative form than from case studies in other forms?

To try to discover what we learn from our case studies and the role that narrative plays, I will first list what seem to me to be the kinds of knowledge being made or claimed in our studies. I will then categorize the studies according to their use of narrative and look for correlations with the kind of knowledge they seem to make.

Kinds of Knowledge

With the help of Robert Stake's book *The Art of Case Study Research* (1995), I have identified five kinds of contributions that case studies make to our field's knowledge. These kinds are to some extent overlapping, and many of our case studies exhibit more than one, but delineating these kinds of knowledge separately helps us appreciate what the studies are accomplishing. Our case studies can

- refute a generalization already current in the field;
- support a generalization developing in the field;
- "sophisticate the beholding" (p. 43) of the phenomena we study;
- identify new phenomena to study (a contribution that Stake does not discuss but is often cited as the purpose of case study research [see Lauer & Asher, 1988]); and
- enable readers to make "naturalistic generalizations," a term coined by Stake and Trumbull (1982), as quoted by Stake (1995, pp. 85–86).

These knowledge-making activities are self-evident except for the third and fifth ones. Stake (1995) comments that the function of case study research "is not necessarily to map and conquer the world but to sophisticate the beholding of it" (p. 43). It seems to me that the primary effect of many of our case studies is to complicate our view of the entities we study. For example, Myers (1985) reveals hidden social processes at work in the composition of two biologists' proposals; Cross (1994) uses the theories of Bakhtin to dissect an act of collaborative writing; McCarthy (1991) shows a psychiatrist's diagnoses to have been heavily determined by a charter document in the field; Shenk (1994) raises questions about what constitutes credibility. As for naturalistic generalizations, these are conclusions that readers make on their own by relating the case study to their own experiences. These generalizations are thus private and unpredictable, rather than being explicitly invited or announced in the study; they take the form of experiential, not propositional, knowledge. As we shall see, they depend more heavily on narrative detail than any of the other forms of knowledge created by case studies, though our use of narrative can also assist in the creation of the other forms.

Use of Narrative

To assess the extent of our studies' use of narrative, I assigned the studies to one of three categories: "A" uses an overall narrative structure and narrative detail, "B" uses a concept-based structure but includes considerable narrative detail in discussing each concept, and "C" uses neither an overall narrative structure nor considerable narrative detail.

These classifications were based only on my own opinion. The task was complicated by the fact that, essentially, all reports of research can be said to use a narrative structure. As Newkirk (1992) points out, "even the experimental research report follows a conventionalized narrative line: Background, Method, Results, Discussion" (p. 134). So to use the word *narrative* meaningfully, I distinguished between those studies whose sense of a plot derived almost solely from the researcher's activity and those that presented the phenomenon under study in a plot-like form. These latter studies were placed in groups A or B, with one exception: In Clark and Doheny-Farina's (1990) case study, the researchers' plot was the central phenomenon, so that study was placed in group A.

"Emplotment," according to Polkinghorne (1988), is what creates narrative meaning (pp. 60, 160); plot "configures" actions and events "into wholes according to the roles [they] play in bringing about a conclusion" (p. 36). Thus, to be considered a real plot, a plot has to have a certain duration over time—but how long a duration? That is a gray area (see Rentz, 1992, for a fuller discussion), and it caused problems as I tried to distinguish between group B and group C studies.

And finally, defining "narrative detail" and distinguishing it from summaries of what happened were difficult. While we do not expect a story to "behave like a video camera set up to record all the particulars" (Talmy, 1995, p. 435), we do expect a certain number of particulars in a narrative. But how particular is a "particular"? And how many are required in order for an account to be a narrative, as opposed to a summary? Narratives exhibit various levels of "granularity," or coarseness/fineness of detail, and "density," or thickness of detail (pp. 436–437), and how I perceived those levels in our cases was, again, a matter of personal judgment.

About half the case studies fell into group A (see Table A.1 in the Appendix). They use narrative as the overarching pattern for presenting the phenomena under study, and they also include a substantial amount of narrative detail in the form of quotes, specifics about persons and settings, and/or reported incidents (Dautermann's [1993] study is perhaps the most coarse-grained of the group). All these cases except Shenk (1994) were examining processes, and the narrative structure seems to have been the natural choice for looking at these phenomena that took place over time.

As we've seen, case studies are apt when the goal is to understand the "complexity of a single case" as it exists within "important circumstances" (Stake, 1995, p. xi). A plot is "able to take into account the historical and social context" and to "articulate and consolidate complex threads of multiple activities" (Polkinghorne,

1988, p. 19). As in literature, the plot in case studies is not always presented in straight chronological order. Nevertheless, the studies in group A can be seen as tracing the story of a person, document, and/or event over time. Showing how and why is what narratives are supremely good for, and these studies do this well (though in my opinion, the more fine-grained the detail, the better they do it).

I deemed 8 of the 34 studies to be Bs. All these studies focused on processes, but rather than tracing the processes with an overarching narrative structure, these studies were organized by concepts, with narratives used to provide background or to illustrate them. For example, the body of Winsor's *Writing Like an Engineer* (1996) is organized not by the four engineers' stories, but instead by the topics "Socialization Through Writers and Genres," "Learning to Construct and Interact with an Audience," and "The Textual Negotiation of Corporate Reality." Within these sections, though, one finds considerable narrative detail, such as the stories of how Jason and Chris produced certain texts. I counted Selzer (1983) as a B study because, while his topics "Planning and Inventing," "Arrangement," "Drafting," and "Revision" do seem to form a chronological sequence, they do not trace any one phenomenon through time.

With one exception, all studies in group B examined processes. The exception, Ice (1991), looks at Union Carbide's rhetoric audience by audience, but the study includes a good many stories about the reasons behind particular damage-control strategies. The question arises, then, of whether these studies' lack of an overall narrative resulted in less successful depictions of processes than occurred in the group A studies. The answer depends on how we define "successful." I will confess that my own preference would have been the tracing of each subject through a particular story. I think I would have acquired a richer and more coherent sense of interacting forces—and would have been able to make more "naturalistic generalizations"—if I had been able to shadow the participants through a complete experience (and to be fair to Paré [1993], whose study I put in group B, one is able to do this with two of his subjects). Spilka (1997) makes a similar complaint in her review of Winsor's (1996) book, when she says, "I was often frustrated when the author would introduce an especially interesting story, and then suddenly begin a new point or story" (p. 345). On the other hand, since the studies were organized as they were, I was able easily to assimilate the findings into my disciplinary knowledge. The specific experiences that these studies reported lent credence to their findings, and probably made some naturalistic generalizing possible.

Seven case studies plus part of another (Doheny-Farina, 1992.3.2) fell into Group C. Four of these studies do not purport to examine processes but instead static entities: Hansen (1996) looks at "links" (p. 308) between employees' perceptions of culture and their technology choices, and the other three studies perform textual analyses. We would not expect much narrative in these cases and, except for some background information or scattered anecdotes, we don't find any. There is, on the other hand, a great deal of detail in these studies to support the claims they make, especially in the form of quoting; we do come away with a vivid sense of the texts under discussion, or, in Hansen's case, of the four individuals' attitudes.

We are left with three studies and a portion of another in group C that purport to focus on processes and yet have neither an overall narrative structure nor substantial narrative detail (Doheny-Farina, 1992.3.2; Huettman, 1996; Kleimann, 1993; Spilka, 1993b). All but Doheny-Farina's go from research methods to summarized findings without any narrative in between to show where the findings came from. Because Doheny-Farina's case is a compilation of interviews organized by topic, there's no sense of observing a process here, either—though numerous quotes support his claims and create some sense of direct observation. In the other studies, we must take the researcher's word that the gathered data did support the findings. While this kind of presentation makes for efficiency, it does not give us a way to assess the researchers' conclusions, and it provides little opportunity for naturalistic generalizations. In commenting on the monovocality of traditional "realist" ethnographies, Van Maanen (1988) points to space limitations imposed by the publication outlet as a contributing factor (p. 53); in the group C cases that we are examining here, the constraints of the article format may well have determined the researchers' choice of a nonnarrative presentation.

Before we go on to see how use of narrative correlates with the kinds of knowledge being made in the studies, we can conclude at this point that narrative is particularly useful when the purpose is to claim something about processes. When that narrative is broken up by conceptual categories, we lose some sense of how components interacted but may gain a more coherent picture of individual components. When virtually all narrative is replaced by summarizing observations, we have a case study that isn't taking advantage of the key virtue of the case study: "particularization" (Stake, 1995, p. 8). We must be given some particular happenings to help us see the process, assess the researcher's conclusions about it, and draw some of our own, or else the "confirmability" (Lincoln & Guba, 1985, as cited by Marshall & Rossman, 1989, p. 147) is weak.

Correlation Between Use of Narrative and Kinds of Knowledge

Our final task is to see how groups A, B, and C correlate with the five kinds of knowledge laid out at the start of this section. We will set aside for the moment the kind of knowledge I have termed "naturalistic generalizations," since these, as it turns out, play a role in all the other forms.

Table 1.2 correlates the studies' use of narrative with the primary kinds of knowledge they make. I could easily have put several of the studies into several categories (and that itself is a testimony to the richness of this research genre), but I tried to determine which of the four kinds of knowledge was most generated by each study, often taking explicit cues from the authors. Judging from this table, we can observe, first, that the degree to which a study uses narrative structure and detail will not necessarily entail a particular kind of knowledge; the B and C studies were fairly evenly distributed across the four kinds of knowledge, though I felt that only one of them supported a generalization as its main kind of knowledge. On the other hand, there

TABLE 1.2.
Cases Grouped by Kind of Knowledge Made and Use of Narrative

Kind of Knowledge	Use of Narrative		
	Group A	Group B	Group C
Refute a generalization	Doheny-Farina (1989) Doheny-Farina (1992.3.1)	Broadhead & Freed (1986) Paré (1993) Selzer (1983)	Doheny-Farina (1992.3.2) Huettman (1996)
Support a generalization	Thralls (1992) Zimmerman & Marsh (1989)		Kleimann (1993)
Sophisticate the beholding	Berkenkotter & Huckin (1993) Burnett (1996) Clark & Doheny- Farina (1990) Cross (1994) Dautermann (1993) Doheny-Farina (1986) Doheny-Farina (1992.1, 1992.2) Locker (1992) McCarthy & Gerring (1994) Myers (1985) Shenk (1994) Yates (1985)	Ice (1991) Winsor (1990) Winsor (1994)	Hansen (1996) Killingsworth & Steffens (1989) Segal (1993)
Identify new phenomena	Alford (1989) Cross (1990) McCarthy (1991) Moore (1992)	Cross (1993) Winsor (1996)	Patterson & Lee (1997) Spilka (1993)

is clearly one category larger than the others: the group A studies that primarily "sophisticate the beholding" of phenomena. This finding correlates well with the unique advantages of the case study—namely, its high level of detail and its ability to examine a complex phenomenon in context. All the studies in this cell (except for Shenk, 1994) examine processes, and it is narrative detail cast in an overall narrative structure that supplies the evidence for the claims. The effect is that we see a complex process in more sophisticated, nuanced ways. Of course, there is a thin line between that effect and another kind of knowledge, identifying new phenomena to study, for often, accounts of processes reveal elements that can then become the subjects of subsequent studies. Four A studies seemed to fall more into this category—for example, Cross's (1990)[2] exposé of counterproductive forces behind an unsuccessful act of collaborative composing and Moore's (1992) identification of intimidation as a factor in organizational communication practices.

And yet, it is also worth noting that, while "the real business of case study is particularization, not generalization" (Stake, 1995, p. 8), our studies are capable of persuasively challenging a widely held belief. Case studies are capable of refuting generalizations because it only takes one case—provided that readers can accept it as an instance of the general class of phenomena in question—to show that a generalization has holes. Selzer's (1983) case study of the engineer and Broadhead and Freed's (1986) study of two management consultants effectively challenged the belief that all composing is recursive; Paré (1993) convincingly shows that a discourse community is not always "rosy" (p. 111); one cannot read Doheny-Farina's (1992) stories of technology transfer and believe any longer that it is a mechanical, conduit-based process.

As for supporting a generalization, it can be said that many of our studies do this to some extent—perhaps all research articles do—but in only three studies did this purpose seem primary. Most of the researchers are overtly cautious about generalizing from their case studies; the word *suggest* is frequently used in these studies' conclusions. As Stake (1995) says, the case study method emphasizes "uniqueness" and therefore is not usually chosen in order to produce generalizations. "Traditional comparative and correlation studies" are better for that purpose (p. 8).

It is interesting, though, that despite the overt caution, the studies sometimes slide lexically from observations about the specific case into observations about a whole class of cases, and they do this so smoothly that we may not notice the movement. Consider, for example, Doheny-Farina's (1986) article "Writing in an Emerging Organization." From the beginning, the phenomenon under study is ambiguous: Is it a particular emerging organization or emerging organizations as a class? And if the latter, on what grounds might "emerging organizations" constitute a class? To cite another example, when he says, "in this instance, the collaborative writing process achieved a balance" (p. 178), is he suggesting that there is such a thing as *the* collaborative writing process, of which the observed process was only an instance, or is he speaking specifically of the particular process he observed? And if the former, on what basis does he see the observed case as an instance of the general phenomenon?

This discussion brings us to Platt's (1992) point that an overt account of "the logic by which we can get "from observed to unobserved cases" (p. 29) is frequently missing in case studies. That is, what the case is a case of and why it can be seen that way are often not spelled out. "The conviction of the reader that the conclusion is appropriate must depend either on her own implicit analysis of the cases or on trust" of the researcher (p. 24). Sometimes our case study researchers explicitly reckon with the issue of typicality; they cite literature that reports similar phenomena or give some other grounds for considering the case representative. Even in these cases, though, the evidence is only suggestive. Ultimately, readers must bring their own frames of reference to bear on the case to decide how plausible it is and what they can learn, not only about it but about other cases.

Propositional generalizations in case studies, then, share this trait with naturalistic generalizations—to turn to the last form of knowledge on our list. Rather than depending on statistical proof, both kinds of generalization depend on the often tacit reasoning processes of any given reader. Polkinghorne's (1988) observation about narrative arguments applies to all case studies, whether in narrative form or not: they "use the ideal of a scholarly consensus as the test of verisimilitude rather than the test of logical or mathematical validity" (p. 176). We may not consider "scholarly consensus" the ideal basis for validity, but if we want to learn anything about complex processes in natural contexts, consensus is the best basis we have (it is important to recall, too, that measures of validity in experimental and correlation studies also depend upon consensus). As for "verisimilitude," it is a more rigorous measure of validity than one might at first think, for it requires that the case in question accord with the many other accumulated cases in the reader's experience.

However, case studies that tell a detailed story draw upon the reader's commonplace reasoning processes better than those that do not. That is, the more narrative-like the study, the stronger its potential to trigger reader-specific conclusions—what we are calling naturalistic generalizations—that reach beyond the study's declared meaning. (The same can be said of ethnographies, which overlap with case studies in many ways.³) Cognitive researchers, discourse analysts, and narrative theorists have several terms for these reasoning processes—for example, "folk psychology" and "common sense" (see Edwards, 1990; Polkinghorne, 1988) and "natural reason" and "practical wisdom" (Fisher, 1987, citing Vico and Aristotle)—but all agree that narrative is critical to everyday learning. Supporting this claim is the widely held belief that we naturally construe our own lived experiences as stories (see review in Rentz, 1992; Widdershoven, 1993). We tend to perceive the events of our lives as plots, with beginnings, middles, and ends and with more or less coherent cause-effect sequences. We learn from both lived and written narratives by adding new stories to old stories; "enduring meanings come from encounter, and are modified and reinforced by repeated encounter" (Stake, 1994, p. 240). This process is the foundation, we might note, of casuistry, or moral reasoning based on cases (Jonsen & Toulmin, 1988). Narratives "optimize the opportunity of the reader to gain an experiential understanding of the case" (Stake, 1995, p. 40). They invite readers to "add their own parts of the story" (p. 86), whereas variable-based research seeks "to minimize the importance of interpretation" (p. 41).

Readers of case study narratives, therefore, will sometimes create "their own alternative interpretation" (Stake, 1995, p. 87). When we look at the cases in our sample that tell the most detailed stories—and I would consider Cross (1994), Doheny-Farina (1989, 1992.1, 1992.2, 1996), Moore (1992), McCarthy (1991), McCarthy and Gerring (1994), Myers (1985), and Zimmerman and Marsh (1989) to be some of these—I think we see that we do wind up with richer data than the conclusions of the studies actually used.

As evidence of this point we might consider Cross's three accounts of how employees at an insurance company wrote a two-page executive letter for an annual report. Cross demonstrates convincingly that this was an example of unsuccess-ful collaboration: Eight people took 77 days to produce the letter, and in its final form it still did not sufficiently take into account the 500,000 policyholders or the media, preparing neither of these audiences for an upcoming rate increase. In his most bare-bones account (1993), a 12-page article in which Cross analyzes the influence of genre on the production of two documents in this organization, we are led to propositional conclusions largely through summaries rather than fine-grained detail, as in the following excerpt:

> Eight people with different perceptions of audience contributed text to the letter and struggled for empowerment. Yet, less that one-third of the changes made by editors ended up in the final version of the letter. In fact, thirty days into the process, the letter was rewritten "from scratch" by three different people, and then two of these letters were quickly rejected. The cause of many rejections was the graduate shift of power and storytelling rights from the CEO and his advisors in Corporate Communications to the new president. (p. 149)

In contrast, Cross's original 30-page account (1990), which focused exclusively on the writing of the letter, is more detailed and therefore creates a more vivid sense of the wasted energy involved in this failed act of collaborative writing. Here, for example, is the account of a significant moment in the process, when, disagreeing over the letter's rhetorical approach, the vice president of corporate communica-tions ("Andy") and his subordinate, the supervisor in the department ("Carol"), take the letter to the company's senior vice president ("Ron") to ask his opinion:

> When the Supervisor and the Vice President met with the Senior Vice President, he supported the Vice President's judgment: nearly half of the changes that the Senior Vice President suggested (9 out of 19, over 47 percent) repeated the Vice President's statements.... The Senior Vice President ... told the Supervisor to discuss problems at the beginning of the letter, ahead of sentences presenting statistics indicating the com-pany's improved financial performance. Yet the CEO had told the Vice President and the Supervisor that the numbers were to be placed first.... After the meeting, the Supervisor communicated her impression of her superiors' revision directions to the Writer and again delegated the writing to her subordinate. Adding another link to the serial chain had it price: Of the 37 directions given by the Vice President and Senior Vice President, 10, over a fourth (27 percent), were not implemented. (pp. 183–184)

Finally, we have the book-length version's blow-by-blow account of the writing of the letter (1994). In this version, the supervisor and vice president's meeting with the senior vice president is covered in nine full pages, not just one long paragraph. Included in the account are details about the plush setting of the senior VP's office 30 stories above the department of corporate communications, as well as lengthy quotations from the dialogue that took place among the three participants. We can see from the quotations that Carol is struggling to explain to her two male supervisors, in the face of largely negative feedback from them, why she and her subordinate, Gail, have written the letter as they have. The two supervisors talk more than she does, and when she tries to assert that she was following the CEO and president's initial advice, she is virtually shouted down. Still, she makes the best of Ron's sudden involvement in the writing process, telling Cross in an interview afterwards that getting Ron's opinions may give the writers "'a little more clout'" (p. 62) with the top executives.

The next paragraph in this account starts out almost identically to the corresponding paragraph from the 1990 version:

> The period of instability continued as Carol next communicated her impression of her bosses' revision directions to Gail on Friday, November 14, and again delegated the writing to her subordinate. Adding another link to the serial chain had its price: Of the 37 directions given by Andy Hamilton and Ron Dewald, over one-fourth (10 or 27%) were neither understood nor implemented. (p. 62)

But then Cross adds this paragraph:

> Gail rewrote the letter in a pressure cooker. When I asked how things were going on Monday, November 17, she replied: "I'm going crazy.... I've got [the news magazine]. I've got the planning document. I've got the annual report. I've got radio spots. That's *this week*." She was displeased about the discrepancy between Ron Dewald's and Carol's understanding of what the executives wanted in the letter and objected to its routing: "It's getting too complicated too early...because this is just the first draft and it's gone through so many revisions already without the input of the people who are doing the actual approval.... [There are] too many chefs." She was unhappy because having to redo the draft was "taking me back a step.... People that I [wrote] the draft for haven't seen it yet.... I feel that this is just an unnecessary revision." (p. 62)

Whereas the earlier, shorter versions had largely conveyed the impression of corporate inefficiency—of wasted time, money, and personnel hours—I came away from this longest account with a sense of how dehumanizing it can be to work in a hierarchical corporate structure, especially if one is a woman on a lower level of a male-dominated company; of how careless executives can be with their underlings' time and how oblivious of their feelings; of how frustrating it is to guess what the powerful want and to have one's best efforts totally disregarded. These "naturalistic generalizations" are not included in Cross's extensive list of conclusions, but they are "in" the case for me because they ring true against similar experiences I've had or learned about. And as I read more stories about corporate life, they will be part of the storehouse of "cases" I bring to bear on my reading. One result of the poststructuralist turn in English studies has been the lesson that carefully wrought fictional worlds can always generate alternative, even subversive, interpretations. The same could be said of our most detailed narrative case studies; they have more knowledge-making power than the researcher can fully control.[4] While imperfect control can ruin an experimental study, the suggestiveness of narrative detail is a major asset in studies of complex, naturally occurring cases, where the primary goal is not control but understanding.

CONCLUSION

The 34 case studies that I examined support the following observations:

- Case studies in professional writing tend to follow the social science model, with some exceptions that derive largely from our interest in texts.
- As an organizing structure, narrative plays an important role in these studies, particularly in studies of processes.
- While narrative detail can be used in the service of several kinds of knowledge, it is particularly critical to the making of experiential knowledge, or "naturalistic generalizations."

In a 1996 article, Blyler calls for a postmodern turn in professional communication research; she urges us "to become more self-reflexive in our thinking about research," more aware of the blurred boundaries "between the researcher and the researched," and more experimental in our forms (pp. 344–346). Ralph Cintron (1993) expresses views similar to Blyler's, but, as he points out, "writing research occurs often in the context of educational research, and the pragmatic needs of education ... inhibit ... experimentation" (p. 401). This inhibition is especially true of education in professional communication. We research, teach, and write in a field that values practical results above self-expression or connectedness to others. This preference is broadly evident in our case studies; by and large, they are "instrumental" (Stake, 1994, p. 237) in that they seek to give us better processes and products in the classroom and workplace. To use Van Maanen's (1988) categories, our case studies are more "realist" than "impressionist"—that is, the author is minimally present in the text, details are included "to serve as instances of something important" rather than being interesting in their own right, and the interpretation of events tends to be univocal (events are not "given meaning first in one way, then another" (p. 52). But because different readers bring different experiences to their reading, there is always more power in a detailed story than the researcher can control. This indeterminacy is what saves many of our case studies from the confines of a narrow instrumentalism. Through narrative, these studies not only create useful disciplinary knowledge; they also sow seeds of disciplinary change.

APPENDIX

TABLE A.1.
Professional Writing Case Studies (Those Receiving 5 or More Positive Votes)

Author, Date	Focus on Process/Entity	Subject of Study	Use of Narrative[a]
Alford, 1989	Process	The separate writing projects of two writers in a trade association	A
Berkenkotter & Huckin, 1993	Process	The rewriting of a biologist's article for publication	A
Broadhead & Freed, 1986	Process	The proposal writing of two management consultants	B
Burnett, 1996	Process	The failed collaboration of student engineers in the workplace	A
Clark & Doheny-Farina, 1990	Process	Two writers rethinking their original interpretation of a case study	A
Cross, 1990	Process	The collaborative writing of an executive letter in an annual report	A
Cross, 1993	Process	The collaborative writing of two documents in two genres in a company	B
Cross, 1994[b]	Process	The collaborative writing of an executive letter in an annual report	A
Dautermann, 1993	Process	Nurses' collaborative writing in a hospital	A
Doheny-Farina, 1986	Process	The collaborative writing of a business plan by executives in a new organization	A
Doheny-Farina, 1989	Process	One adult writing in academic and nonacademic discourse communities	A
Doheny-Farina, 1992[c]	Case 1: Process Case 2: Process Case 3.1: Process Case 3.2: Process	1) Developing the business plans to exploit a technology; 2) the creation of training documents for a medical technology within a three-organization context; 3) the role of technical writers in product design in two companies	1: A 2: A 3.1: A 3.2: C
Hansen, 1996	Entity	The relation of context to choices of communication technology on the part of four product-development team members in an organization	C
Huettman, 1996	Process	The audience considerations of a writer writing one report in a hospitality consulting firm	C
Ice, 1991	Entity	The public relations messages produced by Union Carbide after the Bhopal chemical leak	B
Killingsworth & Steffens, 1989	Entity	Objectifying language in several environmental impact statements	C

TABLE A.1. (continued)

Author, Date	Focus on Process/Entity	Subject of Study	Use of Narrative
Kleimann, 1993	Process	The influence of workplace culture on document review in a government office	C
Locker, 1992	Process	Two acts of collaborative writing in a state agency, one a failure and one a success	A
McCarthy, 1991	Process	A psychiatrist's use of a charter document in her research and writing	A
McCarthy & Gerring, 1994	Process	Psychiatrists' revision of a charter document	A
Moore, 1992	Process	The role of intimidation in the *Challenger* accident	A
Myers, 1985	Process	The production of two biologists' separate funding proposals	A
Paré, 1993	Process	Social workers' use of discourse regulations in their reports	B
Patterson & Lee, 1997	Entity	The rhetoric of "balance" in one environmental impact statement	C
Segal, 1993	Entity	The rhetoric of medicine in a scientific review article	C
Selzer, 1983	Process	The composing processes of an engineer	B
Shenk, 1994	Entity	Credibility of the texts in a controversy over a naval fitness report	A
Spilka, 1993b	Process	The interaction of oral and written communication in six projects in two bureaus of an agency	C
Thralls, 1992	Process	The collaborative nature of writing, as exemplified in one journal article's publication	A
Winsor, 1990	Process	The communication and reasoning that led to the *Challenger* accident	B
Winsor, 1994	Process	Invention in a project of senior engineers	B
Winsor, 1996	Process	Relation between becoming an engineer and forming attitudes toward rhetoric, on the part of four students	B
Yates, 1985	Process	The rise of graphics in a company	A
Zimmerman & Marsh, 1989	Process	The use of storyboarding in the production of a proposal	A

[a] Type A studies use an overall narrative structure and considerable narrative detail. Type B studies use a concept-based structure but considerable narrative detail. And Type C studies use neither an overall narrative structure nor considerable narrative detail.

[b] This study is an extended version of Cross, 1990.

[c] This book-length study consists of three separate cases, and the third consists of two subcases. I will therefore refer to them with the numbers 1992.1, 1992.2, 1992.3.1, and 1992.3.2. Doheny-Farina, 1992.1, is an extended version of Doheny-Farina, 1986.

NOTES

[1] The 19 studies that the panelists wrote in on the survey were Beamer (1995); Berkenkotter and Huckin (1995), which is actually a collection of studies; Burnett (1991); Burnett and Ewald (1994); Freed and Broadhead (1987); Herndl, Fennell, and Miller (1991); Hildebrandt (1985); Locker (1985); Mathes (1986); McIsaac and Aschauer (1990); Ross and Benson (1995); Rymer (1988); Sauer (1994); Schryer (1993); Seiter (1995); Spilka (1990, 1993a); Tyler (1997); and Yates and Orlikowski (1994).

One panelist also wrote in Sypher (1990), a collection of cases for teaching organizational communication (most of which seem to have been based on real cases); and volume 11.3 (1998) of *Management Communication Quarterly*, which contains one research article labeled as a case study and one case written (fabricated?) to spark discussion. I assumed that my panelists would interpret "case study" to mean case study research instead of cases designed for teaching purposes, but this panelist's response, as well as Sypher's introduction, raises the possibility that the two genres are not entirely distinct. To me, they seem to make different truth claims. Case studies claim "this happened," with supporting documentation, while cases for discussion may claim only "something like this can happen" and cite no sources at all. But a fuller inquiry into these two genres' kinds of knowledge-making might well reveal significant similarities.

[2] It may seem strange that I classify Cross (1990) and Cross (1994) differently. The two studies report on essentially the same research project, and both identify new phenomena to study further—unsuccessful collaborative writing and, more specifically, centrifugal and centripetal forces at work in collaborative writing. But the book-length version presents a more detailed, complicated picture, with the result that it seems more to sophisticate our beholding of (unsuccessful) collaborative writing.

[3] Case studies (with origins in several social sciences as well as medicine [see Hamel, 1993]) and ethnographies (which originated in anthropology) both typically examine phenomena within their natural, complex settings. In ethnography, however, the social world itself is often the primary object of study. Many of the case studies in our sample of 34 use ethnographic methods borrowed from anthropology—participant-observation, extended time at the research site, multiple sources of data and triangulation of data, a careful account of the researcher's relation to the subjects, and what Geertz called "thick description," or a superabundance of details. However, only two authors represented in our sample, Cross (1990, 1994) and Doheny-Farina (1986), actually call their studies ethnographic studies. Interestingly, these studies were among the 13 that received the highest number of positive votes from our panelists, who were judging them as case studies. The panelists, then, seem to regard ethnographic studies in professional communication as extended case studies. Perhaps this is because our more ethnographic studies are nevertheless focused, as case studies are, on a particular phenomenon (the writing of a letter or business plan, for instance) within a social world rather than on that world itself.

[4] The exchange of commentary following the publication of Clark and Doheny-Farina's 1990 article in *Written Communication* (Jarratt, 1991; Lunsford & Ede, 1991) is another example of this same point; readers are able to draw different conclusions from Anna's story because it is detailed enough to have its own knowledge-making power apart from the meaning foregrounded by the author.

REFERENCES

Alford, E. (1989). The text and the trade association: A story of documents at work. In C. Matalene (Ed.), *Worlds of writing: Teaching and learning in discourse communities of work* (pp. 136–152). New York: Random House.

Amsden, D., & Amsden, A. (1993). The KIVA story: A paradigm of technology transfer. *IEEE Transactions on Professional Communication, 36,* 190–195.

Anderson, P., Brockmann, J., & Miller, C. (Eds.). (1983). *New essays in technical and scientific communication: Research, theory, practice.* Farmingdale, NY: Baywood.

Bazerman, C., & Paradis, J. (Eds.). (1991). *Textual dynamics of the professions: Historical and contemporary studies of writing in professional communities.* Madison, WI: University of Wisconsin Press.

Beamer, L. (1995). A schemata model for intercultural encounters and case study: The emperor and the envoy. *The Journal of Business Communication, 32,* 141–161.

Berkenkotter, C., & Huckin, T. (1993). You are what you cite: Novelty and intertextuality in a biologist's experimental artice. In N. Blyler & C. Thralls (Eds.), *Professional communication: The social perspective* (pp. 109–127). Newbury Park, CA: Sage.

Berkenkotter, C., & Huckin, T. (1995). *Genre knowledge in disciplinary communication: Cognition/culture/power.* Hillsdale, NJ: Lawrence Erlbaum.

Blyler, N. (1996). Narrative and research in professional communication. *Journal of Business and Technical Communication, 10,* 330–351.

Blyler, N., & Thralls, C. (Eds.). (1993). *Professional communication: The social perspective.* Newbury Park, CA: Sage.

Brown, V. (1994). Facing multiple audiences in engineering and R&D writing: The social contexts of a technical report. *Journal of Technical Writing and Communication, 24,* 67–74.

Brown, V. (1996). Persuasiveness and audience focus in a nonacademic R&D setting. *Journal of Technical Writing and Communication, 26,* 37–55.

Broadhead, G., & Freed, R. (1986). *The variables of composition: Process and product in a business setting.* Carbondale, IL: Southern Illinois University Press.

Burnett, R. (1991). Substantive conflict in a cooperative context: A way to improve the collaborative planning of workplace documents. *Technical Communication, 38,* 531–539.

Burnett, R. (1996). "Some people weren't able to contribute anything but their technical knowledge": The anatomy of a dysfunctional team. In A. Duin & C. Hansen (Eds.), *Nonacademic writing: Social theory and technology* (pp. 123–156). Mahwah, NJ: Lawrence Erlbaum.

Burnett, R., & Ewald, H. (1994). Rabbit trails, ephemera, and other stories: Feminist methodology and collaborative research. *Journal of Advanced Composition, 14,* 21–51.

Cintron, R. (1993). Wearing a pith helmet at a sly angle: Or, can writing researchers do ethnography in a postmodern era? *Written Communication, 10,* 371–412.

Clark, G., & Doheny-Farina, S. (1990). Public discourse and personal expression: A case study in theory-building. *Written Communication, 7,* 456–481.

Creswell, J. (1998). *Qualitative inquiry and research design: Choosing among five traditions.* Thousand Oaks, CA: Sage.

Cross, G. (1990). A Bakhtinian exploration of factors affecting the collaborative writing of an executive letter of an annual report. *Research in the Teaching of English, 24,* 173–203.

Cross, G. (1993). The interrelation of genre, context, and process in the collaborative writing of two corporate documents. In R. Spilka (Ed.), *Writing in the workplace: New research perspectives* (pp. 141–152). Carbondale, IL: Southern Illinois University Press.

Cross, G. (1994). *Collaboration and conflict: A contextual exploration of group writing and positive emphasis.* Cresskill, NJ: Hampton Press.

Dautermann, J. (1993). Negotiating meaning in a hospital discourse community. In R. Spilka (Ed.), *Writing in the workplace: New research perspectives* (pp. 98–110). Carbondale, IL: Southern Illinois University Press.

Denzin, N., & Lincoln, Y. (1994). Introduction: Entering the field of qualitative research. In N. Denzin & Y. Lincoln (Eds.), *Handbook of qualitative research* (pp. 1–17). Thousand Oaks, CA: Sage.

Doheny-Farina, S. (1986). Writing in an emerging organization. *Written Communication, 3,* 158–185.

Doheny-Farina, S. (1989). A case study of one adult writing in academic and nonacademic discourse communities. In C. Matalene (Ed.), *Worlds of writing: Teaching and learning in discourse communities of work* (pp. 17–42). New York: Random House.

Doheny-Farina, S. (1992). *Rhetoric, innovation, technology: Case studies of technical communication in technology transfers.* Cambridge, MA: MIT Press.

Doheny-Farina, S., & Odell, L. (1985). Ethnographic research on writing: Assumptions and methodology. In L. Odell & D. Goswami (Eds.), *Writing in nonacademic settings* (pp. 503–535). New York: Guilford Press.

Duin, A., & Hansen, C. (Eds.). (1996). *Nonacademic writing: Social theory and technology.* Mahwah, NJ: Lawrence Erlbaum.

Edwards, D. (1990). *Discourse and cognition.* London: Sage.

Eiler, M. (1989). Process and genre. In C. Matalene (Ed.), *Worlds of writing: Teaching and learning in discourse communities of work* (pp. 43–63). New York: Random House.

Faigley, L. (1985). Nonacademic writing: The social perspective. In L. Odell & D. Goswami (Eds.), *Writing in academic settings* (pp. 231–248). New York: Guilford Press.

Fisher, W. (1987). *Human communication as narration: Toward a philosophy of reason, value, and action.* Columbia, SC: University of South Carolina Press.

Forman, J. (Ed.). (1992). *New visions of collaborative writing.* Portsmouth, NH: Boynton/Cook.

Freed, R., & Broadhead, G. (1987). Discourse communities, sacred texts, and institutional norms. *College Composition and Communication, 38,* 154–165.

Glaser, B., & Strauss, A. (1967). *The discovery of grounded theory: Strategies for qualitative research.* New York: Aldine.

Hamel, J. (with Dufour, S., & Fortin, D.). (1993). *Case study methods.* Newbury Park, CA: Sage.

Hansen, C. (1996). Contextualizing technology and communication in a corporate setting. In A. Duin & C. Hansen (Eds.), *Nonacademic writing: Social theory and technology* (pp. 305–324). Mahwah, NJ: Lawrence Erlbaum.

Herndl, C., Fennell, B., & Miller, C. (1991). Understanding failures in organizational discourse: The accident at Three Mile Island and the shuttle *Challenger* disaster. In C. Bazerman & J. Paradis (Eds.), *Textual dynamics of the professions: Historical and contemporary studies of writing in professional communities* (pp. 279–305). Madison, WI: University of Wisconsin Press.

Hildebrandt, H. (1985). A sixteenth-century work on communication: Precursor of modern business communication. In G. Douglas & H. Hildebrandt (Eds.), *Studies in the history of business writing* (pp. 53–67). Urbana, IL: Association for Business Communication.

Huettman, E. (1996). Writing for multiple audiences: An examination of audience concerns in a hospitality consulting firm. *The Journal of Business Communication, 33,* 257–273.

Ice, R. (1991). Corporate publics and rhetorical strategies: The case of Union Carbide's Bhopal crisis. *Management Communication Quarterly, 4,* 341–362.

Jarratt, S. (1991). Comments on Clark and Doheny-Farina. *Written Communication, 8,* 117–120.

Jonsen, A., & Toulmin, S. (1988). *The abuse of casuistry: A history of moral reasoning.* Berkeley, CA: University of California Press.

Killingsworth, M., & Steffens, D. (1989). Effectiveness in the environmental impact statement: A study in public rhetoric. *Written Communication, 6,* 155–180.

Kleimann, S. (1993). The reciprocal relationship of workplace culture and review. In R. Spilka (Ed.), *Writing in the workplace: New research perspectives* (pp. 56–70). Carbondale, IL: Southern Illinois University Press.

Lauer, J., & Asher, J. (1988). *Composition research: Empirical designs.* New York: Oxford University Press.

Lindeborg, R. (1990). Faster manuscript publishing: A case study. *IEEE Transactions on Professional Communication, 33,* 7–11.

Lindeborg, R. (1993). The irresistible electronic messages of the 1990s: A case study. *IEEE Transactions on Professional Communication, 36,* 152–157.

Locker, K. (1985). The earliest correspondence of the British East India Company (1600–19). In G. Douglas & H. Hildebrandt (Eds.), *Studies in the history of business writing* (pp. 69–86). Urbana, IL: Association for Business Communication.

Locker, K. (1992). What makes a collaborative writing team successful? A case study of lawyers and social service workers in a state agency. In J. Forman (Ed.), *New visions of collaborative writing* (pp. 37–62). Portsmouth, NH: Boynton/Cook.

Louhiala-Salminen, L. (1997). Investigating the genre of a business fax: A Finnish case study. *The Journal of Business Communication, 34,* 316–333.

Lunsford, A., & Ede, L. (1991). Comments on Clark and Doheny-Farina. *Written Communication, 8,* 114–117.

Marshall, C., & Rossman, G. (1989). *Designing qualitative research.* Newbury Park, CA: Sage.

Matalene, C. (Ed.). (1989*). Worlds of writing: Teaching and learning in discourse communities of work.* New York: Random House.

Mathes, J. (1986). *Three Mile Island: The management communication failure.* Ann Arbor, MI: University of Michigan, College of Engineering.

McCarthy, L. (1991). A psychiatrist using DSM-III: The influence of a charter document in psychiatry. In Bazerman, C., & Paradis, J. (Eds.), *Textual dynamics of the professions: Historical and contemporary studies of writing in professional communities* (pp. 358–378). Madison, WI: University of Wisconsin Press.

McCarthy, L., & Gerring, J. (1994). Revising psychiatry's charter document DSM-IV. *Written Communication, 11,* 147–192.

McIsaac, C., & Aschauer, M. (1990). Proposal writing at Atherton Jordan, Inc.: An ethnographic study. *Management Communication Quarterly, 3,* 527–560.

Miles, M., & Huberman, A. (1984). *Qualitative data analysis.* Beverly Hills: Sage.

Miles, T. (1989). The memo and "disinformation": Beyond format and style. *Issues in Writing, 2*(1), 42–60.

Moore, P. (1992). Intimidation and communication: A case study of the *Challenger* accident. *Journal of Business and Technical Communication, 6,* 403–437.

Myers, G. (1985). The social construction of two biologists' proposals. *Written Communication, 2,* 219–245.

Newkirk, T. (1992). The narrative roots of the case study. In G. Kirsch & P. Sullivan (Eds.), *Methods and methodology in composition research* (pp. 130–152). Carbondale, IL: Southern Illinois University Press.

Odell, L., & Goswami, D. (Eds.). (1985). *Writing in nonacademic settings.* New York: Guilford Press.

Ostroff, D., Donelly, D., & Fried, A. (1992). The business environment, demographics and technology: A case study. *IEEE Transactions on Professional Communication, 35,* 31–37.

Paré, A. (1993). Discourse regulations and the production of knowledge. In R. Spilka (Ed.), *Writing in the workplace: New research perspectives* (pp. 111–123). Carbondale, IL: Southern Illinois University Press.

Patterson, R., & Lee, R. (1997). The environmental rhetoric of "balance": A case study of regulatory discourse and the colonization of the public. *Technical Communication Quarterly, 6,* 25–40.

Platt, J. (1992). Cases of cases… of cases. In C. Ragin & H. Becker (Eds.), *What is a case? Exploring the foundations of social inquiry* (pp. 21–52). Cambridge, England: Cambridge University Press.

Polkinghorne, D. (1988). *Narrative knowing and the human sciences.* Albany, NY: State University of New York Press.

Ragin, C., & Becker, H. (1992). *What is a case? Exploring the foundations of social inquiry.* Cambridge, England: Cambridge University Press.

Rentz, K. (1992). The value of narrative in business writing. *Journal of Business and Technical Communication, 6,* 293–315.

Ross, D., & Benson, J. (1995). Cultural change in ethical redemption: A corporate case study. *The Journal of Business Communication, 32,* 345–362.

Rymer, J. (1988). Scientific composing processes: How eminent scientists write journal articles. In D. Jolliffe (Ed.), *Writing in academic disciplines* (pp. 211–250). Norwood, NJ: Ablex.

Sauer, B. (1994). Dynamics of disaster: A three-dimensional view of documentation in a tightly regulated industry. *Technical Communication Quarterly, 3,* 393–419.

Schryer, C. (1993). Records as genre. *Written Communication, 10,* 200–234.

Segal, J. (1993). Writing and medicine: Text and context. In R. Spilka (Ed.), *Writing in the workplace: New research perspectives* (pp. 84–97). Carbondale, IL: Southern Illinois University Press.

Seiter, J. (1995). Surviving turbulent organizational environments: A case study examination of a lumber company's internal and external influence attempts. *The Journal of Business Communication, 32,* 363–382.

Selzer, J. (1983). The composing processes of an engineer. *College Composition and Communication, 34,* 178–187.

Shenk, R. (1994). Gender bias in naval fitness reports: A case study on gender and rhetorical credibility. *Journal of Technical Writing and Communication, 24,* 367–387.

Spilka, R. (1990). Orality and literacy in the workplace: Process- and text-based strategies for multiple-audience adaptation. *Journal of Business and Technical Communication, 4,* 44–67.

Spilka, R. (1993a). Collaboration across multiple organizational cultures. *Technical Communication Quarterly, 2,* 125–145.

Spilka, R. (1993b). Moving between oral and written discourse to fulfill rhetorical and social goals. In R. Spilka (Ed.), *Writing in the workplace: New research perspectives* (pp. 71–83). Carbondale, IL: Southern Illinois University Press.

Spilka, R. (Ed.). (1993c). *Writing in the workplace: New research perspectives.* Carbondale, IL: Southern Illinois University Press.

Spilka, R. (1997). [Review of the book *Writing like an engineer: A rhetorical education*]. *Technical Communication Quarterly, 6,* 343–346.

Stake, R. (1994). Case studies. In N. Denzin & Y. Lincoln (Eds.), *Handbook of qualitative research* (pp. 236–247). Thousand Oaks, CA: Sage.

Stake, R. (1995). *The art of case study research.* Thousand Oaks, CA: Sage.

Sypher, B. (Ed.). (1990). *Case studies in organizational communication.* New York: Guilford Press.

Talmy, L. (1995). Narrative structure in a cognitive framework. In J. Duchan, G. Bruder, & L. Hewitt (Eds.), *Deixis in narrative* (pp. 421–460). Hillsdale, NJ: Lawrence Erlbaum.

Thralls, C. (1992). Bakhtin, collaborative partners, and published discourse: A collaborative view of composing. In J. Forman (Ed.), *New visions of collaborative writing* (pp. 63–81). Portsmouth, NH: Boynton/Cook.

Trimbur, J., & Braun, L. (1992). Laboratory life and the determination of authorship. In J. Forman (Ed.), *New visions of collaborative writing* (pp. 19–36). Portsmouth, NH: Boynton/Cook.

Tyler, L. (1997). Liability means never being able to say you're sorry: Corporate guilt, legal constraints, and defensiveness in corporate communication. *Management Communication Quarterly, 11,* 51–73.

Van Maanen, J. (1988). *Tales of the field: On writing ethnography.* Chicago: University of Chicago Press.

Widdershoven, G. (1993). The story of life: Hermeneutic perspectives on the relationship between narrative and life history. In R. Josselson & A. Lieblich (Eds.), *The narrative study of lives* (pp. 1–20). Newbury Park, CA: Sage.

Winsor, D. (1990). The construction of knowledge in organizations: Asking the right questions about the *Challenger. Journal of Business and Technical Communication, 4,* 7–20.

Winsor, D. (1994). Invention and writing in technical work: Representing the object. *Written Communication, 11,* 227–250.

Winsor, D. (1996). *Writing like an engineer: A rhetorical education.* Mahwah, NJ: Lawrence Erlbaum.

Yates, J. (1985). Graphs as a managerial tool: A case study of DuPont's use of graphs in the early twentieth century. *The Journal of Business Communication, 22,* 5–33.

Yates, J., & Orlikowski, W. (1994). Genre repertoire: The structuring of communicative practices in organizations. *Administrative Science Quarterly, 39,* 541–574.

Yin, R. (1984). *Case study research: Design and methods.* Beverly Hills, CA: Sage.

Zimmerman, M., & Marsh, H. (1989). Storyboarding an industrial proposal: A case study of teaching and producing writing. In C. Matalene (Ed.), *Worlds of writing: Teaching and learning in discourse communities of work* (pp. 203–221). New York: Random House.

2

Narrative, Rhetoric, and Lives: Doing Ethnography

Jane Perkins
A.T. Kearney, Inc.

> We can, and have been, vexing each other with profit, the
> touchstone of interpretive advance.
> Geertz, cited in Rabinow, 1986, p. 256

Narrative has the potential to put lives into our research and, therefore, our knowing and our teaching. Most commonly, narrative is differentiated from other kinds of writing by the dimension of time (see, for example, Perkins and Blyler's Introduction, in this volume). Narrative also depends on characterization: individual characters, the character of the narrator(s), and, to varying degrees of recognition, the reader(s) or audience. Characterization may be the most important aspect of "the local"—the focus and result of anthropology's narrative/rhetorical turn; it is also missing in much of our research and writing. When our "subjects" are generalized into quantities and decontextualized classifications, their voices and stories vanish. When as researchers we objectify our roles and relationships with cultural others, details of our research lives are also lost. When readers are persuaded by knowledge-making strategies of counting or classifying, they lose out on individuals' stories.

It isn't that one method of knowledge-making is better than others; they are, of course, rhetorical. The problem is that for professional communication, the choice of narrative, complete with characterization, has not been an option. In one sense, researchers and their readers miss out on a level of detail that will potentially engage, delight, and stimulate thinking. The detail—for example, a unique character or a character's unique idea—may not show up in quantified results; it may elude the survey response form or fall between sense-making classifications. If told, it could be the catalyst for new thinking or approaches. While detailed characterization is important for professional communicators because of what we can learn, it is also important because of how we learn. Research that includes localized, character-filled stories demands discerning methodological and theoretical understanding, which helps to build our discipline.

In our field and others, research discussions, both methodological and theoretical—questioning what and how we know—continue to teeter between objectivity and subjectivity, between quantitative and qualitative, between methodological rigor and critical theory, between functionalism and interpretation...and the sorting and naming go on. Because in professional communication we are yet identifying and defining our developing field and our research approaches, this discussion has been invaluable for broadening the scope and increasing the sophistication of our research. Throughout, the discussion fulcrum has most often been ethnography. I want, therefore, to tell you a story (not The Story or a complete story) in three chronological parts of professional communication's appropriation of ethnography as a methodology for making some of our disciplinary knowledge. This story unfolds against an aside of anthropological experience and cautions, which foreground narrative, rhetoric, and lives. Because as our discussions and our research continue the balancing—the who's up and who's down—individuals or characters are most often left out. This story moves from a distinct beginning, through our grapplings for authority, to our awareness of ideological complexities, and continues with speculations.

BEGINNINGS

The publication of Odell and Goswami's *Writing in Nonacademic Settings* in 1985 introduced professional communication to ethnography. With his chapter in this landmark collection, Faigley enticed us with opening vignettes, classified our research perspectives as three types, and then called for ethnographic research in composition and professional communication studies. He argued for and helped to create a social perspective for our research. He also pointed us to relevant work in the collection: an early ethnography, "Writing at Exxon ITD: Notes on the Writing Environment of an R&D Environment," by Paradis, Dobrin, and Miller; and the basics for conducting ethnographic research, "Ethnographic Research on Writing: Assumptions and Methodology," by Doheny-Farina and Odell. At about the same time, Doheny-Farina (1986) published his first ethnography, "Writing in an Emerging Organization." We were intrigued by the dramatic story Doheny-Farina told of the significance of writing in the formation of the organization he studied. Ethnographies like his could take us inside businesses, industries, and social organizations, providing heretofore unresearched understanding of professional communication. Beyond survey responses (and their interpretations), we could learn about contexts, interrelationships of writing to events and actions, and more of the stories.

We were also provided with instructions that made this research methodology seem pretty straightforward: basically, observe a culture and write down what you see. Although individual characters, including the researcher/narrator—usually in what anthropologists refer to as the obligatory arrival story—peek through in these early ethnographies, their emphasis is on findings, not on characterization. We were introduced to what anthropologists call "realist" ethnography.

Anthropological Experience and Cautions: Ironically, while these innovators were introducing ethnography to the professional communication field (that is, to writing experts), some anthropologists were realizing that ethnography is writing. For anthropology, Geertz (1988) says, "A hundred and fifteen years (if we date our profession, as conventionally, from Tylor) of asseverational prose and literary innocence is long enough" (p. 24). With acknowledgment of Geertz as the forerunner, anthropologists typically mark their field's interpretive turn with the publication of Clifford and Marcus's (1986) *Writing Culture: The Poetics and Politics of Ethnography.* In his introduction to the collection, Clifford distinguished interpretive ethnography from realist ethnography, asserting that the most distinguishable aspect of interpretive ethnography is "the present dominant interest...about how interpretations are constructed by the anthropologist, who works in turn from the interpretations of his informants" (p. 26). Anthropologists also realized that they are part of the research, not neutral observers of cultures, but participants in cultures and most assuredly in the writing of the cultures. They had started to talk about their work as, for example, no longer just about cataloging cultural artifacts and features in the tradition of Boas, or about discovering cross-cultural generalizations in the tradition of Levi-Strauss. For these anthropologists, cultural knowing was now about "informants"—the individuals who comprise their research. Anthropologists also began to talk about the rhetorical influence of their readers and the academic considerations and constraints of publishing. Looking back at this turn in anthropology, Van Maanen (1995) summarized the realist approach that was common before the turn: "All that was required, it seemed, was a steady gaze and hand, a sturdy and thick notebook, and plenty of time to spare," and contrasted it to the after, in which "ethnography is no longer pictured as a relatively simple look, listen, and learn procedure but, rather, as something akin to an intense epistemological trial by fire" (p. 2). For interpretive anthropologists, writing ethnography became increasingly complex.

GRAPPLINGS FOR AUTHORITY

In the years that followed, professional communicators (researchers, teachers, and practitioners)—often by way of composition studies—quickly counted ethnography among our acquired research methodologies. Composition as a research field, complete with methodologies, was new, and professional communication, even newer. Over the years, the seesawings between, for example, methodological rigor and theoretical awareness have helped us assimilate ethnography and extend the field of professional communication through research innovations.

Methodological Rigor

On one side, for example, in 1987, North discussed ethnography in *The Making of Knowledge in Composition: Portrait of an Emerging Field*, and in 1988, Lauer and Asher included it among the methodologies they detailed in *Composition Research: Empirical Designs*. Overall, these influential works adopted ethnography in the "how-to," realist vein, holding it up to standards of objectivity and replicability. While included, the research methodology wasn't heralded with much confidence. North cautioned that ethnography "may reduce our puzzlement about the people and places studied, though, these fictions have their limits as knowledge" (p. 278) and that "among users and consumers alike [there is] considerable confusion about what sort of authority it has" (p. 313). Lauer and Asher also raised many realist questions, such as "Will the same variables be gleaned from new settings by other observers? Will these variables remain stable over time?" (p. 48). Thus in these early discussions, narration and characterization were considered to be part of the problem with this new-to-us research methodology, not as part of its distinct advantage. With North assuming Geertz's interpretive way of discussing ethnography as story but puzzling over it, and with Lauer and Asher attempting to vanish the individual (or variable), ethnography was a difficult methodological configuration when measured against realist evaluative criteria.

The 1992 special issue of *Technical Communication*, Research in Technical Communication, is also a significant part of the story. While many of the contributors included ethnography as an appropriate methodology for professional communication, their implicit guidelines for good research methodologies assessed ethnography against realist criteria. For example, the author of one article, MacNealy, suggested that data must be gathered by asking the same questions of all interviewees and that the data collected should result in records that can be reviewed by outsiders. Both methodological activities erase individual stories—the stories of individual interviewees or cultural others and the storied narrator.

Theoretical Awareness

During this time, ethnography's assimilation was balanced by the work of many professional communication theorists. Among those furthering the discussion and our understanding with arguments often born of interpretive anthropologists were Halpern (1988) with "Getting in Deep: Using Qualitative Research in Business and Technical Communication" and Brodkey (1987) with "Writing Ethnographic Narratives." Rather than being concerned, as North (1987) was, that "ethnographic inquiry produces stories, fictions" (p. 277), they addressed the narrative issue by dividing the research methodology into types. Halpern adopted Van Maanen's categories, which he used to describe ethnographic approaches in anthropology and to claim that ethnographers employ "alternative modes of presentation" (p. 37). She identified significant differences of writing and theorizing among the three alternatives: traditional realistic narrative, confessional narrative, and impressionistic narrative.

Brodkey (1987) also distinguished between ethnographic approaches, arguing that the differences between realist ethnography and interpretive ethnography[1] exemplify in practice much of the academy's then current debate. Her argument was built on differences between the "rhetoric of demonstration and (ethnographic) analysis [which] deals with certainty, that is, offers proofs that presume not simply that certainty is desirable, but attainable" and the "rhetoric of dialectics and (ethnographic) interpretation [which] deals with uncertainty, that is, offers arguments that display rather than obviate doubt." These differences, Brodkey explained, are also apparent in attitudes about the role and "interference" of the ethnographer and indicate basic "epistemological issues" (p. 27); their presence is either considered "intrusive" and "problematic" or as necessary for "constructing" information (p. 31).

In relation to these ethnographic differences, Brodkey raised concerns about narrativity. She categorized narrative stances as "perception," "conception," and "interest" (p. 38), identifying narratives of perception with realist ethnography. These ethnographic narratives are "a guided tour in which reader-tourists more or less willingly accept the narrator or analyst's decisions about what in the data is worth looking at" (p. 39). For a narrative stance of conception, the focus is on the narrator's ideology. And for a narrative stance of interest, "readers are in the scene as if they were themselves the narrator" (p. 39). While Brodkey's main point focused on the rhetorical constraints of telling stories in the academy (even as she pleads for their importance), her detailed explanation of narrative differences, and corresponding ethnographic choices, introduced some of the complex concerns of interpretive anthropologists. Between descriptions of realist (objective) and interpretive (subjective) ethnography, characterization, especially in the role of narrator, edged into our methodological/theoretical discussions through narrative.

In response to these descriptive classifications of ethnography, Kent (1993) attempted to shift our focus away from the binary opposition of "objectivity/subjectivity" (p. 74). By arguing against a "master narrative of objectivity," he aimed to collapse the objective/subjective split, which for ethnography raises concern for establishing objectivity in research in order to acquire validity. This possibility, he explained, depends on "an alternative vocabulary [that] is beginning to emerge that allows us to talk about discourse production without stumbling over the contradictions and paradoxes inherent in a language game controlled by the master narrative of objectivity" (p. 66). An alternative vocabulary means talking about "coherence strategies" rather than objectivity. These coherence strategies, such as fieldwork methodology, "enable us to weave the ethnography's claim into our own webs of belief" (p. 69).

Although the binary split—most easily summarized as objective/ subjective—
that fueled much of this discussion was valuable for merging theory with methodology and for increasing fieldwork and presentation sophistication, it also obscured
other ethnographic issues. For Kent, these issues included identifying coherence
strategies for gaining rhetorical acceptance, in other words, for establishing new
evaluative criteria for this research. For others, as the third part of my story explains,
the obscured issues are about ideology and power. And for me, of most importance
is awareness and responsibility in our research for individuals, for lives. In professional communication, the objective/subjective tottering has not gone away.
Perhaps the debate is continued as a rhetorical strategy for supporting contrasting
ways of doing ethnographic research. There are, after all, so many possibilities and
aspects to consider, including access to sites and people; a rhetorical rationale for
studying particular cultures; day-to-day fieldwork decisions of where to be, whom
to talk with, and whom to listen to; when and how to take notes and record; degrees
of participation with cultural others; and ways of writing the stories.

While methodologists and theorists talked about ethnography, a few professional communication researchers had by this time ventured to do it. In this retrospective of ethnography in professional communication, I'll continue to focus on a
storyline of issues, rather than describing or analyzing specific ethnographies,
although such analyses add value to our discussions. (Refer to Rentz's chapter in
this collection on case study research for a comprehensive list of ethnographic titles
in our field.)

Anthropological Experience and Cautions: While professional communicators
debated what counts as knowing and became more comfortable with ethnographic
methodology and theoretical issues, anthropologists agonized, in the most real and
immediate sense, about how to do it—how to represent cultures, how to write them.

By 1995, in his introductory chapter, "An End to Innocence," Van Maanen
claimed the Interpretive or Rhetorical Turn accepted throughout anthropology: "this
reversal is not a terribly controversial issue these days—at least among practicing
ethnographers" (p. 16). The result, he claimed, presented "troublesome epistemological issues with which we as writers must in some fashion deal" (p. 16). No
longer did most anthropologists believe that culture is "an object to be described,"
but rather, as Clifford (1986) states, it is always "contested, temporal, and emer-
gent" (p. 19). As these researchers developed more focused spins and concerns, the
broad covering term of interpretive ethnography became subdivided: "experimental," "radical," "participatory," "critical," and so forth. For Marcus and Fischer
(1986), the unrest and change was positive: "'What is happening' seems to us to be
a pregnant moment in which every individual project of ethnographic research and
writing is potentially an experiment. Collectively, these are in the process of recon-
structing the edifices of anthropological theory from the bottom up" (p. ix).

Part of anthropologists' challenge related to textualization, or, in other words, to
an awareness that ethnographers make knowledge by writing—narratively and
rhetorically. Because of their awareness of their writing and of what they are doing

with their writing, many anthropologists have consciously crafted their writing in ways other than what is considered traditional ethnographic presentation. They aim to reconfigure genres, especially ethnographic genres, and to push their writing in creative directions that announce to readers its impact rather than its neutrality. For Tyler (1986), the problem was not with a realist methodology: "It is instead a failure of the whole visualist ideology of referential discourse, with its rhetoric of 'describing,' 'comparing,' 'classifying,' and 'generalizing,' and its presumption of representational significance" (p. 130).

These innovators' motives, however, were not just to distinguish themselves from the ethnographic writing that had proceeded them, nor to signal attention to their writing; their purpose was, as Clifford (1986) explained, much more complex:

> Once cultures are no longer prefigured visually—as objects, theatres, texts—it becomes possible to think of a cultural poetics that is an interplay of voices, of positioned utterances. In a discursive rather than a visual paradigm, the dominant metaphors for ethnography shift away from the observing eye and toward expressive speech (and gesture). The writer's "voice" pervades and situates the analysis, and objective, distancing rhetoric is renounced. (p. 12)

Issues of textualization or the responsibility of representation are intimately tied to narrative and to characterization. Ethnographers were no longer comfortable with writing words to represent or symbolize a culture, but instead they believed an ethnography to be "a (morally charged) *story* about that" (original emphasis, Geertz, 1988, p.100). Therefore, along with issues of textualization and narration, which implicate the narrator and readers as characters in new ways, came characterization of the cultural others as coparticipants in ethnographies. For anthropology, Geertz could claim that "one of the major assumptions upon which anthropological writing rested until only yesterday, that its subjects and its audience were not only separate but morally disconnected, that the first were to be described but not addressed, that the second informed but not implicated, has fairly well dissolved" (p. 132).

The implication of the researcher with cultural others brought ethical issues to the foreground. Ethics has always been a part of ethnographic research (as it is for all research); however, without the assumed shroud of objectivity separating researchers from cultural others, ethics became ethnographers' primary concern. Because interpretive ethnography "foregrounds dialogue as opposed to monologue, and emphasizes the cooperative and collaborative nature of the ethnographic situation in contrast to the ideology of the transcendental observer" (p. 126), Tyler (1986) asserted that fieldwork and relationships with cultural others are fundamentally changed. The ethics of a participant rather than of an observer are much different because the implications of the researchers' actions, words, and presence are always immediate in this relationship. The relationship, as Tyler explains, is not based on the "ideology of 'observer-observed,' there being nothing observed and no one who is observer. There is instead the mutual, dialogical production of a discourse, of a story of sorts" (p. 126).

Anthropology's Interpretive, Narrative, Rhetorical Turn left ethnographers puzzling, on a day-to-day basis, about the "relations of power whereby one portion of humanity can select, value and collect the pure products of others" (Rose, 1990, p. 38).

IDEOLOGIES AND LIVES

Professional communicators were also starting to discuss issues of power. Raising many of the same issues troubling anthropologists, Herndl (1991) focused on the future of ethnographers in our discipline and "the reflexivity of postmodern ethnographic theory [that] conflicts with the demand of a professional, institutional practice" (p. 320). He suggested that "as members of the research community, we need to understand the way our disciplinary discourse appropriates the experience of the research subject and represents it in our institutions" (p. 320). From his ideological perspective, he touched on dimensions of characterization—cultural others, narrator(s), readers—in writing about "how the writer establishes a stable relation between herself and the 'other world' she describes, but also how she constructs a relationship between herself as an author and the representation she offers readers" (p. 324). Although he offered hope for experimental ethnographies because of the diversity of new and more reflexive ethnographic texts, his argument is weighted by an ideology powerless to foster change: "Since discourse and the knowledge it generates reproduce ideological structures, it will be difficult to impose a radical rhetorical practice in an existing institutional context" (p. 327).

Additionally, Dobrin and Doheny-Farina, two of the researchers who introduced ethnography to professional communication, discussed issues of power and representation as they reflexively contemplated their early research. Dobrin (1987) reflected on disciplinary boundaries that are enforced by discipline-specific and generalizable research. With great candor, he destroyed the generalities of his early "ethnography," alluding to the real "facts" he learned in his research and his wish that he and his coauthors could have written a different report: "Such a report would have been nothing more than an intelligent, knowledgeable account of the situation there, one that was both true to the complexities and removed from the quotidian...[it] would be successful only if, like good fiction, it allowed people to recognize themselves in it" (p. 7). Although he didn't actually say "narrative," "rhetoric," or "lives," the concepts were implicit in his regret of not being able to write personal, anecdotal stories that resonate with readers. He also envisioned the implications of such experimental ethnographic writing, citing the "risk" as "an admission that the academic forms of generalization, those which are designed to create disciplinary knowledge, are not appropriate here.... It would rip off the protective coloration we've been trying to put on for many years" (p. 7–8).

Responding to issues of ideology, Doheny-Farina (1993) reflected on his 10 years of ethnographic work to explain his ethical beliefs and actions. Rather than voicing concern about disciplinary constraints, as Herndl (1991, 1993) and Dobrin (1987) have, Doheny-Farina described those restraints as audience considerations. He reminded us that all research is rhetorical and concluded that "if writers of field studies of writing in nonacademic settings make clear to themselves from the start that their research processes—from entering sites through publishing research reports—are rhetorical enterprises that should be identified as such, then those researchers can act ethically" (p. 267). The ethical position he described has two strands: authoritative, which he calls "practical validity," and personal decision making and action. He linked practical validity—"determined through a range of readings by audiences located within the researcher's discipline, as well as those located within the research sites"—to the ethnographer's "ethical stance in the construction of research texts" (p. 261). This ethical stance, he explained, depends on researchers being "consistent with the claims that their studies ultimately make" (p. 258). Doheny-Farina's ethics of personal decision-making and action are apparent in his honest reflection on his fieldwork: "I begin exerting control by trying to obtain things: I want access. I want information. I want documents.... As my place becomes more secure—as I gain control—I seek conflict. I look for it and probe it.... And when I do not find conflict, I subtly create it. How? Through some of our best methods, such as discourse-based interviews ... and compose aloud protocols" (pp. 264–265). Integral to Doheny-Farina's ethical position is the necessity of negotiating rhetorical tensions of doing ethnography—tensions among all of the participants, including cultural others, ethnographers, and readers.

We continue, in Geertz's words (cited in Rabinow, 1986), to benefit as researchers, teachers, and practitioners by "vexing each other with profit" (p. 256). The profit comes with our reflexiveness, which helps us with our decision making and actions in doing research; hopefully makes our research a valuable experience for cultural others; and provides readers, and especially students, with needed understanding. Recent, thoughtful, and impassioned arguments have continued to do so. Blyler (1995) has added critical interpretive research as an avenue for our learning, emphasizing the ideological and value-laden nature of all research and arguing that "we in professional communication would do well to think long and deeply about this alternate ideology as a guide to our research endeavors" (p. 309) because of the potential for emancipation and social change. Charney's (1996) response and her subsequent interchanges with Cooper (1997) have also refined our research understanding, especially in blurring the division of ideological camps. The teetering continues as we circle around the important issues, focus on key aspects, turn to additional reflexive voices, name and rename. Ethnography continues to be central to these methodological and theoretical discussions because of our need to know Others, how they communicate, and what communication does in and for their lives.

Anthropological Experience and Cautions: Interpretive ethnographers' interactions with cultural others are guided by their efforts to respect cultural others, to include their voices in their ethnographic writing, to be responsible participants in their cultures, and to give back meaningfully. Ethnographers have not only become aware of the impact of textual issues and ethics—they also realize that they are responsible for doing and experimenting. For anthropologists (and for all ethnographers) a vivid and powerful history directs current research and inspires efforts for methodological change. Our experimentation is spurred by efforts to avoid colonialistic or neocolonialistic research habits and representation. In their efforts to know and help Others, Marcus and Fischer (1986) described a colonialistic research philosophy as the belief that "'the white man's burden' was to rescue these latter-day people from centuries of decay, disease, ignorance, and political corruption. Their own views were of interest only in the same way as was a child's whom one wished to educate as a means of teaching them the truth" (p. 2).

As anthropologists agonize about knowing Others (individual and cultural lives), they connect narrative (writing and textual imperatives) with the power of rhetoric. Marcus and Fischer (1986) caution that "rhetorical totalitarianism" results when "these subjects, who must be spoken for, are generally located in the world dominated by Western colonialism or neocolonialism; thus, the rhetoric is itself an exercise in power, in effect denying subjects the right to express contrary views, by obscuring from the reader recognition that they might view things with equal validity, quite differently from the writer" (original emphasis, p. 1). They remind us not only of our need to be rhetorically and ideologically aware but also that we are situated outside of Others' cultures and, therefore, must suspect our assumptions and even our good motives. They remind us that tensions, teeterings, vexings, and self-reflection are safeguards in the difficult work of knowing others when we realize that all of our research is participatory.

Questioning our assumptions in the making of ethnographic knowledge is, as in any hermeneutic communication, an interaction in which the Other is valued. Moreover, Rose (1990) suggests that as ethnographers we need to place ourselves in *"unfolding situations, to live through complex ongoing events—the stuff of stories*—rather than looking alone for the meaning of gestures, the presentations of selves, class relations, the meaning of rituals, or other abstract, analytical category phenomena on which we historically have relied" (original emphasis, p. 58). He also encourages us to do radical ethnography that "gets you closer to those you study at the risk of going native and never returning; it is hoped, at least, that you will not again embrace the received assumptions with which you, inheriting your academic texts, methods, and corporate academic culture, began" (p. 12). Anthropologists' long ethnographic history and their reflections upon it provide professional communication researchers with much to consider and apply—not only in our methodological/theoretical vexings but also as a reminder that assumptions and knowing need also to be weighed and balanced.

SPECULATIONS

My story of ethnography in professional communication takes us to an appreciation for what we have gained and can continue to learn from the rhetorical vexings of researchers in professional communication and anthropology, to an understanding and valuing of the ethical tensions that are necessary for ethnographers to negotiate their meaning-making and assumptions, and to connections between these points and the significance of narrative and characterization. With narrative and characterization, we have increased research opportunities and responsibilities for the lives that are included or excluded in what we write and how we write—lives of cultural others, researchers, and readers. What might these ethnographies be like?

Others' Cultures

When ethnographers are less concerned with identifying cultures as holistic entities with discrete boundaries and with classifying cultural attributes according to generalized categories, they realize that cultures comprise individuals who belong to layers of multiple cultures. For example, a corporation might be considered a culture, and in fact, that organization's leaders probably try to promote a unified cultural image, what they would term their brand. Within that corporation, however, individuals are members of departments or divisions; they may belong to teams within those divisions or that cross functions; they might have cultural membership that depends on geography, or gender, or tenure in the organization. The characters who populate our ethnographic stories will force us to listen to the significance of their cultural belongings, especially as these differences relate to communicating.

Professional communicators, then, will benefit from understanding interactions and communications among these multiple cultures. For example, corporate cultures typically include identifiable subcultures of marketing and R&D. Professional writers might be grouped, at least by the corporate org chart, within either of these departments or sometimes as a separate group. In the startup software development company of one of my ethnographic studies, marketers fostered the company's success with promises of new products and early delivery, software engineers were squeezed to deliver features they had not always developed, and professional writers were usually caught between the two. The cultural others in these three groups told stories important for professional communicators; their stories provided details about changing roles of these professional writers, of communication tools and strategies to promote product development, of communication processes that failed and some that succeeded, and so forth. Ethnographers and their cultural others determine the cultures and subcultures of their stories. Localized, characterized ethnographies will be about multiple cultural memberships and what those differences mean.

Present Narrator(s)

Our ethnographic stories might also be more about narrator(s). These stories could take the form of reflexive accounts in any number of venues. Before the interpretive turn, anthropologists often wrote, in addition to their sanctioned, academic ethnographies, unofficial, first-person accounts of their fieldwork (for example, Rabinow's (1977) *Reflections on Fieldwork in Morocco*) or told their stories in introductions, prefaces, or lengthy endnotes. Now, more often, these reflections are central to ethnographies as researchers experiment with their storytelling.

Reflexive narrators are important because they not only are aware of the role they play in the stories they tell and their influence on cultural others, they also teach researchers by example. Because doing ethnography is complex, we need to hear about our difficulties and our outcomes; we need reflexive narratives to learn ways to act and ways to write. For example, I've learned much from Rabinow's (1977) telling of his initial fieldwork uncertainties and his detailed and human actions that marked his coming to terms with his anthropology, from Geertz's (1995) autobiographical musings that span four decades, and from other narrators' stories. In our ethnographies, narrators may be increasingly reflexive and experimental.

Relationships

I also speculate that as ethnographies are enriched by characterization of cultural others with their complex cultural belongings and of reflexive narrators, our work and writings will be more about relationships. The importance of relationships isn't new to ethnographic research; relationships get us in the door and provide access to information. However, for interpretive ethnographers, relationships have changed and, therefore, the stories are also different. From relationships come the "plural present" that Goodall (1991) describes: "Ethnography is no longer about 'you' in the quest or conquest of 'them.' It is about the voice that emerges from the context(s) you share; it is about the choices you both make in the relational territory you jointly develop" (p. 219). The plural present, he explains, is a way of writing "the always contested nature of context, self, and Other. It is a step in the direction of narrative progress ... to try to get at the dignity of the Other in the same ways that we try to get at the dignity of self" (p. 217).

Readers, too, have a character part when they act on their rhetorical position. Professional communicators can encourage research that includes interpretive ethnographies—those aware of narrative, rhetoric, and lives. Readers then will encourage disciplinary tolerance and experimentation in formats and characterization, connect our discipline with cultures new to our studies, and through those cultures expand the scope of our professional and societal issues. Our ethnographies have the potential to be rewardingly diverse and innovative because communication is central to lives and cultures.

NOTE

[1] Brodkey (1987) uses the terms "traditional (analytical)" and "experimental (interpretive)" to describe these two ethnographic approaches.

REFERENCES

Blyler, N. R. (1995). Pedagogy and social action: A role for narrative in professional communication. *Journal of Business and Technical Communication, 9,* 289–320.

Brodkey, L. (1987). Writing ethnographic narratives. *Written Communication, 9,* 25–50.

Charney, D. (1996). Empiricism is not a four-letter word. *College Composition and Communication, 47,* 567–593.

Charney, D. (1997). Paradigm and punish. *College Composition and Communication, 48,* 562–565.

Clifford, J. (1986). Introduction—partial truths. In J. Clifford & G. E. Marcus (Eds.), *Writing and culture: The poetics and politics of ethnography* (pp. 1–26). Berkeley, CA: University of California Press.

Clifford, J., & Marcus, G. E. (Eds.). (1986). *Writing and culture: The poetics and politics of ethnography.* Berkeley, CA: University of California Press.

Cooper, M. (1997). Distinguishing critical and post-positive research. *College Composition and Communication, 48,* 556–561.

Dobrin, D. (1987) Writing without discipline(s). *Journal of Business and Technical Communication, 1,* 5–8.

Doheny-Farina, S. (1986). Writing in an emerging organization: An ethnographic study. *Written Communication, 3,* 158–185.

Doheny-Farina, S. (1993). Confronting the methodological and ethical problems of research on writing in nonacademic settings. In R. Spilka (Ed.), *Writing in the workplace: New research perspectives* (pp. 253–267). Carbondale, IL: Southern Illinois University Press.

Doheny-Farina, S., & Odell, L. (1985). Ethnographic research on writing: Assumptions and methodology. In L. Odell & D. Goswami (Eds.), *Writing in nonacademic settings* (pp. 503–535). New York: Guilford Press.

Faigley, L. (1985). Nonacademic writing: The social perspective. In L. Odell & D. Goswami (Eds.), *Writing in nonacademic settings* (pp. 231–248). New York: Guilford Press.

Geertz, C. (1988). *Works and lives: The anthropologist as author.* Stanford, CA: Stanford University Press.

Geertz, C. (1995). *After the fact: Two countries, four decades, one anthropologist.* Cambridge, MA: Harvard University Press.

Goodall, H. L. (1991). *Living in the rock 'n roll mystery: Reading context, self, and others as clues.* Carbondale, IL: Southern Illinois University Press.

Halpern, J. W. (1988). Getting in deep: Using qualitative research in business and technical communication. *Journal of Business and Technical Communication, 2,* 22–39.

Herndl, C. (1991). Writing ethnography: Representation, rhetoric, and institutional practices. *College English, 53,* 320–331.

Herndl, C. (1993). Teaching discourse and reproducing culture: A critique of research and pedagogy in professional and non-academic writing. *College Composition and Communication, 44*, 349–363.

Kent, T. (1993). *Paralogic rhetoric: A theory of communicative interaction.* Lewisburg, PA: Bucknell University Press.

Lauer, J., & Asher, W. (1988). *Composition research: Empirical designs.* New York: Oxford University Press.

MacNealy, M. S. (1992) Research on technical communication: A view of the past and a challenge for the future. *Technical Communication, 39*, 533–551.

Marcus, G., & Fischer, M. (1986). *Anthropology as cultural critique: An experimental moment in the human sciences.* Chicago: University of Chicago Press.

North, S. (1987). *The making of knowledge in composition: Portrait of an emerging field.* Portsmouth, NH: Boynton/Cook.

Odell, L., & Goswami, D. (Eds.). (1985). *Writing in nonacademic settings.* New York: Guilford Press.

Paradis, J., Dobrin, D., & Miller, R. (1985). Writing at Exxon ITD: Notes on the writing environment of an R&D organization. In L. Odell & D. Goswami (Eds.), *Writing in nonacademic settings* (pp. 281–307). New York: Guilford Press.

Rabinow, P. (1977). *Reflections on fieldwork in Morocco.* Berkeley, CA: University of California Press.

Rabinow, P. (1986). Representations are social facts: Modernity and post-modernity in anthropology. In J. Clifford & G. E. Marcus (Eds.), *Writing and culture: The poetics and politics of ethnography* (pp. 234–261). Berkeley, CA: University of California Press.

Rose, D. (1990). *Living the ethnographic life.* Newbury Park, CA: Sage.

Tyler, S. (1986). Post-modern ethnography: From document of the occult to occult document. In J. Clifford & G. E. Marcus (Eds.), *Writing and culture: The poetics and politics of ethnography* (pp. 122–140). Berkeley, CA: University of California Press.

Van Maanen, J. (1995). An end to innocence: The ethnography of ethnography. In J. Van Maanen (Ed.), *Representation in ethnography* (pp. 1–35). London: Sage.

part II
Narrative and Science Writing

3

Getting the Story, Telling the Story: The Science of Narrative, the Narrative of Science

Cheryl Forbes
Hobart and William Smith Colleges

Darwin knew how to tell a good tale, and 19th-century readers responded just as we do today. Poincaré was no mean raconteur, either, mathematically speaking. Booksellers in France couldn't keep his books in stock. Primo Levi brought the elements to life in *The Periodical Table*, which my ninth grade science teacher could have used to excite us students about the properties of copper, zinc, and titanium. Book reviewers raved.

What made the books of these scientists bestsellers? What made these scientists good writers? Each had a sense of narrative or story, which is important in fiction, memoir, and biography—but in science, in professional communication? Certainly when we professors prepare students to write scientific reports, we don't usually emphasize narrative; if anything, we forbid it, perhaps because, like second-hand smoke on hair and clothes, the odors of subjectivity, invention, and triviality, and "dumbing-down" cling to the word *narrative*. We want our science presented objectively, with the appropriate authorial distance, sobriety, factuality; or so we instruct students.

Yet the style we teach makes a subtle epistemological argument. When we insist that students write objectively, dispassionately, in the third person, using the passive voice, avoiding metaphors, similes, analogies—in other words, in prose devoid of voice or humanity—we are arguing that science is not what human beings make, but something human beings merely report as having been made or discovered.

Science is the way to find what is Out There, objective, eternal, unchanging. It gives readers an inaccurate perception of the messy, chaotic, contingent, accidental, disputatious nature of scientific inquiry and discovery—which makes science so exciting. The objective style keeps readers at arm's length and reifies science, or, as Alan G. Gross claims, such a style "creates a sense that science is describing a reality independent of its linguistic formations" (1990, p. 17).

That so few rhetoricians of science tackle narrative discourse or the discourse of popular science indicates how reified the objective style is. For example, though Gross considers analogy in scientific discourse and analyzes Watson's *The Double Helix* as a fairy tale (1980, p. 58 ff), he does not put his discussion in the large context of narrative itself (later in this essay I return to Watson and Crick's paper on DNA). Or consider Rom Harré's article, "Some Narrative Conventions of Scientific Discourse" (1990), in which the discussion of narrative focuses on the "story" in academic prose: the scientist as hero, the presentation of results as a linear, logical progression from a set of hypotheses, and the final inductive work. Harré's point is that the scientific article presents a fiction, a fairy tale because the reality of scientific research is nothing like that described in the literature (Greg Myers makes a similar argument in "Making a Discovery: Narratives of Split Genes" [1990]).

Although I agree, this is not the kind of narrative I am talking about, as I make clear below. Nor am I (primarily) concerned with the discourse of the academic scientific journal article, even though I would like to urge that most, if not all, scientific discourse forego an objective style in favor of the narrative style I explore here. I would like to read such discourse in articles in disciplinary journals and not just in *Harper's* or *The New Yorker*. I would like scientists to tell me stories, but though my heart lies with this suggestion, my head does not (and of course it would merely replace one kind of discourse requirement for another, when what we need are multiple kinds of discourse). For busy scientists who need to read succinct, highly coded discourse, narration could well conflict—and the typographic and formatting requirements of many disciplinary journals are designed to make articles quickly understandable (for instance, the abstract, subheadings that outline contents, the conclusion, tables, and figures).

Nevertheless, and keeping this caveat in mind, a scientist could introduce narrative elements into an objective style (through choice of verbs, for instance, or through metaphor), without sacrificing succinctness or shifting the focus from the scientific information to the scientist herself. However, my purpose here is not to discuss the academic scientific journal article and its narrowly focused readership. Rather, I am concerned with professional communication written by scientists or science journalists for a general, "liberally" educated audience. Why this focus, when most recent work on scientific prose has centered on the academic article? (In addition to those already cited above, see, for instance, *Understanding Scientific Prose*, edited by Jack Selzer [1993]; *Textual Dynamics of the Professions: Historical and Contemporary Studies of Writing in Professional Communities*, edited by Charles Bazerman and James Paradis [1991]; Bazerman's *Shaping Written*

Knowledge: The Genre and Activity of the Experimental Article in Science [1988]; and *The Rhetorical Turn: Invention and Persuasion in the Conduct of Inquiry*, edited by Herbert W. Simons [1990]).

I focus on scientific discourse for a general, educated audience because, like Selzer (1993), I believe that scientific prose is a central discourse in our culture (this goes beyond Selzer's "especially important"), but I disagree with Selzer's claim that "scientific discourse today is typically carried out not in public but in more private communities..." (p. 7). On the contrary, the scientific discourse that is "especially important" in and for our culture is precisely that carried out in public: through newspapers, news magazines, scientific periodicals, and "public service" brochures and advertisements, whose readership is the generally educated public, and over the air and radio waves (though I limit myself here to scientific discourse in print, I could well and fruitfully apply my argument to broadcast scientific discourse).

To return, then, to the scientists cited at the outset, we need to understand that their discourse is effective because of the narrative elements. We need to answer our students who read Darwin or Poincaré (often at our request) and then ask why those scientists write one way when they have been told to write in another. And, finally, we need to graduate more scientists who can write for a broad audience, precisely because science and its discourse is so important in and for our culture. Stephen Jay Gould himself calls for this in the introduction to *Bully for Brontosaurus* (1992).

So in thinking about stories and science and whether Darwin, Poincaré, and Levi are exceptions and exceptional among scientists or writers of science, I conducted an experiment. I pulled from my bookshelves several volumes of contemporary scientific discourse, most of them marketed to a general, educated audience, as were Darwin's, Poincaré's, and Levi's. (These volumes were not chosen with forethought or because I thought they would support my position; they simply happened to be the science books on my shelf; in this sense, I chose them randomly.)

I opened the introduction or preface and the first chapter of each book to find out how the author starts out because the beginning of any discourse sets the tone, establishes the style, and prepares readers for what follows. For scientific discourse, the lead, to use a journalistic word, is crucial, and for a general audience, the more technical the subject, like astrophysics, quantum mechanics, or DNA research, the more attention a writer must pay to the opening words in order to keep readers reading, to engage them at the outset in the adventures they are about to participate in. In other words, from the opening sentences, a writer wants readers to participate in the journey, to be part of the discovery, to catch the excitement of the adventure, as if they had been in on things from the beginning. Thus, I read the introductory matter as well as opening chapters. I studied the pronouns each writer used, what verb forms, what adverbials, all of which are significant discourse markers for narrative. I wondered how (or whether) writers establish a sense of plot and character (pronouns), of drama and comedy (passive or active verb forms), of place and time (the function of adverbials). Here, then, are seven samples, with a few brief comments after each, to begin the discussion of narrative in "popular" scientific discourse; each book was written for a general audience (broadly defined, sometimes *very* broadly):

- Dennett, *Darwin's Dangerous Idea: Evolution and the Meanings of Life* (1995). "We used to sing a lot when I was a child, around the campfire at summer camp, at school and Sunday school, or gathered around the piano at home. One of my favorite songs was 'Tell Me Why'" (p. 17). Dennett says in the preface that he is writing about science, not writing science *per se*, so it might be unfair to point to his use of the first persons singular and plural or the sense of place and time he establishes. But *Consciousness Explained* (1991) is science, and there he begins his preface with another personal story and the first chapter with a "supposition": "Suppose evil scientists removed your brain from your body while you slept, and set it up in a life-support system in a vat" (p. 3). A supposition by any other name is a story, and he uses the second person to engage our attention, to involve us in his story.
- Sacks, *An Anthropologist on Mars* (1995; Sacks, a neurophysiologist, uses the word *anthropologist* metaphorically). "I am writing this book with my left hand, although I am strongly right-handed" (p. xv). There it is again, the first person singular. His first chapter begins, "Early in March 1986 I received the following letter" (p. 3). Although Sacks could have begun this sentence also with the first person singular, he chooses to begin with an adverb of time (undoubtedly for a smoother transition into the letter he is about to quote). But the emphasis remains on the first person.
- Johnson, *Fire in the Mind* (1995). "Several years ago, on a visit home to New Mexico from my self-imposed exile in New York City, I was driving through the predominantly Catholic village of Truchas, on the high road from Santa Fe to Taos, when I rounded a corner and was startled to see..." (p. 1); this sentence, the first of the Introduction, continues for four more lines. The first chapter begins, "In the evening, just as their planet is about to complete another revolution, small bands of earthlings" (p. 11). He tells a story from his point of view, and though this sentence doesn't contain the first person singular (he does use it in the course of the chapter), Johnson nevertheless makes it clear to readers that we are hearing the story from his perspective. (Here is a good example of the way writers can present a first person perspective without actually using "I.")
- Gould, *Dinosaur in a Haystack* (1995). "I have always seen myself as a meat-and-potatoes man. You can take your ravioli stuffed with quail and...well, stuff it somewhere (I am also quite capable of releasing my own ground pepper from a shaker)" (p. ix). In the first sentence of the first essay, Gould writes that "Galileo described the universe in his most famous line: 'This grand book is written in the language of mathematics, and its characters are triangles, circles, and other geometric figures'" (p. 3). No first person singular, to be sure, but we do find narrative: In 29 words, Gould cleverly packs a story within a story.
- McPhee, companion books *In Suspect Terrain* (1983) and *Assembling*

California (1993). "The paragraph that follows is an encapsulated history of the eastern United States, according to plate-tectonic theory and glacial geology" (1983, p. 3) and "You go down through the Ocean View district of San Francisco to the first freeway exit after Daly City, where you describe, in effect, a hairpin turn to head north past a McDonald's to a dead end in a local dump" (1993, p. 3). Although neither sentence includes the first person singular, like the second passage cited from Gould above, we do have narrative. We have stories. We have "encapsulated history," and history is by definition a narrative. McPhee is promising to tell us the geological story of one part of our country, and throughout the rest of the book, he tells us the story as narrated by scientists who hold or dispute plate tectonic theory (thus also narrating and explicating the theory iteself). In the second quotation, McPhee uses the even-more-frowned-upon and forbidden second person singular (think of the many admonitions professors give students about using "you"), which I noted in Dennett and found again in Gould. "You" automatically implies "I."

- Angier, *The Beauty of the Beastly* (1995). "When I was a girl"—more first person singular—"I had a terror of cockroaches that bordered on pathological" (p. ix). What about the beginning of the first chapter? "Ah, Romance. Can any sight be as sweet as a pair of mallard ducks gliding gracefully across a pond" (p. 3). Angier does not use the first person here or throughout the chapter. Nevertheless, who could deny that she establishes a strong narrative voice or that the first person singular is lurking suspiciously close to the surface of her discourse? Does she not invite readers to stand shoulder to shoulder with her and watch those mallards "glide gracefully" as she tells us their story?
- Nuland, *How We Die* (1994). "Every life is different from any that has gone before it, and so is every death. The uniqueness of each of us extends even to the way we die" (p. 3). Not what I'd call a scintillating start for a story. I may have found my one real exception, but then the second paragraph (and the acknowledgments, of all things) changes my initial response: "The first time in my professional career that I saw death's remorseless eyes, they were fixed on a fifty-two-year-old man, lying in seeming comfort between the crisp sheets of a freshly made-up bed, in a private room at a large university teaching hospital" (p. 4). Death is no longer an abstraction, but a character in a narrative. As with Gould's opening line about Galileo, here is a story within a story. In Chapter 2, Nuland gives readers the medical story of heart disease, the story that lies underneath the first two he tells.

Let me repeat. I am putting forward the case that good science writing, particularly (though not exclusively) for a general, liberally educated audience, depends on the conventions of narrative—place, time, characters, dialogue, dramatic tension, humorous incongruity, suspense, mystery, intrigue, plot, and a believable, reliable narrator.

Sometimes the story reads like a whodunit, sometimes like an Aesop's fable or folktale, sometimes like slapstick comedy, but regardless of the (sub)genre, at the heart of good science writing for an educated audience—an audience not narrowly specialized—what drives the writing and the writer and what engages readers, what makes the text succeed, is narrative. And without narrative—or with mishandled, inconsistent narrative—the text fails to fulfill the expectations of readers and the goals of the writer.

Let's look a little more closely at the few sentences I have quoted in my sample list of books, before moving to an extended analysis of the narrative elements in two scientific essays. Although not every quotation contains every item in my narrative catalogue (place, time, characters, dialogue, dramatic tension, suspense, mystery, intrigue, plot, humorous incongruity, and a believable, reliable narrator), we do find several in most of them. Take place, for example. Johnson and McPhee and Nuland give us place, as does Dennett. Gould, Sacks, Angier, and Johnson emphasize time, also introducing characters and dialogue, even if they do it by citing letters or other writing. McPhee subtly includes dialogue by paraphrasing a scientific theory, which makes his first book on plate tectonics, *In Suspect Terrain* (1983), a conversation with that theory (and the scientists who hold or reject it); in the second book, he establishes a conversation with the reader by his emphatic use of the second person singular.

Although dramatic tension, suspense, mystery, and intrigue can all be subsumed under plot and seen as synonymous, I list them separately to emphasize their importance, for every sentence cited above evidences these characteristics: Something is about to happen to someone, and we'd better keep our eyes open.

Because such discourse has tension, contains mystery, and suspends or delays the main point, readers ask questions, our curiosity is peaked, and we continue to read. Humorous incongruity can work similarly, and though not all the writers cited above use humorous incongruity, several do, among them Gould and Angier. Welcome to the seriously playful side of science.

The narrator in science writing deserves a separate paragraph (if not a separate article). Every writer, even McPhee, establishes a distinctive narrative voice, usually with the first person singular (McPhee creates a narrator by his use of "you" and the implied "I"), which affects verb choice. The result is an active, not passive, voice. For of all the characteristics of narrative, the credible, personable, reliable, conversational presence of the teller of the tale is the most important. We might do without an unambiguous sense of place or humorous incongruity (many narratives have neither), but we cannot do without the narrator, who provides presence and perspective and establishes empathy and connection with the reader (and not, coincidentally, with the subject). So although the narrator comes last in the list, she initiates the rest, for without a narrator we cannot have a narrative: cause and effect.

Given the above list of characteristics of narrative and to further develop the theory that there is a narrative of science and a "science" (or system) of narrative, I want to look closely at two quite different but well-known writers of science, a journalist who specializes in science and a scientist who writes journalism. Both kinds of writers direct their discourse at a general, educated audience, and this audience (I am included in it) needs both kinds of writers for a rich understanding of science and scientific inquiry. The biological essays of journalist Angier have been praised as "science writing at its best," and she has been compared to writers from Aristotle to Lewis Thomas. Gould's collections on evolution, culled from his monthly column for *Natural History* magazine, have consistently landed on the bestseller lists. I have chosen them, therefore, because they are highly respected, widely read, and representative of the two types of writers who publish in the field today.

Angier's "The Scarab, Peerless Recycler," in *The Beauty of the Beastly* (1995), takes an unlikely subject and through narrative changes our presuppositions. Gould's "Creation Myths of Cooperstown" from *Bully for Brontosaurus* (1992), the collection Gould himself considered his best to date, interrogates the nature of story itself to ask fundamental epistemological questions: How do we know what we know; What counts as or constitutes science? His essay (and indeed the whole book), therefore, exposes the heart of writing science as narrative.

ANGIER

Recycling, Superfund cleanup, landfills, supertankers trolling the waters with garbage and no port or harbor willing to accommodate the trash: Such issues form the backdrop for Angier's Aesop-like essay, "The Scarab, Peerless Recycler" (1995). Implicitly she asks what humans might learn (about ourselves?) from studying the scarab. She also implicitly asks us to reconsider our value system—a kind of "least of these" approach to understanding nature.

Therefore, from her opening lines, Angier wants to jar us. We might think that we are superior to the Egyptians, who might have worshiped the dung beetle, but perhaps they recognized how important the dung beetle was, unlike us. We would rather avoid beetles altogether—just as we would rather keep our dung out of sight and out of mind.

So Angier says to readers, "Don't think you're wiser than the Egyptians. Listen to this story." She uses phrases like "stamp of nobility," compares a beetle head to a diadem and a beetle body to "glittering mail of bronze or emerald or cobalt blue," and catalogues a beetle's symbolic significance: "rebirth, good fortune, the triumph of sun over darkness" (1995, p. 109). All this for a creature that feeds on feces. How many women sporting an emerald or ruby scarab brooch know the real story? Angier's essay reminds me of Primo Levi's tale about lipstick, for which manufacturers need, among other ingredients, a goodly supply of chicken shit (the Anglo-Saxon, which is his, has delighted students every time I include it on a syllabus); as Levi discovers, it isn't all that easy to come by.

Angier (1995) tells a story at once medieval, magical, and masculine, for her words conjure up images of jousting tournaments, damsels in distress, the courtly love tradition. The adjective *majestic* and the adverb *romantically* reinforce such images so that readers write a particular kind of narrative as they read, not one normally associated with science in general or with dung beetles in particular. Angier's metaphors, almost a requirement for narration in science because of the implied story inherent in any metaphor, create a singular (that is, unique) voice, even though she does not use the first person singular. They also create the humorous incongruity of dung beetles as knights in shining armor doing battle against the forces of evil: They "assiduously clear away millions of tons of droppings, the great bulk of it from messy mammals like cows, horses, elephants, monkeys, and humans." Yes, Angier assures us readers, dung beetles do us a favor, work nobly for our good, and, she implies, it's about time we give credit where it is due. (Angier sneaks in the revelation that we are among the messiest of mammals—and by listing humans last she implies that we are, actually, *the* messiest. A climax comes at the end of the sentence; we know and are not surprised by cows and elephants being messy, but humans? She nails us by surprising us.)

In other words, what a story this is.

Every sentence, every paragraph in Angier's (1995) succinct essay contributes to the story, at the same time that each is a story in miniature, making the whole far greater than the sum of its parts. In terms of narrative, what do we find?

- A protagonist—the quintessential youngest son, the lowly dung beetle
- A problem—too much waste material on our overcrowded planet
- Dramatic tension—thousands and thousands of dung beetles descending on a large pat of dung and eating it sometimes within minutes; or the story within the story about how Australia in the 1960s began to solve its dung problem by introducing several varieties of beetles
- Romance—"singles bars," "courtship dances," dung beetles mating and forming families
- Artistry—those dung beetles that shape their food into beautiful geometric forms
- Exotic locations—the savannahs of Africa, the deserts of India, the Himalayan meadows, the Panamanian jungles, the redwood forests
- Time—early bird beetles to late night revelers
- Costumes—some beetles don disguises, for instance, looking like sticks; and
- Competition and crime—fighting for the first bite.

About the only narrative element Angier lacks is dialogue, for though she unabashedly and unapologetically loves to anthropomorphize, she stops short of writing explicit beetle conversations the way a writer of beast fables might (where beasts have human language and even human characteristics). Nevertheless, in what she *does* narrate we can write the dialogue she only implies, as in the following: "Robber beetles sneak in and try to steal balls painstakingly shaped by others. Joining the fray are many species of dung-eating flies. The scene resembles a fast-food outlet at lunchtime, with all the patrons grabbing something to bring back to their desk" (1995, p. 112). Because she uses an analogy from readers' everyday experience, it is easy to imagine the dialogue:

"Your money or your life."

"Stick 'em up."

"I'll take a Big Mac and a large fries."

"Hey you—whaddya mean, butting into line like that?"

"Jeez, it's late. I've gotta get back to work or the boss'll *kill* me."

We can do this because we know what happens at a fast-food franchise during a frantic American worker's lunch hour. And we now also have a pretty good idea of the feeding frenzy that hits dung beetles when yet another cow drops a pat.

Angier writes economically, tells the story vividly, and helps us participate enthusiastically. Will we agree with her that beetles are "key organisms in the environment?" (1995, p. 113). Absolutely, thanks to her skill as a storyteller. Will we think of beetles the same way after reading her story? Never.

GOULD

When we think of scientists who write today, Gould is the first name to come to mind. Yet he stands in a contradictory place when it comes to science, to writing, and to scientific discourse, and for this very reason he is worth studying. He brings a great deal to the table. Like Angier, Gould takes writing science for a general audience as a high calling, almost a priestly vocation. He deplores the equation of popular writing with pap and distortion: "Such a designation imposes a crushing professional burden on scientists (particularly young scientists without tenure) who might like to try their hand at this expansive style" (1992, p. 11).

Yet Gould also dislikes journalism that gives "instant fact and no analysis...for the dumb-downers tell us that average Americans can't assimilate anything more complex or pay attention to anything longer" (1992, p. 91; Angier, who never provides facts without analysis, does not fall within Gould's critical scope). Nevertheless Gould boldly urges young scientists to imitate him, and practice and perfect *good* science writing for average Americans: "We must all pledge ourselves to recovering accessible science as an honorable intellectual tradition" (p. 12).

Whom does Gould mean to include with the first person plural? Scientists? Science journalists? Professors of science? Professors of scientific and technical writing? He doesn't say, other than that "several of us are pursuing this style of writing in America today. And we enjoy success if we do it well" (1992, p. 12). I would, therefore, include all the writers mentioned above, and many, many more; and I would make the case that Gould wants teachers to instruct all students of science in the same "style of writing" he and his cohorts are practicing (which does not imply that it should be the *only* style students learn). It's about time, he implies, to put this "honorable intellectual tradition" back in the curriculum for the benefit of students, professors, and the public.

Although Gould does not define his style of writing as narrative, nevertheless he hints at two narrative strands in the history of science writing, which he labels the Franciscan and the Galilean. Angier (1995) lies in the Fransciscan tradition, the poetic, exultant celebration of nature's glory and quirkiness—as her comparisons, analogies, similes, metaphors, and whimsy in "Scarab, Peerless Recycler" demonstrate. Although Gould loves a good Franciscan narrative, he refuses to tread that trail because he claims he would fall on his face. Instead, as he documents the human effort to understand nature, he follows the Galilean tradition. Using words like *history*, Gould explains that he loves "the puzzles and intellectual delights" nature provides (1992, p. 13). It is not stretching narrative to the breaking point to say that a "puzzle" is just another name for a "mystery" or that an "intellectual delight" implies a search for the telling incongruity.

If we readers don't find a fully expressed theory of scientific narrative in the opening pages of *Bully for Brontosaurus* (1992), by studying Gould's discourse we can infer one, for instance in the third chapter, "The Creation Myths of Cooperstown." This essay is remarkable on two grounds: It provides another example of narrative, and its subject is, ultimately, narrative itself—the narratives that compete for our attention. Thus, he implicitly addresses why scientists should write in this way.

Gould juxtaposes the scientific hoax of the Cardiff Giant (which he compares to Piltdown Man) and its story of human origins to the Abner Doubleday hoax about the founding of baseball, which is immortalized in Cooperstown (itself the repository of numerous stories, town as book, so to speak) and to the story of evolution, the only story that Gould credits with telling the scientific truth. It doesn't give the plot away to quote from the end of Gould's intricate tale:

> And why do we prefer creation myths to evolutionary stories?...Yes, heroes and shrines are all very well, but is there not grandeur in the sweep of continuity? Shall we revel in a story...that may include the sacred ball courts of the Aztecs.... Or shall we halt beside the mythical Abner Doubleday...thereby violating truth and, perhaps even worse, extinguishing both thought and wonder? (1992, p. 58)

Because Gould understands the pull of stories, as he admits here, he wants evolutionary stories to hold their own with other stories, which he calls myths. And how can they hold their own in the popular imagination—to return to Gould's first chapter—without writers who know the story and how to tell it well, Gould asks? I would add, where will these informed, skillful writers come from, unless students learn how to write narrative?

Because opening lines tell us so much, as I pointed out above, consider the opening lines of "Cooperstown": "You may either look upon the bright side and say that hope springs eternal, or, taking the cynic's part, you may mark P.T. Barnum as an astute psychologist for his proclamation that suckers are born every minute" (1992, p. 42). Gould's second person singular establishes a narrative voice and, indeed, a narrator, who says, in effect, Let me tell you about..., or, Do you recollect the time that...? Any time a writer directly addresses the audience, readers find a story about to commence, if not already in progress, which is the impact of Gould's opening words. We readers feel as if we have arrived in the middle of a story, and though we don't know what the narrator has already said, we sense that it won't take us long to figure out what's going on. To help us, Gould uses many of the same narrative elements as Angier:

- Mystery and dramatic tension—how the Cardiff Giant succeeded in fooling people
- A problem—why origins of anything fascinate people and why we like to believe in "myths"
- A villain—George Hull
- A hero—Gould himself?
- Romance—our love of baseball and Cooperstown, and
- Stories within stories within stories—from Abner Doubleday to A. G. Spaulding to Henry Chadwick to the Civil War to the Victoria and Albert Museum in London and then back to Lower Manhattan and Alexander Joy Cartwright.

Unlike Angier, Gould does use the first person. He wants readers to come with him as he stalks his prey, as he unravels the ultimate story, as he tries to discover why people love myths. And here occur some hints at a theory: "Creation myths...identify heroes and sacred places, while evolutionary stories provide no palpable, particular object as a symbol for reverence, worship, or patriotism" (1992, p. 57).

Can scientists compete with mythic tales? Are evolutionary stories deficient as stories because they lack heroes whom readers can turn into symbols, objects to revere? (Stories, as I noted above, do have heroes and villains.) Does Gould's claim undercut the very argument I have been making? Or is Gould in this passage being disingenuous or subtle or modest?

Let me answer my questions by calling Gould himself as witness in my defense and against himself:

- "We care deeply about Darwin's encounter.... The details do not merely embellish an abstract tale moving in an inexorable way. The details are the story itself" (1992, p. 29).
- "We are bombarded with too much.... If we cannot sort the trivial from the profound, we are lost in terminal overload. The criteria for sorting must involve context [the story] and theory—the larger perspective that a good education provides" (p. 91).
- "The full story... contains lessons" (p. 212).

And most tellingly and directly in the final essay of the collection, "The Horn of the Triton," Gould rejects his earlier declaration about science lacking heroes and sacred places:

- "This essential tension...has been well appreciated by historians, but remains foreign to the thoughts and procedures of most scientists. We often define science (far too narrowly, I shall argue) as the study of nature's laws and their consequences" (p. 500).
- "We are truly historians by practice, and we demonstrate the futility of disciplinary barriers between science and the humanities" (p. 501).
- "They [the planets] are objects in the domain of a grand enterprise—natural history—that unites both styles of science in its ancient and still felicitous name" (p. 508).

Science and story, heroes and heroines, good guys and bad guys, events and the places where they occur—on earth, inside the earth, above the earth—how can Gould assert on the one hand that scientists have no story to tell, that scientists shouldn't surrender "science to the domain of narrative" (p. 506), and then write so persuasively that science is story?

Gould narrates the story that is involved in the scientific fact, demonstrating theory and revealing assumptions by writing about particular people in particular places doing particular things at particular times. Scientific discovery, as I said at the outset, does not come fully formed from on high. Often the best way to understand a fact or theory is to know how it came to be known—in other words, what people did.

Gould also writes with one of the strongest narrative voices in the science-writing business. For instance, he directly engages readers through his use of parenthetical asides, which are ubiquitous (I cite one example, above), and by telling us directly of his passions, his curiosities, his questions: "I confess that I have always viewed..." (1992, p. 331); "I read Stewart's letter and sat bolt upright with attention and smiles" (p. 389); "I find something enormously ironical in this old battle" (p. 412); "I need hardly remind everybody" (p. 181); "My odd juxtapositions sometimes cause consternation; some readers might view this particular comparison as outright sacrilege" (p. 122).

If we are to take Gould at his word that he practices the kind of science writing that he wants others to practice as well, and if we find in his discourse every element that constitutes narrative, as we do, then we can only conclude that, despite the few paradoxical passages that appear to reject the very style of discourse he is writing and recommending, he nevertheless believes that successful science writing means narrative. We don't need less narrative, we need more. We don't need fewer narrators of science, we need more of them.

To return to the point I made at the beginning, my focus is on scientific discourse for a general, educated audience. However, as I also indicated at the beginning, I think it possible for scientists writing in disciplinary journals to use some of the narrative elements I identify. A case in point is one of this century's seminal scholarly papers in biology, which announced the discovery by Watson and Crick of the double helix DNA.

Not only do Watson and Crick use the first person, but they use it throughout their two reports. They also use the active voice and strong verbs. For instance, here is their opening paragraph: "We wish to suggest a structure for the salt of deoxyribose nucleic acid (DNA). This structure has novel features which are of considerable biological interest (1980, p. 237). Later they write, "We wish to put forward a radically different structure....we have made the usual chemical assumptions" (p. 238). And near the end of their short, tight paper, we find, "It has not escaped our notice that..." (p. 240).

Although I cannot claim that Watson and Crick completely fit the stylistic model demonstrated here, their reports do reflect a sense of mystery and intrigue intended to peak readers' interest and curiosity; they do use some narrative elements: "In our opinion, this structure is unsatisfactory for two reasons" (1980, p. 237), which leads them into their "radically different structure." They are saying, in effect, that many people have been working to unravel a mystery, some good attempts have been made, but they have fallen short, and we now know why.

Here is another example from Watson and Crick's second paper, which also incorporates a sense of mystery and uses the first person: "Despite these uncertainties we feel that our proposed structure..." (1980, p. 246). Therefore, there may well be a place for narrative, even in articles for disciplinary journals. In fact, last year the editors of Science announce that they wanted to make their articles more readable, more jargon-free, less arcane—and, their examples indicated, more narrative-like.

Narrative, then, isn't simply a way to dress up, entertain, or sweeten science for nonscientists—not the Mary Poppins approach to broad, ongoing education. Rather, in Gould's words, "The details [and he means the narrative details] are the story itself": people, places, conversation, serendipitous mistakes (who did what and why). We professors need to teach our science students to imitate Gould, Angier, McPhee, Dennett, Johnson—and Darwin, Einstein, Poincaré, and others. For as Berthoff, a teacher and researcher of composition theory has put it, "how we construe is how we construct" (1983, p. 166). How we conceive of a discipline—our epistemology—is defined or revealed by the discourse we write.

REFERENCES

Angier, N. (1995). *The beauty of the beastly: New views on the nature of life.* Boston: Houghton Mifflin.

Bazerman, C. (1988). *Shaping written knowledge: The genre and activity of the experimental article in science.* Madison, WI: University of Wisconsin Press.

Bazerman, C., & Paradis, J. (Eds.). (1991). *Textual dynamics of the professions: Historical and contemporary studies of writing in professional communities.* Madison, WI: University of Wisconsin Press.

Berthoff, A. E. (1983). How we construe is how we construct. In P. L. Stock (Ed.), *Fforum: Essays on theory and practice in the teaching of writing* (pp. 166–170). Upper Montclair, NJ: Boynton/Cook.

Dennett, D. C. (1991). *Consciousness explained.* Boston: Little, Brown.

Dennett, D. C. (1995). *Darwin's dangerous idea: Evolution and the meaning of life*. New York: Simon & Schuster.

Gould, S. J. (1992). *Bully for brontosaurus: Reflections in natural history*. New York: W. W. Norton.

Gould, S. J. (1995). *Dinosaur in a haystack: Reflections in natural history*. New York: Harmony Books.

Gross, A. G. (1990). *The rhetoric of science*. Cambridge, MA: Harvard University Press.

Harré, R. (1990). Some narrative conventions of scientific discourse. In C. Nash (Ed.), *Narrative in culture: The uses of storytelling in the sciences, philosophy, and literature* (pp. 81–101). London: Routledge.

Johnson, G. (1995). *Fire in the mind: Science, faith, and the search for order*. New York: Vintage.

McPhee, J. (1983). *In suspect terrain*. New York: Farrar, Straus and Giroux.

McPhee, J. (1993). *Assembling California*. New York: Farrar, Straus and Giroux.

Myers, G. (1990). Making a discovery: Narratives of split genes. In C. Nash (Ed.), *Narrative in culture: The uses of storytelling in the sciences, philosophy, and literature* (pp. 102–126). London: Routledge.

Nuland, S. B. (1994). *How we die: Reflections on life's final chapter*. New York: Vintage.

Sacks, O. (1995). *An anthropologist on mars: Seven paradoxical tales*. New York: Vintage.

Selzer, J. (Ed.). (1993). *Understanding scientific prose*. Madison, WI: University of Wisconsin Press.

Simons, H. W. (Ed.). (1990). *The rhetorical turn: Invention and persuasion in the conduct of inquiry*. Chicago: University of Chicago Press.

Watson, J. D. (1980). *The double helix: A personal account of the discovery of the structure of DNA* (G. S. Stent, Ed.). New York: W. W. Norton.

FOR FURTHER READING

The following list, by no means exhaustive, is intended as a supplement to the works cited in the text. With one exception, I have not included other titles by authors named there; certainly any reading list should contain additional books by Gould, McPhee, and Sacks. In putting the list together, I wanted breadth in terms of scientific discipline and writing style.

Broad, W. J. (1998). *The universe below: Discovering the secrets of the deep sea*. New York: Touchstone.

Grice, G. (1998). *The red hourglass: Lives of the predators*. New York: Delacorte.

Hubbell, S. (1993). *Broadsides from the other orders: A book of bugs*. New York: Random House.

Lopez, B. (1986). *Arctic dreams: Imagination and desire in a northern landscape*. New York: Scribner's.

Nuland, S. N. (1997). *The wisdom of the body*. New York: Knopf.

Quammen, D. (1997). *The song of the Dodo: Island biography in an age of extinctions*. New York: Touchstone.

Wallace, D. R. (1980). *Idle weeds: The life of an Ohio sandstone ridge*. Columbus, OH: Ohio State University Press.

4

The Limits of Narrative in The Construction of Scientific Knowledge: George Gaylord Simpson's *The Dechronization of Sam Magruder*

Debra Journet
University of Louisville

The role of narrative in the physical sciences has become the focus of recent attention by philosophers (e.g., Goudge, 1961; Hull, 1989; Ruse, 1988), and scientists (e.g., Gould, 1989; Mayr, 1982, 1988), as well as by rhetoricians (e.g., Journet, 1991, 1995; Miller & Halloran, 1993; Myers, 1989). In particular, narrative has been critical in differentiating what are sometimes characterized as two kinds of science. They have been variously named, but I will use Gould's (1989) terms and call one "experimental-predictive" and the other "historical science." Experimental-predictive sciences such as chemistry or physics aim to formulate general or covering laws that are invariant in space and time, for example, laws that explain chemical interactions or molecular structures. On the other hand, historical sciences such as geology, astronomy, and evolutionary biology offer narrative explanations of unique and unrepeatable events, such as why the dinosaurs became extinct. Historical sciences, argue theorists, thus have their own objects of concern, their own methods and modes of argument, and accordingly present a kind of knowledge unattainable by experiment and prediction. Specifically, historical sciences offer narrative accounts of the past—narratives similar, in many ways, to those produced by social, cultural, and other historians (Nitecki & Nitecki, 1992).

This chapter deals with the role of narrative in the historical science of paleontology. Specifically, I examine the responses of noted paleontologist George Gaylord Simpson (1902–1984) to the difficulties of constructing narrative accounts of distant evolutionary history. Simpson's work reveals, I believe, the rhetorical and epistemic power as well as limitations narrative has for the construction of knowledge in scientific and professional communication.

Simpson was, perhaps, the most renowned and influential paleontologist of this century (Laporte, 1991): the author of over 750 publications and a key figure in the evolutionary synthesis that united Darwinian theory with Mendelian genetics to transform scientific understanding of the mechanisms of evolutionary change. Foucault's claim in *The Archeology of Knowledge* (1969/1972) that the Darwinian affirmation "species evolve" constitutes a different "statement," belonging within a different "discursive formation," or a different system of knowledge, after Simpson (p. 104), attests to the epistemic power Foucault saw Simpson wielding.

Late in his life, Simpson wrote a short novella, *The Dechronization of Sam Magruder* (1995), published posthumously,[1] in which he symbolically revisits the achievements of his career and reevaluates the limits of what paleontologists could know about the evolutionary past. While Simpson clearly understood the potential of narrative in historical sciences such as paleontology, his turn to a fictional genre also provides an interesting perspective on what a scientist realized could *not* be narrativized, even as it dramatizes his need to construct a coherent story of evolutionary history.[2]

SIMPSON AND THE POWER OF NARRATIVE IN THE BIOLOGICAL SCIENCES: THE HISTORICAL FACTOR IN SCIENCE

As narratives, historical explanations—whatever their focus of attention—must answer the questions: *What* happened? and *Why* did it happen this way? That is, on one level historians must establish a chronological sequence of events, and on another they must interpret the cause-and-effect relations among those events. Furthermore, they must answer those questions in ways that are credible to other historians or scientists. In an essay written in the middle of his career, "The Historical Factor in Science" (1964), Simpson describes these three essential tasks as 1) describing phenomena, 2) seeking theoretical explanatory relationships among those phenomena, and 3) testing and establishing confidence regarding observations and theories.

Simpson (1964) calls the first of these objectives "plain story," the description of the real and individual events that make up the universe at a given time. Using analogous terms, historiographer White (1973, 1987) calls this the historical "chronicle": the identification of a central subject and the arrangements of events pertaining to that subject into chronological order. Plain story, the "straight description of what is there and what occurs," is a traditional goal of paleontology, which concerns itself in part with uncovering and dating the fossil record. Establishing a plain story is in itself an interpretive act, involving choices taken from the unprocessed historical or fossil record about what is relevant and significant to the central subject (Kitts, 1992). But by itself, neither chronicle nor plain story is a fully historical or scientific explanation. For that, the historian needs the other component of narrative—what White calls "plot" and Simpson calls "explanatory relationships among phenomena." The historian transforms chronicle into emplotted narrative through greater selection and exclusion, emphasis and subordination. Plots enable the historian to place a temporal boundary around the sequential events of the chronicle, so that there is a beginning, middle, and end, and to establish causal connections so that earlier events lead to later ones. The resulting narrative endows events with a meaning or significance they would not have as mere sequence (White, 1973, 1987).

Simpson does not speak in detail about the third component of historical science, testing and establishing confidence regarding observations and theories, but it poses an important epistemic challenge that has been a source of debate for philosophers of science and history. Essentially, historians and biologists often recognize, as Simpson also seems to acknowledge late in his career in *The Dechronization of Sam Magruder* (1995), that historical accounts of the past will never be complete or definitive.

Since there is no direct access to the past—no point at which someone can definitively say "*this* is the way things *really* happened"—and since there is no critical experiment that tests evolutionary predictions, the knowledge claims produced by evolutionary biologists, like those of other historians, are never completely established and always open to further interpretation. Molecular biologist Stent argues (1986) that "understanding the complex interactions that produce historical phenomena" requires modes of analysis similar to hermeneutics. Like the interpretation of any complex text, the analysis of complex biological systems is open-ended: "It is this evident unattainability of universal and eternal truth in interpretation that seems to make hermeneutics different from the Greek conception of science, for which the belief in the attainability of objectively valid explanations of the world is metaphysical bedrock" (p. 215). Lacking "metaphysical bedrock," historical scientists must rely on other ways of establishing their readers' confidence. The hermeneutic nature of historical narrative thus raises a number of rhetorical and epistemological challenges—challenges Simpson explores in *Sam Magruder* (1995).

SIMPSON AND THE LIMITS OF NARRATIVE IN THE BIOLOGICAL SCIENCES: THE DECHRONIZATION OF SAM MAGRUDER

Simpson was, by all accounts, a remarkable man. Not only did he write several major scientific works, he also wrote numerous essays and books, connected with all aspects of his career as a scientist, and addressed to a variety of audiences.

Recently discovered 10 years after his death, *The Dechronization of Sam Magruder* (1995) extends Simpson's achievements into fictional genres. A time-travel book, *Sam Magruder* is a meditation on, among other things, human loneliness, dinosaurs, and the nature of historical narrative.

Sam Magruder, the novel's main character, is a chronologist, a scientist of the future (the year is 2162) who is working on a machine designed to discover the nature of time. One day, as he works on this machine, he is accidentally thrust out of time, suffering, in the book's terminology, "dechronization" or "time-slip." When he "bounces" back into time, he lands not in his present but, as he later discovers, in the late Cretaceous period of 80 million years ago, the age of the dinosaurs. There Magruder finds himself completely alone, separated from human society (that has not yet evolved). In an urge to communicate his experiences, however, he carves his story on several stone slabs. They are discovered and read an unspecified number of years later by a group of readers who, like characters in Wells's *The Time Machine*, bear labels rather than names. Gathered to ponder Magruder's experiences are the Universal Historian, who has prepared the "definitive annotated text for publication" (p. 29); the Pragmatist; the Ethnologist; the Common Man; and later Pierre Précieux ("precious stone"), a geologist who is part of the team that found Magruder's slabs.

Simpson and the Challenges of Historical Representation

Sam Magruder is about history: How we come to know and understand the past. One of the characters in *Sam Magruder* says that "the past has a reality, an objective and eternal existence, even more truly than does the present. It *produces* the present" (p. 12). The difficulty, however, is that we know the past not directly but only through its reconstruction.[3] The consequences of this difficulty are central to *Sam Magruder*. Most immediately, the challenges of attempting to narrate the past are explicit concerns for Magruder and his later readers, as I will discuss below. Furthermore, in the novel's formal qualities, particularly the way *Sam Magruder* constantly calls attention to its own status as a textual object, Simpson also dramatizes the difficulties of historical representation—the complex relation among what Danto (1985) calls history-as-actuality, history-as-record, and history-as-thought. Like other self-referential works (both fictional and nonfictional), it reminds us, over and over again, that every textual scenario we witness is a reconstruction of some prior reality and is open to multiple interpretations. As Magruder himself acknowledges, his own picture of dinosaurs is the product of earlier textual constructions, in this case "comic-book and scientification stories involving dinosaurs." "Reality," Magruder says in this Chinese box of a novel, is "quite different" (p. 74).

The textual nature of the reality with which *Sam Magruder* deals is most complexly rendered in the novel's narrative structure, particularly the series of multiple nested narratives that Simpson interweaves and asks his readers to negotiate. All these narratives, we are reminded, are reconstructions—products of authorial arrangement, omission, and emphasis. The effect of these nested narratives and multiple interpretations is to suggest the problematic nature of historical representation and interpretation and to defer, in an almost deconstructive sense, any kind of analytic certainty or finality.

Forming the heart of the novel is the story of Magruder's dechronization: a transcript of the eight slabs recorded in the past but discovered an unspecified number of years in the future—sometime after Magruder's 2162 disappearance. Framing Magruder's narrative is the story of the people who have come together, in the unspecified future, to read and explain the recovered slabs. And framing that story are the thoughts of the novel's unnamed first-person narrator, who is present at these conversations and who decides in what order he will present information about Sam Magruder, as well as what he will include and omit from "the text of Magruder's narrative" (p. 9). Finally, appearing implicitly throughout the novel is the story of Simpson himself. As Gould (1996) explains, *Sam Magruder* is highly autobiographical: Simpson is easily recognizable not only in the novel's portrayal of his "particular interests, pleasures, and concerns," but also in the portrayal of "his most profound fears" (p. 119).[4]

All these narratives offer different perspectives on Magruder's original experience. The story told on Magruder's slabs is itself an interpretation and summary of the events of his Cretaceous life; on several occasions Magruder reminds the reader that he is recording "not each day of [his] long stay here" but only "the most crucial ones" (p. 59), those most pertinent to his interests and concerns. In the framing narrative, each member of the group that gathers to listen to Magruder's story offers his own evaluation of Magruder's experiences, an evaluation that fits the speaker's representative nature. Supplementing those evaluations are the interpretations of other scientists, including those of the palaeontologist Saurier (lizard), present in the editorial comments or annotations added to Magruder's text. Gould (1996) explains that much of this "commentary consists of paleontological in-jokes and subtle sendups of professional practice" (p. 108), textual parody that further emphasizes the book's self-referentiality and intertextuality. And the unnamed narrator offers comments not only on Sam Magruder but also on his various interpreters.

The complexity of the narrative structure is intensified by the number of temporal levels with which the book deals: the unspecified future in which Magruder's slabs have been found and transcribed; the specified future (for Simpson's readers) of the year 2162, when Magruder suffers his dechronization; and the past of 80 million years ago. There is constant confusion about these levels of time in the book, particularly for Magruder, who is often unsure of which verb tense to use; his personal past (2162) is in the future in relation to his personal present (the late Cretaceous).

Further complicating the attempt to understand the past is the problem of historical evidence, all of which is, to some degree, unreliable. To try to explain what really happened to Magruder and the dinosaurs he observed, the book offers a number of different kinds of evidence: first-person accounts (Magruder's recollections), documentary evidence (newspaper accounts of the 2162 accident in which Magruder disappeared), and scientific data and theory (the interpretations offered by later paleontologists and geologists). None of these, the book reveals, can provide a definitive answer.

The Dechronization of Sam Magruder (1995) suggests that issues of historical representation are problematic even when the events have been documented and are not in the distant past. The novel begins with the question of what really happened to Magruder in 2162. In the first four chapters, the Universal Historian describes his attempts to uncover the truth about Magruder's dechronization, and Pierre Précieux relates the discovery in the San Juan basin[5] of the stones on which Magruder's subsequent history was narrated. In this respect, the challenges of uncovering and revealing Magruder's history are those typically faced by historians. Like other historians, the Universal Historian must depend on documents, in this case a newspaper account that emphasizes the lapses and uncertainties of memory: The two first-hand witnesses cannot agree on what they heard, and one has no memory of making a statement the other heard him say. The "veritester" can only ascertain "that they were telling the truth as they saw it" (pp. 20–21). These difficulties, and the inevitable likelihood of error, are further dramatized in the historical mistakes and misstatements made by those living in 2162 when they speak of Simpson's late 20th century (e.g., "marteeny," the "Province of New Mexico," etc.).

As a novel (and as unrealistic science fiction), *Sam Magruder* exaggerates the problems of historical representation in general and those of historical sciences, such as paleontology, more particularly. Nevertheless, the book's convoluted structure and its attempts to resist any privileged position from which to relate the past provide a suggestive context for Simpson's consideration in *Sam Magruder* of the more concrete and realistic challenges faced by writers who are narrating evolutionary history. Specifically, the novel calls attention to the constructed nature of historical scientific knowledge—including the multiple interpretive possibilities created by unreliable, incomplete, or unobservable data and processes.

Simpson and the Challenges of Narrating Evolutionary History

The difficulties faced in trying to represent recent human history are even greater in attempts to narrate paleontological history. *Sam Magruder* is about, among other things, what paleontologists can and cannot reveal about the passage of evolution. While dramatizing the desire of scientists to know and understand that past, the book also confronts the past's ultimate inaccessibility. Although I have argued above that evolutionary narratives have analogues with human cultural narratives,[6] they also differ from them in several significant ways. Through time travel, Simpson allows Magruder an opportunity, which modern scientists will never have, to correct misconceptions about dinosaurs. In reality, paleontologists necessarily construct narratives made up of chronicles that contain more gaps and plots that are more speculative than the narratives constructed by many other historians. These differences are exemplified in the novel by the contrast between the coherent story enscribed on Magruder's slabs and the fragmentary, disconnected story present in the fossil rocks.[7]

The chronicle from which paleontologists work is almost always called the fossil *record*. Darwin (1859/1964), taking the metaphor of reading the fossils from Lyell, describes the fossil record as

> a history of the world imperfectly kept and written in a changing dialect; of this history we possess the last volume alone, relating only to two or three countries. Of this volume, only here and there a short chapter has been preserved; and of each page, only here and there a few lines. (pp. 310–311)

The hermeneutic challenge for scientists is to rewrite the history of the world from this very imperfect text. In a similar vein, one of *Magruder's* readers says that the goal of paleontology is to take the "rocks...which carry the time record of dinosaurian history" (p. 25) and use them for the "reconstruction of this scene and its integration into the long, long history of Earth and life" (p. 27). But despite the metaphor, the fossil record is not a *written text*.

One of the key differences between large-scale evolutionary narratives and human cultural narratives is that there was never any human observer of most of the evolutionary past, which means there are no written documents. Even the most austere medieval chronicles that White describes are interpretive textual artifacts: selections and arrangements constructed from a particular point of view. The fossil record, however, is an accident: the result of the parts of the organism that happened to or were capable of fossilizing. Because certain characteristics of organisms either cannot survive or have very little chance of surviving as fossils, paleontologists must infer characteristics of anatomy, physiology, and behavior from incomplete traces. These inferences are, themselves, the products of guiding assumptions, as Magruder realizes when he is surprised to find that the teeth of a dinosaur "gleamed white":

> "But your teeth should be dark brown!" I had often seen the tyrannosaur skull in the Universal Natural History Museum, and its teeth were deeply colored. I had never stopped to think that the discoloration was the result of mineralization and that in the living animal the teeth would be white, as they are. (p. 51)

Constructing narratives from the fossil record causes historical scientists a number of interpretive problems, problems vividly dramatized when Magruder sees his first dinosaur. Magruder has immediate difficulty identifying this dinosaur, first because he has no context for his discovery, and second because the colors are not what he expected. When Magruder first sights the dinosaur, he thinks it is a "bright green, oversized fire hose" (p. 37). He is unable to identify it as a "sauropod" because, as he says, "I had not yet located myself even roughly in time.... And I had no frame of reference for any more explicit expectation" (p. 38). Without a context, a narrative of the past, observations make no sense. Even more disconcerting is the fact that his visual frame of reference is misleading. Colors—along with all kinds of physical characteristics—do not survive as fossils and thus can only and must always be speculative. As Magruder records:

> The colors of prehistoric animals are unknown. Playing it safe, artists have not dared to use the emerald-green hue of the creature I now saw before me. They show the eyes as brown or black, not the startling crimson of the reality before me. My mental image from student days was all the wrong colors. Would you immediately recognize a bright red, stripeless tiger or a purple-spotted squirrel? (p. 38)

Magruder's certainty about the dinosaurs' colors emphasizes the differences between fictional and scientific narratives. Although Simpson can, in a novel, resolve this question, no scientist will ever definitively know the colors of dinosaurs. The interpretive problems caused by these inevitable gaps are also demonstrated for modern readers by another element of Magruder's narrative. At one point, Simpson appears to resolve a controversy very important during his career: whether dinosaurs were warm-blooded or, as he believed, cold-blooded. While Magruder is emphatic that they are cold-blooded and sluggish, most scientists now believe that the dinosaurs were warm-blooded (Gould, 1996).

The lack of a written chronicle, produced by a human observer—one who is able to select and interpret events—provides one of the key differences between evolutionary and other kinds of historical narratives. Although, because of interpretive commitments, the author of the chronicle necessarily leaves things out, chronicles inevitably provide a picture of the past more relevant to *our* needs than do the chance processes of nature. Yet the presence of human observers would not alone resolve the problems of historical reconstruction of the evolutionary past. That is, even if paleontologists had what Danto (1985) calls an "Ideal Chronicle," a complete and perfect description of everything that ever happened, there would still be work for the historian, whose further task is to introduce what Danto calls "narrative sentences": statements that—like Simpson's concept of "theoretical explanatory relationships among phenomena" and White's of "plot"—establish causal relationships among events.

Danto (1985), like Simpson and White, emphasizes that narrative accounts must not simply present the past; they must also organize it. This imperative creates particular problems in evolutionary history, however, because of the time scale. Human history, at least as passed down through written records, is within our comprehending grasp. Though no one observer can see all prior circumstances leading to specific occurrences or foresee future consequences, many historical events are witnessed within the life span of individuals or groups of individuals. This is not true of evolution, where processes unwind through millions of years. Thus, though evolutionary biologists try to piece together discrete pieces of evidence, a completely coherent account of evolution's sequences will always be unattainable.[8]

Magruder recognizes this limitation when he tries to resolve the question of why the dinosaurs because extinct. He goes through a number of theories (warming climates, mammals eating dinosaur eggs, disease) but is forced to admit that no single observation, even performed at a key moment, can solve this mystery: "In short, I know no more about the causes for [the dinosaurs'] disappearance than if I had never seen one" (p. 81). This inability to explain the dinosaurs' extinction suggests the difficulties of establishing accurate plots, as well as chronicles, for the construction of paleontological historical narratives. To understand the plot, or mechanisms, of evolution—mechanisms of adaptation as well as extinction—is to understand processes that typically unwind through long periods of time. While scientists can model or theorize causes and effects of evolutionary processes, they are not, except in very unusual cases, able to observe them directly.[9]

Sam Magruder dramatizes the rhetorical and epistemological challenges faced by evolutionary historians, particularly paleontologists: challenges that involve both historical chronicle and plot. Paleontologists not only have incomplete evidence to build stories on; they are unable to establish definitively, through observation or experimentation, the causal relations among events separated in what geologists call "deep time." Both sets of difficulties limit the kinds of historical narratives palaeontologists are able to construct.

SIMPSON AND THE SOCIAL NATURE OF SCIENCE: WHY MAGRUDER WRITES

The Dechronization of Sam Magruder (1995) was not published during Simpson's lifetime. In fact, the manuscript's existence was unknown until Simpson's daughter, Joan Simpson Burns, discovered it among those papers not sent to Simpson's archive, and there is no evidence that Simpson ever intended to publish it. It is thus interesting to speculate, as do Burns and Gould, on why Simpson wrote the novella. Simpson provides no answer to that question, but he does raise a similar question in regard to his character, Sam Magruder, who is compelled to write the story of his life despite the fact that there is no one to read it.

Isolated in the late Cretaceous, Magruder is powerfully aware of his solitude: His loneliness is a major and pervasive motif in the book. Lacking anyone to talk to, he slowly and laboriously inscribes his story on stones, even though there is very little chance anyone will ever read them and even though he will never know if they have been found. With no audience, why does Magruder feel the need to construct this narrative? Simpson's answer, through his character Sam Magruder, suggests the social nature of science, indeed of all meaning-making activities.

The answer to why Magruder writes is connected to the reason he struggles to survive. Before being thrust into solitude, Magruder thought that the "deep purpose" of his life lay not in "merely surviving" but in "learning, investigating, probing the secrets of nature and making her workings known for the benefits of mankind"

(p. 43). But these tasks have value, Magruder realizes, only because he exists in a community: "It is *mankind* that has survived, not any one man. The fitness includes and depends on social organization, on cooperation, on division of labor, on the building up and passing on of knowledge, of tools and methods" (p. 45).

To endow existence with meaning, Magruder must somehow recreate, even if only imaginatively, this social organization. This he does by talking to himself, "almost constantly" (p. 46), and by constructing an audience for his slabs. The audience is made up of himself and of later readers, who he (despite the odds) invokes:

> My real purpose in engraving these slabs is a search for comprehension. Primarily, the search is for my own sake. I want to understand what has happened to me and why I have reacted as I have. I am exploring my own nature, and perhaps also the nature of mankind, of the great species of which I stand here as an advance sample. Secondarily, I cannot entirely abandon hope that these words will sometime be read by other humans. I know how slight is this possibility. I also realize that I am never to know whether this message reaches others of my kind. Yet I take some small and irrational comfort from the bare chance that my desperate voice will be heard, that someone, sometime, will be aware of Sam Magruder and will feel interest in, perhaps sympathy for, his fate. (p. 83)

The epistemological and rhetorical goal of historical sciences is to recover, not create, the past. Simpson's extensive career as a scientist suggests that recovery of the past was his goal as well. But *Sam Magruder* also suggests Simpson realized that, in many ways, historical narratives are our constructions. When asked to consider "what you are and why," one of Magruder's readers responds, "The questions *are* the answer" (p. 94). Magruder ends his own tale with the assertion, "I have often wondered why I kept going. That, at least, I have learned and I know it now at the end. There could be no hope and no reward. I always recognized that bitter truth. But I am a man, and a man is responsible for himself" (p. 104). Set against the vastness of geological time is the need to tell a coherent story—and for someone to share that story with—even if the story is inevitably incomplete.

The Dechronization of Sam Magruder (1995) underlines the difficulties writers encounter when rendering unique historical events—a task important in much scientific and professional communication. Simpson's realization that historical sciences produce narratives and those narratives will always be contingent to some degree is an important epistemological claim in the philosophy of biology (Hull, 1989; Mayr, 1988; Ruse, 1988). The epistemological status of scientific narratives also presents significant rhetorical challenges: Without direct observation or critical experiment, historical scientists must depend on other ways of making narratives persuasive. Blurring the lines between fiction and science, Simpson allows Magruder the kind of rhetorical authority not open to other evolutionary historians: the opportunity to say he has "been there." Lacking that opportunity, writers of historical and professional narratives need to be aware not only of what can and cannot be narrated, but also what kind of rhetorical resources they need to employ in the construction of disciplinary and professional narratives.

NOTES

[1] Because *The Dechronization of Sam Magruder* (1995) refers to the argument about whether the dinosaurs were warm-blooded or cold-blooded, Gould (1996) explains that it would have been written after 1968, when the controversy first arose.

[2] Gould (1996) provides a more positive reason for why Simpson wrote fiction: "Ironically, fiction can often provide a truer and deeper account of empirical subjects than genres supposedly dedicated to factual accounting. This situation arises because many modes of nonfiction develop strong constraints and traditions that prevent (unintentionally in most cases) any approach to factual adequacy—whereas fiction, under its protective guise of storytelling, remains free to be inclusive.... In particular, the requirements of sobriety, for caution, for 'sticking to inferences properly drawn from known facts,' preclude the reasoning speculations, even the flights of potentially rewarding fancy, that all creative minds must employ" (pp. 106–107).

[3] Most neurobiologists and psychologists believe that reconstruction, even of those past events we have directly experienced, is a part of our memory (Edelman, 1992).

[4] In the published version, framing Simpson's text, are several more interpretations, an introduction by Arthur C. Clarke, an afterword by Stephen Jay Gould, a memoir of Simpson by Joan Burns, acknowledgments, notes about the authors, and a note about the dinosaur names used in the book.

[5] This area is itself rich in paleontological history. It is one of the locations in which the famous 19th-century paleontologist Edward Drinker Cope, and later Simpson himself, found many of their most important fossils (Simpson, 1951).

[6] I explore these analogues more thoroughly (Journet, 1995) in relation to *Tempo and Mode in Evolution*, one of Simpson's most important biological texts.

[7] Both the fossil record of the San Juan Basin and Magruder's contemporary account of his "life" at this site are, of course, very different from the disciplinary narrative Simpson produced for paleontological specialists (e.g., Simpson, 1948).

[8] This is not a failing of science, but, rather, an inevitable consequence of science's attempt to describe and explain the history of evolutionary—particulary large-scale evolutionary—change.

[9] Mechanisms of evolution, particularly adaptation, present major questions in evolutionary theory. Part of the scientific consideration of the role of adaptation has been a debate about what constitutes an appropriate narrative explanation of evolutionary change. In Lewontin's terms, are narratives of adaptation "just so-stories," that is "plausible stories, things that *might* be true," or are they "true stories, things that actually have happened" (1993, p. 100)?

REFERENCES

Danto, A. C. (1985). *Narration and knowledge.* New York: Columbia University Press.

Darwin, C. (1964). *On the origin of species.* Cambridge, MA: Harvard University Press.

Edelman, G. (1992). *Bright air, brilliant fire.* New York: Basic Books.

Foucault, M. (1972). *The archeology of knowledge* (A. M. Sheridan Smith, Trans.). New York: Pantheon. (Original work published 1969)

Goudge, T. A. (1961). *The ascent of life.* Toronto: University of Toronto Press.

Gould, S. J. (1989). *Wonderful life.* New York: W. W. Norton.

Gould, S. J. (1996). Afterword. In G. G. Simpson (Ed.), *The dechronization of Sam Magruder* (pp. 105–120). New York: St. Martin's Press.

Hull, D. L. (1989). *The metaphysics of evolution.* Albany, NY: State University of New York Press.

Journet, D. (1991). Ecological theories and cultural narratives. *Written Communication, 8,* 446–472.

Journet, D. (1995). Synthesizing disciplinary narratives. *Social Epistemology, 9,* 113–150.

Kitts, D. B. (1992). The conditions for a nomothetic paleontology. In M. H. Nitecki & D. V. Nitecki (Eds.), *History and evolution* (pp. 131–145). Albany, NY: State University of New York Press.

Laporte, L.L. (1991). George G. Simpson, paleontology, and the expansion of biology. In K. R. Benson, J. Maienschein, & R. Rainger (Eds.), *The expansion of American biology* (pp. 80–106). New Brunswick, NJ: Rutgers University Press.

Lewontin, R. (1993). *Biology as ideology.* New York: Harpers.

Mayr, E. (1982). *The growth of biological thought.* Cambridge, MA: Harvard University Press

Mayr, E. (1988). *Toward a new philosophy of biology.* Cambridge, MA: Harvard University Press.

Miller, C., & Halloran, S. M. (1993). Reading Darwin, reading nature. In J. Selzer (Ed.), *Understanding scientific prose* (pp. 106–126). Madison, WI: University of Wisconsin Press.

Myers, G. (1989). *Writing biology.* Madison, WI: University of Wisconsin Press.

Nitecki, M. H., & Nitecki, D. V. (Eds.). (1992). *History and evolution.* Albany, NY: State University of New York Press.

Ruse, M. (1988). *Philosophy of biology today.* Albany, NY: State University of New York Press.

Simpson, G. G. (1948). The Eocene of the San Juan Basin, New Mexico. *American Journal of Science, 246,* 363–385.

Simpson, G. G. (1951). Hayden, Cope, and the Eocene of New Mexico. *Proceedings of the Academy of Natural Sciences of Philadelphia, 103,* 1–21.

Simpson, G. G. (1964). The historical factor in science. In *This view of life* (pp. 121–148). New York: Harcourt, Brace & World.

Simpson, G. G. (1995). *The dechronization of Sam Magruder.* New York: St. Martin's Press.

Stent, G. (1986). Hermeneutics and the analysis of complex biological systems. In D. J. Depew & B. H. Weber (Eds.), *Evolution at a crossroads* (pp. 209–225). Cambridge, MA: MIT Press.

White, H. (1973). *Metahistory.* Baltimore, MD: John Hopkins University Press.

White, H. (1987). *Tropics of discourse.* Baltimore, MD: John Hopkins University Press.

part III
Narrative and Managerial Communications

5

Management Discourse and Popular Narratives: The Myriad Plots of Total Quality Management

Mark R. Zachry
Utah State University

In 1980, NBC broadcasted the story of W. Edwards Deming to America. Their documentary *If Japan Can, Why Can't We?* "touted Deming's role in the revival of Japanese industry" (Gabor, 1990, p. 223), capturing the attention of business leaders and sparking a national corporate "quality revolution" (Aguayo, 1990, p. 253). The story of how Deming, an American statistician, revolutionized Japan's postwar manufacturing industry and earned an esteemed position in that country's culture of quality is often used in management literature to introduce the total quality movement.[1] A revered figure in American industry, Deming is remembered for his role in General Douglas MacArthur's plan to rebuild Japan and for his celebrated "Detroit debut" (Gabor, 1990, p. 30) as a high-profile management consultant at both the Ford Motor Company and General Motors. During the 1980s, Deming inspired a large following of converts, who rallied under his call to move America "out of the crisis" (Deming, 1986). These followers, including management consultants and academics, organized the quality-related management philosophies of Deming and other management gurus under the rubric of Total Quality Management (TQM)[2] in 1985.

Inspired by the publicized efforts of Deming and the developing rhetoric of total quality in managerial discourse, a number of major American companies committed themselves to reversing "declining quality" trends (Weaver, 1991, p. 4). Many people in the manufacturing sector of America's economy are familiar with the "success stories" of "Xerox, Allen-Bradley, Motorola, Marriott, Harley-Davidson, Ford, and Hewlett-Packard" (Grant, Shani, & Krishnan, 1994, p. 25). As industry journals report, "thousands of companies...enthusiastically embraced" the principles of TQM in their efforts to improve production (Grossman, 1994, p. 57). From 1980 until the present, managerial discourse has been oriented toward continuous quality improvement, forming a normative ideology for contemporary organizational cultures (Barley & Kunda, 1992).

Stories of total quality, however, have also emerged in settings far removed from industrial enterprise. Following the lead of manufacturers, several organizations outside industry have adopted total quality principles to improve their own processes. Educational and government institutions, for example, have embraced TQM and are advocating the free exchange of TQM implementation stories so that more organizations can share the success of those who are leading the quality revolution (Del Valle, 1994; MacRitchie & Sinn, 1998; Schmoker, 1993). Major American corporations are pushing for closer ties between industry and academia, suggesting that total quality could serve as the common language that these two institutions share "to better prepare graduates for corporate America" (Walker, 1995, p. 104). The TQM University Challenge, for example, is a cooperative program between industrial and academic organizations for bringing the principles of total quality into the university classroom. Additionally, several primary and secondary schools have embraced the principles of total quality, supported by the argument that "TQM in education is good for individuals, the economy, and society" (Smialek, 1995, p. 71). The widespread adoption of total quality principles since the 1980s has given rise to what Wendt (1994) calls "the epoch of total quality management" (p. 5).

Despite the rapid expansion of total quality discourse into the organizations where professional communicators work and even to some of the classrooms where they are trained, TQM has received little attention in our disciplinary literature. This lack of critical discussion is surprising because many of the practices described in TQM literature overlap with those discussed in professional communication. Deming, for example, theorizes connections between communication and bad news, logic, and evidence. Subsequent total quality theorists discuss countless additional themes of interest to scholars studying professional communication: teamwork (Katzenbach & Smith, 1994), corporate culture (Berry, 1991), authority (Weaver, 1991), affective language and semantics (Shiba, Graham, & Walden, 1993), consensus and technology (Creech, 1994), and ethics (George & Weimerskirch, 1994). The connections between TQM and workplace communication are often explicit in the popular literature produced for industry professionals. As one author explains, a total quality program directly affects the "documents produced for and by a company...such as the quality manual, quality procedures and working procedures, as well as all development plans, drawings, specifications, test instructions, training documents, commercial procedures, management directives and the associated records" (Lock, 1994, p. 146). Likewise, TQM implementation stories—a commonplace in popular management literature—reveal that coherency between the multiple forms of communication in the workplace is frequently at the core of total quality business practices. In one such account, Roosevelt (1995) tells the story of Merix, "a quality-award winning electronics company" that credits its success to a strategic planning process that involves an intricate web of documents. As part of its total quality program, the company composes its annual business plan and capitalization plan, which in turn prompt every department to write functional plans, which are eventually tied to all "employees' performance plans," ensuring "a direct link between employee goals and company goals" (pp. 35–36).

Examining the emergence and proliferation of TQM in companies such as Merix would provide professional communication scholars with an opportunity to study the interplay between the stories that circulate in the workplace and the practices associated with workplace communication. As Mumby (1987) notes, the stories told in any given workplace are closely tied to that organization's "meaning systems" (p. 114). The total quality program at Merix, for example, affected communicative practices at multiple levels within the organization's documented "meaning system." These changes in Merix's documents are indicative of what Roosevelt (1995) calls "the cultural change required to become a 'TQM company'" (p. 35). As the cultural change at Merix suggests, management practices are an integral part of the communicative acts we study and teach as well as of the environments in which we live and work. In this chapter, therefore, I want to extend our understanding of the interplay between management discourse and professional communication by focusing on the discourse associated with total quality programs. I argue that TQM should be examined as a narrative—or, more accurately, an assemblage of narratives. To make this argument, I first describe TQM as it is presented in both popular management and academic literature. Next, I present a theoretical framework for connecting management, organizations, and narrative. Finally, I examine the narratives of TQM, accounting for their widespread appeal and discussing how they operate in the workplace.

COMING TO TERMS WITH TOTAL QUALITY MANAGEMENT

Since TQM was popularized in the 1980s, several attempts have been made to identify its defining characteristics. As I describe below, these efforts have been largely frustrated by competing understandings of what total quality means and by the varied TQM programs developed in far-flung organizations.

The Values of Total Quality

In management literature for workplace professionals, TQM is often associated with a loosely connected set of organizational values. Some of these values are refinements of participatory management theories, such as an emphasis on employee empowerment and a reliance on the knowledge-making activities of teams. Other values are taken from earlier versions of the industrial quality control movement that started "in the late 1930s and 1940s as a science of manufacturing" (Dickson & Barton, 1996, p. 41). Building on the managerial discourse of quality control, TQM literature is predicated on the belief that measured improvement is possible and a confidence that the right mixture of quantitative and qualitative tools will enable the organization to realize its quality visions. In addition to these values, TQM theorists frequently call for organizations to commit themselves to continuous improvement and to customer satisfaction. This cluster of values is repeated in countless variations in TQM literature, helping constitute a new managerial discourse of corporate culture and quality. Reviewing academic and management publications about TQM, Barley & Kunda (1992) identify three underlying "tenets" of this culturally focused discourse:

1. Economic performance in turbulent environments requires the commitment of employees who make no distinction between their own welfare and the welfare of the firm.
2. Strong cultures can be consciously designed and manipulated.
3. Value conformity and emotional commitment...foster financial gain. (pp. 382–383)

The corporate values associated with TQM are complemented by a collection of organizational practices designed to help make a total quality culture possible. As a consultant, Deming challenged the wisdom of relying on traditional quality-control techniques to change an organization, and his series of anecdotes about the failure of those techniques led subsequent management theorists to focus less on conventional approaches to management (e.g., inspection, quotas, time standards) and more on participatory management practices. Such practices include team building (Katzenbach & Smith, 1994), training leaders at all levels within organizations (Creech, 1994), and achieving customer satisfaction in transactions outside *and* inside organizations (Shiba, Graham, & Walden, 1993). TQM consultants and corporate trainers responsible for reforming organizational behaviors translate these underspecified participatory management practices into concrete activities that can be used to alter workplace culture. The activities they advocate present workplace participants with alternative narratives for making sense of the new management values. For example, Shiba and colleagues report teaching participants in MIT's Leaders for Manufacturing program a ritual called "yo-one" as part of their TQM training. Note particularly how this ritual (one of many cited in discussions of total quality training) is designed to reinforce the values of participatory teamwork as well as to govern workplace behavior.

> The mechanics of the ceremony are simple: Once a task has been completed, everyone stands in a circle, so that they can all see each other. The leader starts by saying

"yo-oh" (in two syllables). Other people join in, and then the group says the word "one" in a louder voice, and everyone claps their hands together once, simultaneously. The rhythm of this chant is approximately "one, two, THREE." A group needs only a couple of rehearsals to learn how to perform this ceremony. The yo-one ceremony signifies completion and agreement. It is typically used when a phase of a team activity is finished. Yo has no meaning, and one simply means one. The chanting of those words provides closure to an activity. The time just before the yo-one ceremony, when people are asking "are we ready to yo-one?" is explicitly designed to give people an opportunity to voice final doubts. If no one speaks up and the group goes ahead with the yo-one ceremony, everyone observes everyone else clearly and forcefully saying "yo-one" and clapping. Thus there is no doubt that each person is unambiguously committed to making their work or their decision final. If someone tries to reverse or rework a position, the group can remind that person firmly that he or she has "yo-oned" and is therefore violating a publicly made commitment. As an added value, a cheer at the end of hard work is invigorating and acknowledges a task successfully done. It makes people feel good. (pp. xxiv–xxv)

The yo-one ceremony departs dramatically from conventional management techniques such as those associated with Taylorism. Whereas the "many narratives" (Banta, 1993, p. 14) of Taylorism encouraged activities associated with bureaucratic control, systemization, and numerical analysis, TQM stories often emphasize social interaction. Like Taylorism, however, TQM incorporates multiple stories, posing a fundamental problem for scholars who have attempted to systematically study TQM.

Competing Conceptions of Total Quality

Although patterns of values and practices associated with TQM are evident in popular management literature, TQM remains a difficult entity to study because each application of TQM reconfigures those values and practices in an ad hoc fashion. As TQM consultants observe, a program "succeeds only through applied knowledge" rather than through systematic approaches "to every problem." Management must "find a plan that will fit the company's culture and workforce" (Hoover, 1995, pp. 85–86). Consequently, there is no single, coherent definition of TQM. In popular management literature, it is variously referred to as a movement, a management program, a way of life, a doctrine, a frame of mind, and an evolving system. Management scholarship offers still another set of tenuously connected concepts to characterize TQM. Klimoski (1994), editor of *The Academy of Management Review*, devoted an entire issue to examining the nature of TQM, with each author proposing significantly different understandings of total quality. As Dean and Bowen (1994) observe, "total quality remains a hazy, ambiguous concept" (p. 394). In another journal, *Sloan Management Review*, a group of management and marketing professors extend this view, noting that "business schools have been unable to comprehend TQM's power and potential" because "it appears intellectually insubstantial" (Grant, Shani, & Krishnan, 1994, p. 30).

Scholars in managerial and organizational communication have suggested still other ways of understanding TQM. Based on a case study of a manufacturing organization implementing a total quality system, Fairhurst (1993) contends that TQM is a type of "frame" that "produces behavior that is consistent with the [corporate] vision" (p. 362). She argues that for TQM to be a meaningful vision within an organization, management must pay "[a]ttention...to the internal campaign [it will use] to manage the vision" (p. 366). In essence, this campaign involves a carefully developed and complementary set of texts—both written and oral—that will guide the organization. In another study, Wendt (1994) notes the potential for manipulation via discourse associated with TQM. Examining the language that circulated during the implementation of TQM at a university, Wendt discovered that "TQM hegemony" is apt to "reify linear and dualistic thinking" so that "passive, bounded, regimented, and efficiency-focused thinking tends to be privileged over critical, self-reflexive, strategic, and creative thinking" (p. 5). He observes that the language of TQM is characterized by "[p]owerful tropes, clichés, and pat answers [that] often control...the quality organization" (p. 39). His Foucauldian reading of the discursive practices associated with TQM complements critical studies of the quality movement by scholars in rhetoric (Dickson & Barton, 1996) and management (Boje & Winsor, 1993). Additional organizational communication scholarship suggests that total quality programs depend on underarticulated definitions of key terms (Fairhurst & Wendt, 1993).

The absence of a refined, single identity for TQM, despite the multiple publications that purport to describe the system and guide organizations in their implementation, frustrates efforts to pin TQM down. Its "ambiguous" and "insubstantial" nature persists. I contend that the continued attempts to define TQM reveal that the classification systems theorists have applied to this management discourse are insufficient. TQM cannot be reduced to a clearly defined set of workplace practices—as writers have attempted in popular guidebooks, academic texts, journals, television broadcasts, advertising campaigns, and workplace literature—because every instantiation of TQM is (re)formed by the culture in which it exists. Rather than examining TQM as a definable system of practices, I contend that TQM should be examined as a shifting collection of narratives that emerges in popular and workplace genres. These narratives provide insight into the way different practices are (re)arranged at specific sites. The theoretical basis for my argument is drawn from studies that discuss the role of narratives in management and organizational communication.

MANAGEMENT, ORGANIZATIONS, AND NARRATIVE

Scholars in both management communication (Fairhurst & Sarr, 1996; Mitroff & Kilmann, 1975) and organizational communication (Mohan, 1993; Mumby, 1987; Witten, 1993) have examined the functions of narratives in the workplace. Their research, by illustrating how widespread the use of narrative is and how it functions in the workplace, suggests that narrative is not a minor or incidental concern for scholars studying professional communication.

Management communication researchers discuss the use of stories as managerial tools for solving organizational problems (Mitroff & Kilmann, 1975) and for "framing" meaning in order to lead more effectively (Fairhurst & Sarr, 1996, p. 82). In this scholarship, managers are discussed as storytellers who make things happen through the discourse they introduce to organizations. Storytelling thus becomes a tool for orienting organizational action by providing textual touchstones to unify corporate goals. A function of management, then, is the construction of visionary narratives: "The tellers of stories about ideal situations are not obliged to stick to reality or to account for it. Their images of the ideal are purer and simpler than their images of the real world could ever be" (Mitroff & Kilmann, 1975, p. 20). Furthermore, managers can tell "a single story [to] manage meaning around several subjects" (Fairhurst & Sarr, 1996, p. 117). Thus, narratives are extremely flexible tools for organizing diverse resources and identities into an ordered discourse like TQM. Management consultants rely on storytelling to introduce total quality discourse to organizations (Luther, 1997), and managers turn to the multiple stories of total quality as a tool when they must account for current circumstances *and* move toward an organizational goal. Enactment of the yo-one ceremony, for example, provides participants with a symbolic conclusion to a single team project, while reinforcing organizational goals through a carefully plotted ritual of mutual commitment.

Placing less emphasis on management, organizational communication scholars focus their attention on what the stories that circulate in institutions tell us about organizational control and cultural identity. Much of this scholarship is concerned with theorizing a linguistic basis for organizational norms, and storytelling—a fundamental organizational habit—is cited as a mechanism for perpetuating workplace ideologies: "The everyday use of narrative in organizations is one of the means by which the power structure of an organization is produced and reproduced" (Mumby, 1987, p. 125). The quotidian repetition of workplace narratives reinforces the logic of current practices and discourages change, thereby yielding a type of organizational control. Such "covert" control, Witten (1993) observes, "is accomplished as certain interpretive patterns and strategies of action are made to seem more salient, appropriate, natural, useful, and legitimate than others" (p. 99). Workplace narratives contribute to a self-enforced discipline that eliminates the need for many more overt controls (for example, the shop floor disciplinarians that Frederick Winslow Taylor describes as part of a scientifically managed shop). The narrative of the yo-one ritual, for example, is not predicated on the manager-as-champion plot so common in conventional management narratives. In a fundamental sense, the ritual is the celebration of disciplined cooperation among participants, and through the celebration they are committing themselves to observe the agreements they have reached in unison.

In addition to establishing control, the stories that circulate in the workplace form identities for individuals by introducing subject roles that can be occupied by organizational participants. These narratives, as symbolic artifacts, "assume an energy controlling mode as they function to attract and inspire new members while repelling 'undesirable outsiders'" (Mohan, 1993, p. 50; see also Wells, 1996, p. 33). Narratives about teamwork are a commonplace in contemporary management discourse and are particularly prevalent in the total quality workplace, where they sometimes take the form of ritual, as in the yo-one ceremony, or build on a sports metaphor, as I will describe later.

THE NARRATIVES OF TOTAL QUALITY MANAGEMENT

TQM is constructed and perpetuated through narratives ranging from the heroic lore of total quality's pioneers to the success stories of revitalized companies, from the plotted rituals that those in the total quality culture share to the anecdotes with which consultants entertain initiates. As I discussed above, a TQM program involves more than stories—it includes a variety of tools and practices upon which its participants may draw—but these varied resources become meaningful to organizations only when they occupy positions in the oft-told tale of an organization rising to the challenges of the contemporary marketplace in pursuit of Total Quality Management. Thus, while many of the tools and practices associated with TQM are not innovative (for example, collaborating, brainstorming, charting, and planning), the way they are (re)arranged in TQM narratives is. This is why TQM is frequently characterized as a "revolution" (Shiba, Graham, & Walden, 1993) or as a fundamental system change (Creech, 1994).

As I will discuss below, we can gain a great deal of insight into the popular appeal of this managerial discourse and how it structures workplace practices by examining TQM as a collection of narratives that circulates through several social settings. Rather than treating the workplace as a closed system, my analysis assumes that the workplace is shaped by (and shapes) the networks of social activities that surround it. Both academic and popular management literature, for example, bring stories into play about the workplace and how it should operate. Conversely, the principles of TQM developed in the workplace have become a part of the academic curriculum in many universities (Dickson & Barton, 1996). Stories shared in varied social settings thus provide a populist rationale for the values and practices of TQM, even as these stories are remade to fit specific organizational visions, power structures, and identities.

Popular Stories and the Appeal of Total Quality Management

TQM offers a generic tale of continuous improvement that ends in total quality. The dynamic collection of individual narratives that have been generated in the name of total quality brings together the lore, success stories, instructive anecdotes, and testimonies of organizational participants. The most common iteration of this tale is the heroic story of Deming, though many people are familiar, too, with the financial turnaround of prominent companies during the 1980s. In academic and popular literature, case studies (e.g., Oakland & Porter, 1994) make the story of TQM more concrete, helping readers identify with the plot of organizational change. These widely shared stories help unify TQM organizations in a culture of quality with recognizable heroes and communal wisdom about how challenges have been met.

Stock Scenarios

As TQM is represented to the public via broadcasts and advertising and as it is introduced to organizations through management consultants and literature, it typically takes the form of stories with common narrative scenarios such as the exercise of patriotic duty, the resurrection of the fallen, the survival of the fittest, and the rise of the oppressed (see Table 5.1). These dramatic stock scenarios offer an affective appeal that is not often associated with managerial discourse, though the use of such simple stories in public discourse has been theorized by Bormann (1985). The stock scenarios associated with TQM often converge with stories that are already familiar to many people in American culture. This familiarity makes the stories powerful tools for creating shared visions.

The patriotism scenario, for example, is featured prominently in many TQM narratives, connecting TQM to a sense of national duty. Popular management literature, in particular, draws on patriotic visions of America's dominance in the world market as a standard scenario to bolster the appeal of this managerial discourse. Several writers (Creech, 1994; Deming, 1986, 1994; Shiba, Graham, & Walden, 1993;

TABLE 5.1.
A Sample of Narrative Scenarios Associated with TQM

Scenario	Description
Resurrection	The rebirth of companies that had become stagnant or were on the brink of dissolution figures prominently in many TQM narratives. The extraordinary turnaround of major companies (Oakland & Porter, 1994) provides persuasive testimony for those considering implementing a TQM program.
Survival	TQM narratives often refashion the Darwinian survival-of-the-fittest plot to demonstrate the urgency of implementing a new managerial program. These narratives focus on crises that endanger organizational existence (Weaver, 1991) and encourage organizations to become more fit to ensure survival (Berry, 1991; Deming, 1986).
Empowerment	TQM is frequently presented as a means of giving employees more control over their work, thereby tapping the wisdom of everyone in the organization. This scenario is often embedded in stories about leveling bureaucratic hierarchies (Creech, 1994) or heroic tales of a sole employee taking responsibility and solving a problem (Deming, 1994).

Weaver, 1991) demonstrate the exigency of a return to quality through variations of a story about the United States leading the industrial world in the "good old days," but in recent years allowing other countries to usurp its position in manufacturing. They warn that unless we stem this tide, virtually nothing will be made in America. For example, the first chapter of Deming's *The New Economics* (1994) is a complex matrix of stories about why the United States is "not doing well" in comparison to rising economic powers around the world (p. 3). Weaver (1991), a management professor and consultant, connects several of these narratives in the beginning of his book for practitioners, setting a patriotic tone and drawing his audience into the unfolding events: "If you're like me, you grew up believing the United States is the greatest country in the world. You like to think the United States dominates the world in everything. Although this certainly used to be true in most areas, things have changed" (p. 1). To convince the reader that there is a "quality crisis" in America, Weaver then tells several stories (each with a rather simple story line) about truck owners, a university secretary, a grocery store consumer, a carpet retailer, service mangers, and a milk supplier. Creech (1994), a retired four-star general who became a management consultant, elevates this patriotic appeal by explaining the efficiency of the American forces in the Gulf War as evidence of TQM practices at work.

Thematic connections among TQM's narratives provide a sense of unity in managerial discourse. Although these scenarios become more subtle in the day-to-day practices of TQM, they nevertheless continue to operate as standards when organizational tales are represented to others through managerial discourse. These stock scenarios, however, are only one of the narrative devices employed in the (re)presentation of TQM. This discourse derives additional appeal by drawing on popular culture via metaphor.

Cultural Metaphors

TQM exhibits characteristics of populist thought, as opposed to the modernist rationale that underpins management discourses such as bureaucratic rationalism and Taylorism. In its ability to accommodate diverse stories from popular culture, TQM advances participatory management to a new level. It draws on the language of diverse social spheres, connecting organizational discourse more closely with the language of participants. And, with its team-based practices and empowerment programs, TQM seems to invite organizational participants to contribute to developing workplace stories.

Demonstrating rhetorical savvy, the authors of TQM management literature typically connect their narratives via metaphors to large-scale social institutions with which it is easy to identify, including sports, science, religion, the military, and education. Deming (1994), for example, explains employee motivation through a story about his son's development as an athlete. Another author explains Motorola's quality improvement program with a story about seeking statistically measured process perfection (Creech, 1994). A third author discusses team building as laying seige to "heavily fortified bunkers of resistance" (Berry, 1991, p. 32). A fourth author tells the story of how "a creative but undisciplined young school girl" becomes successful via the patient encouragement of her schoolmaster (Shiba, Graham, & Walden, 1993, pp. 496–497). TQM's ability to accommodate tales from such diverse sources (coupled with the success stories of prominent organizations) offers insight into the widespread appeal of this managerial discourse. Fusing explanatory metaphors such as team, score, and coach from sports; plots about scientific methods and statistical proofs from science; tales of conversion, redemption, and baptism from religion; war stories from the military; and accounts of pedagogy, TQM keeps an odd collection of stories at play in managerial discourse.

TQM Narratives and Workplace Practices

Within organizations, the shared stories of TQM—with their easily recognized scenarios and popular appeals—provide instructive examples for those who wish to make the success-through-quality story their own. Addressing this impulse, TQM practitioner literature offers several "practical" tools to plot organizational practices so they will yield similar results. After establishing a "quality vision" (a type of prophetic organizational tale), practitioners may select from a variety of discursive tools—such as deployment charts, cause-and-effect diagrams, and flow charts—that will help organizational groups generate stories about desired workplace changes. These stories, in turn, will help manage the change by identifying roles for participants and actions for them to follow.

In many cases, these tools are refined into detailed forms that are carefully explained by consultants or authors. For example, Plan-Do-Check-Act cycle charts (also called Shewart cycle charts) are a frequently discussed tool (Berry, 1991; Creech, 1994; Deming, 1986, 1994; Shiba, Graham, & Walden, 1993) that provides a simple plot for structuring activities while at the same time providing guidelines for the storytelling practice. Participants, as empowered organizational storytellers, fill predefined slots (plan, do, check, act) in the tool's generic storyline. Within total quality narratives, tools such as these cycle charts encourage "people to organize their behavior around a particular rule system" (Mumby, 1987, p. 115). As workplace participants repeatedly employ these tools in multiple variations across space and time, the narrative logic of total quality discourse becomes more deeply embedded in the order of organizational activities. Such a widespread dispersion of total quality discourse is applauded by many TQM advocates who envision "quality as a way of life" (Stratton, 1997, p. 28).

CONCLUSION

In this chapter, I have argued that professional communication scholars should be aware of the narratives of organizational culture and quality that dominate managerial discourse. To better understand this discourse and its effects on rhetorical practices in the workplace, scholars should investigate TQM as a collection of narratives that circulates inside and outside organizations in a variety of genres. This approach foregrounds the stock scenarios and elements of popular culture that TQM employs to appeal to potential participants and to create shared cultural values. It also provides insight into how these stories are reconstructed within organizations to serve as touchstones that unify participants in their pursuit of total quality visions. Through these stories, TQM communicates desirable behaviors in the workplace, organizing disparate activities into a coherent plot.

As I have suggested, the managerial and organizational functions of workplace narratives are complex. Closer examination of the stories that circulate within and around managed organizations would expand our understanding of professional communication by refocusing our attention on the networks of social practice in which professionals communicate. Specifically, researchers might examine where such stories originate and how they come to be circulated. To pursue such research, scholars would need to examine how management is constituted through workplace communication. Such research would not merely focus on managers, however; as several scholars (e.g., Banta, 1993; Mumby, 1987; Witten, 1993) have demonstrated, managers are not the sole storytellers at work—the managed are also participants in the storied exchanges that constitute workplace rationality. The interplay between the stories of managers and managed, particularly in participatory management organizations where such distinctions are minimized, merits additional study.

NOTES

[1] The genealogy of TQM is contested. However, while its critics and proponents trace TQM's lineage to a variety of origins—extending as far back as Aristotle—their lines almost inevitably intersect on the work of Deming.

[2] Although not all practitioners use the phrase "Total Quality Management" to describe their quality- and continuous-improvement programs, the TQM acronym has gained widespread acceptance. It serves as a useful generic identifier under which we may group the multiple participatory quality programs that have emerged since the early 1980s.

REFERENCES

Aguayo, R. (1990). *Dr. Deming: The American who taught the Japanese about quality.* Secaucus, NJ: Carol Publishing Group.

Banta, M. (1993). *Taylored lives: Narrative productions in the age of Taylor, Veblen, and Ford.* Chicago: University of Chicago Press.

Barley, S. R., & Kunda, G. (1992). Design and devotion: Surges of rational and normative ideologies of control in managerial discourse. *Administrative Science Quarterly, 37,* 363–399.

Berry, T. H. (1991). *Managing the total quality transformation.* New York: McGraw-Hill.

Boje, D. M., & Winsor, R. D. (1993). The resurrection of Taylorism: Total quality management's hidden agenda. *Journal of Organization Change Management, 6* (4), 58–71.

Bormann, E. G. (1985). *The force of fantasy: Restoring the American dream.* Carbondale, IL: Southern Illinois University Press.

Creech, B. (1994). *The five pillars of TQM.* New York: Truman Talley Books.

Dean, J. W. Jr., & Bowen, D. E. (1994). Management theory and total quality: Improving research and practice through theory development. *Academy of Management Review, 19,* 392–418.

Del Valle, C. (1994, October 31). Total quality management: Now, it's a class act. *Business Week,* 72.

Deming, W. E. (1986). *Out of the crisis.* Cambridge, MA: MIT Center for Advanced Engineering Study.

Deming, W. E. (1994). *The new economics for industry, government, education.* Cambridge, MA: MIT Center for Advanced Engineering Study.

Dickson, B., & Barton, E. (1996). Leaving science and technology for business and management: Quality control as a discourse on the move. *Rhetoric Society Quarterly, 26* (4), 41–63.

Fairhurst, G. T. (1993). Echoes of the vision: When the rest of the organization talks total quality. *Management Communication Quarterly, 6,* 331–371.

Fairhurst, G. T., & Sarr, R. A. (1996). *The art of framing: Managing the language of leadership.* San Francisco: Jossey-Bass.

Fairhurst, G. T., & Wendt, R. F. (1993). The gap in total quality: A commentary. *Management Communication Quarterly, 6,* 441–451.

Gabor, A. (1990). *The man who discovered quality: How W. Edwards Deming brought the quality revolution to America: The stories of Ford, Xerox, and GM.* New York: Times Books.

George, S., & Weimerskirch, A. (1994). *Total quality management: Leadership and management.* New York: Wiley.

Grant, R., Shani, M. R., & Krishnan, R. (1994). TQM's challenge to management theory and practice. *Sloan Management Review, 35,* 25–35.

Grossman, S. R. (1994, January 3). Why TQM doesn't work and what you can do about it. *Industry Week, 243,* 57–62.

Hackman, J. R., & Wageman, R. (1995). Total quality management: Empirical, conceptual, and practical issues. *Administrative Science Quarterly, 40,* 309–342.

Hoover, H. W. Jr. (1995). What went wrong in U.S. business's attempt to rescue its competitiveness? *Quality Progress, 28,* (7) 83–86.

Katzenbach, J. R., & Smith, D. K. (1994). *The wisdom of teams: Creating the high-performance organization.* New York: HarperCollins.

Klimoski, R. (Ed.). (1994). A "total quality" special issue [Special issue]. *Academy of Management Review, 19*(3).

Lock, D. (Ed.). (1994). *Gower handbook of quality management.* Hampshire, England: Gower.

Luther, D. B. (1997). Storytellers, science, and continuous improvement. *Quality Progress, 30*(11), 77–78.

MacRitchie, G., & Sinn, J. W. (1998). The 2 + 2 enhancement process. *Quality Progress, 31*(1), 55–58.

Mitroff, I. I., & Kilmann, R. H. (1975). Stories managers tell: A new tool for organizational problem solving. *Management Review, 64*(7), 18–28.

Mohan, M. L. (1993). *Organizational communication and cultural vision*. Albany, NY: State University of New York Press.

Mumby, D. K. (1987). The political function of narrative in organizations. *Communication Monographs, 54*, 113–127.

Oakland, J. S., & Porter, L. J. (1994). *Cases in total quality management*. Oxford: Butterworth-Heineman.

Roosevelt, B. (1995). Quality and business practices: Essential ingredients for success. *Quality Progress, 28* (7), 35–40.

Schmoker, M. J. (1993). *Total quality education: Profiles in schools that demonstrate the power of Deming's management principles*. Bloomington, IN: Phi Delta Kapa Educational Foundation.

Shiba, S., Graham, A., & Walden, D. (1993). *A new American TQM: Four practical revolutions in management*. Portland, OR: Productivity Press.

Smialek, M. A. (1995). Total quality in K-12 education. *Quality Progress, 28*(5), 69–72.

Steingard, D. S., & Fitzsimmons, D. E. (1993). A postmodern deconstruction of total quality management (TQM). *Journal of Organizational Change Management, 6*, 72–87.

Stratton, B. (Ed.). (1997). Quality as a way of life [Special issue]. *Quality Progress, 30*(7).

Walker, H. F. (1995). Texas Instruments' and Iowa State University's experience with the university challenge program. *Quality Progress, 28* (7), 103–106.

Weaver, C. N. (1991). *TQM: A step-by-step guide to implementation*. Milwaukee, WI: ASQC Quality Press.

Wells, S. (1996). *Sweet reason: Rhetoric and the discourses of modernity*. Chicago: University of Chicago Press.

Wendt, R. F. (1994). Learning to "walk the talk": A critical tale of the micropolitics at a total quality university. *Management Communication Quarterly, 8*(1), 5–45.

Witten, M. (1993). Narrative and the culture of obedience at the workplace. In D. K. Mumby (Ed.), *Narrative and social control: Critical perspectives* (pp. 309–330). Newbury Park, CA: Sage.

6

Strategic Communication as Persuasive and Constitutive Storytelling

Janis Forman
University of California at Los Angeles

In the fall of 1996, I was the management communication faculty advisor to a group of executive MBA students (full-time managers at midcareer) who were conducting their capstone project for the MBA: a 20-week strategic study for an Austrian-based company involved in the construction of large industrial plants. As is commonly done for other executive-level strategic studies, the MBAs formed a kind of temporary consulting firm composed of several groups, each of which studied one facet of a set of strategic issues faced by their client. One faculty member had responsibility for the overall direction of the project—as would a senior partner in a consulting firm—and four other faculty members worked as specialists in management subjects relevant to the study focus. As a faculty member of this consulting firm and the only expert in communications, I was assigned to articulate for the students the communication challenges of their strategic work and to help the class manage and produce their client communications.

By design, a strategic study such as this one results in recommendations that have broad organizational impact. The executive MBA students' strategic communications consist of their written and oral communications on these strategic issues. (The use of the term "strategic communications" is, then, not to be confused with its more common generic use to mean any communication intended to achieve a particular goal [or goals] with one or more constituencies.) These communications represent the fruition of the students' work and the tasks in which I was most involved as coach and expert.

During the first half of the final presentations in Austria, the students carefully laid out for the organization what they called an "evolutionary framework" for strategic change that moved, in successive stages, from the concerns of engineering to project management, and, finally, to a fully realized marketing strategy for growth. At a lunch break, the most senior manager of the company arrived. As we had known beforehand, his major concern was something called "balance of plant," or BOP, an acronymn that appeared frequently in senior-level communications with the force of a corporate mantra. By BOP, the senior executive meant those auxiliary processes and activities that go into the construction of large chemical or electrical plants. This executive wanted to find the best ways for his organization to bid for BOP contracts.

At lunch, I urged the student master of ceremonies to rework his prepared remarks, which introduced the second half of the presentations, to include a brief summary in order to provide the senior executive with an understanding of the evolutionary framework that had been so carefully worked out in the morning session; the student was successful in doing so, collapsing the 3-hour story into a 10-minute review. But when subsequent presenters took the stage, they were unable to make necessary adjustments in their stories and, instead, made scant reference to BOP as they elaborated upon the evolutionary framework identified earlier in the day. Not surprisingly, the senior person kept interrupting: "How does this apply to BOP? Can this framework accommodate our interest in extending BOP?" Tension among the MBAs rose with each interruption—as did their rigidity. None of the speakers was willing (or perhaps able) to adjust his or her presentation—a story they had labored over for weeks—to handle the senior manager's questions. Finally, one of the most experienced speakers among the students, someone who was not assigned to a formal speaking role, got up and did an extemporaneous speech that bridged the senior manager's concerns with BOP and the students' carefully crafted story about an evolutionary framework; however, despite this student's intervention, the dominant feeling in the group seemed to be something like this: "I tell you my story, dear senior manager, and it's the one and only master narrative, so don't you dare break in with yours."

The students' final presentation in Austria, and especially their rigid attitude toward story, led me to conduct the investigation presented in this chapter. As a result of my participation in the Austrian project, I saw the need to develop a framework for understanding the potential role of story in strategic communications, and I used my participation in a strategic study that followed the effort in Austria, a study for a high-tech firm with regional headquarters in Germany, to devise the framework.

The purpose of this chapter is first to identify my framework for strategic communications as a kind of persuasive and constitutive storytelling and the theoretical underpinnings for this framework. Then I use my observations of, participation in, and assessment of the high-tech study to illustrate the disparity between this framework—an idealized vision of what students should do—and the students' tendencies either to resist constructing a story or to produce a single storyline unresponsive to shifts in the rhetorical situation, that is, to changes in goals and audience. Finally, I speculate about why the students produced reports and presentations without a story line or refused to adjust the story they did produce to address client concerns.

A FRAMEWORK FOR UNDERSTANDING STRATEGIC COMMUNICATION AS PERSUASIVE AND CONSTITUTIVE STORYTELLING

Although the students' communications for their strategic studies may be characterized as a form of argumentation—they argue first (phase 1 of the study) for the importance of investigating a particular strategic question and then (phase 2) for a set of recommendations that address this question—story is, in fact, the more basic discourse that underlies the students' communications. Their strategic communications may be thought of as narratives of exigency, of a company's need to act strategically in certain ways in light of its strengths and weaknesses and of the competitive forces in the marketplace.

Research in educational psychology, communication, and rhetoric, as well as my experience as a faculty advisor in over 10 strategic studies, support the idea that story lays the foundation for other kinds of discourse. For instance, educational psychologist Applebee's work (1978) on the cognitive development of children from ages 2 to 17 shows that storytelling is at the root of people's increasingly sophisticated understanding of coherence in discourse. Communication theorist Fisher (1987) asserts that humans are storytellers—*homo narrans*—and believes that "all forms of human communication need to be seen fundamentally as stories—symbolic interpretations of aspects of the world occurring in time and shaped by history, culture and character" (p. xi). Business communication specialist Rentz (1992) argues that we would be well advised to consider "the extent to which it [narrative] lurks behind our every utterance" (p. 299). Perhaps most akin to my focus on strategic communications as persuasive and constitutive storytelling, researchers in the rhetoric of public policy analysis and planning, who look at the strategic communications of public sector organizations (e.g., public utilities, city governments), argue for the importance of narrative (Fischer & Forester, 1993; Throgmorton, 1996). For Throgmorton, "planning can be best thought of as a form of persuasive and constitutive storytelling that occurs in a web of relationships—and partial truths" (p. xiv). In his view, "planners can be regarded as *authors* who write *texts* (plans, analyses, articles) that reflect awareness of differing or opposing views and that are normally *read and interpreted* in diverse and often antagonistic ways" (original emphasis, p. 49).

In addition, from my perspective as a communication specialist for strategic studies, a notion of story is the common framework that my colleagues, who are specialists in other disciplines, and I evoke to guide students in developing a coherent, compelling argument out of a wealth of data and analysis. "What's your story?"

is the prompt repeatedly used to get students to think about the arguments they need to construct for their clients. From these perspectives, then, story appears to be at the root of argument.

THE STORY PATTERNS IN THESE STRATEGIC STUDIES: THE TWO-PART STUDY

For the first phase of the study, students' strategic communications consist of an interim report and presentation for the client that discuss the class's work to date and identify the strategic question that should shape the second phase of the study. The story for part 1 might run something like this: "On the basis of our assessment of the company's strengths and weaknesses and the competitive situation, here's the strategic question that the company should want to address to assure its long- and short-term growth." For instance, for the Austrian firm, the strategic question concerned what kind of organizational structure might best allow for the company's growth. The MBAs' story has a persuasive aim: to argue for the worth of a particular strategic question to be investigated in the second half of the project, based on their preliminary analysis of the company and the industry.

At the end of the second phase of the study, the strategic communications consist of a final report and presentation to the client that argue for a set of recommendations. The story here might be something like this: "On the basis of our research and analysis, here are our recommendations for addressing the strategic question." For the Austrian study, these recommendations revolved around an evolutionary framework for strategic change.

THE FRAMEWORK: STORY ELEMENTS IN STRATEGIC COMMUNICATION

There are elements common to story and to strategic communications: the writer's or speaker's point of view, the coherence of the discourse, and the audience. (White, 1987, discusses the first of these and pays special attention to the issue of coherence) In strategic communications, these story elements are recreated to meet persuasive and constitutive ends, that is, to convince an organization to change and, in doing so, to add something substantial to the company's strategic reality.

Using these elements of story as modified for strategic communications, I formulated several goals for the MBAs as persuasive and constitutive storytellers, both as broadly conceived in their roles as strategic consultants to multinational organizations, and, more specifically, in their performances as strategic presenters and report writers. These goals are prescriptive—what I'd like the MBAs to do. Along with my observations of students' discourse for the high-tech study, these goals are largely based upon the literature on narrative and professional communication; my cumulative experience and vantage point as a coach and expert in 10 earlier strategic studies; and notions drawn from postmodern and narrative theories. (Although a highly contested term [see, for instance, Best & Kellner, 1991], "postmodern" is a label applied to Lyotard, Barthes, and Bakhtin, theorists discussed here, among others.) Although the story framework was not fully developed until the end of the study, I presented its major points to the students as early as the study orientation.

Writer's or Speaker's Point of View

Over the course of a study, the students' point of view should be their working hypotheses about the client and its strategic issues and their preferred interpretive models for analysis of company and competitor data; taken together, these hypotheses and models should form the position from which the students tell their story and should enable them to make their understanding of the client's situation explicit to others. Point of view should not be static; instead, it should be modified, elaborated, or even abandoned as the students move through their research and analysis, testing their point of view against new data and changing it as a result of new information or analysis. At the end of the study the students' point of view consists of their recommendations: "Here is what the client should do on the basis of our data gathering and analysis."

In expressing their point of view, students should assume multiple roles both over the course of the study and in their presentations and reports. Most obviously, students are consultants to a client, and, in this role, they must articulate and solve a set of strategic problems of great consequence to the client. Equally important, they are learners who identify and apply key academic models in their strategic work, and they learn about the client organization and its industry. By the end of the study, they are also advocates for a particular set of strategic directions based upon their growing expertise as industry consultants. Fisher's description (1984) of the expert in public policy best summarizes the multi-faceted roles that strategic consultants should assume:

> From the narrative perspective, the proper role of the expert…is that of a counselor, which is…the true function of the storyteller. His or her contribution to public dialogue is to impart knowledge like a teacher, or wisdom, like a sage. It is not to pronounce a story that ends all storytelling. The expert assumes the role of public counselor whenever she or he crosses the boundary of technical knowledge into the territory of life as it ought to be lived. Once this invasion is made, the public [the client organization in the case of strategic studies], which then includes the expert, has its own criteria for determining whose story is most coherent and reliable as a guide to belief and action. (p.13)

In a particular performance with a client, the student may shift roles; sometimes, she is an earnest demonstrator of knowledge about the client and industry, sometimes an interpreter of a particular framework for analysis, sometimes a listener taking note of client needs, sometimes an advocate for a set of recommendations, sometimes a careful and informed respondent to questions, sometimes a distraught, embattled defender of unpopular views. The roles students enact may be held simultaneously or in succession.

Coherence of the Discourse

In light of the students' changing point of view over the course of the study and the multiple roles they enact, their story should have ample play. That is, like the multiple versions of Sleeping Beauty in Robert Coover's (1996) postmodern novel *Briar Rose*, a set of facts about the client's situation should yield multiple versions, depending upon the students' point of view. Over the course of the study, it is important for students to suspend closure about which version, or which story, to tell. Early on in the project, this suspension of closure may mean for them to hold tentatively to one position (for instance, such and such is the best strategic question or the best framework), but to be receptive and thoughtful about other positions and make adjustments in their story when the data or analysis warrant them.

At the end of the study, the coherence of the students' story results from the linking of claims—the students' strategic recommendations—and support for those claims. Yet, even as they have resolved to offer a single story—a master narrative—they must also realize that the coherence of their story may be "broken into" by various constituencies within the client organization when they see fit to do so, and that the students' story is one of several *"petits recits"* (Lyotard, 1979/1984) among competing stories.

Audience

If the "performance [of a story] is seen as a site of strategic interaction, sometimes competitive, sometimes cooperative" (Langellier & Peterson, 1993, p. 62), then the audience for strategic communications are participants in the discourse in that they judge the students' claims against their own knowledge and agendas—whether or not they voice their views. In effect, the audience may offer competing stories, alternative interpretive frameworks to the one voiced by the students.

In his study of a tale by Balzac, *S/Z*, Barthes (1970/1974) presents a notion of the "writerly" text (p. 4) that applies here too. According to Barthes, the writerly text has a plurality of entrances—places where the reader "enters" the text (p. 5)—and a plurality of meanings as constructed by the reader. (Barthes, then, argues against the notion dear to New Critics that a text has internal coherence independent of readers' responses.) The client stakeholders break into the students' story at points of the client's choice. Think of the senior manager at the Austrian firm constantly interrupting to ask, "How does BOP fit into the evolutionary framework?" Because the audience—the key stakeholders in the client organization—judges the students' story against what the audience knows and believes, students need to plan their discourse taking into account as much as they can about what the audience has said about the issue and anticipating how the audience will respond. (See Bakhtin, 1979/1986, on the active collaboration of the reader or listener in the text of the writer or speaker.) Once the storyline is set, the students must also be capable of expanding or collapsing it as the audience shifts in composition and in point of view.

The audience tends to be unstable and ambiguous. As with the Austrian company, the audience may literally change over the course of a presentation, making their entrances and exits as topics of discussion relate to their work. The client's key stakeholders may literally change over the course of the project too; for instance, a vice president in charge of the project may be promoted to another division and a new principal client contact is then assigned to the class. Key concerns of the client's stakeholders may also change over the course of the project, whether or not there is a shift in personnel, because the project unfolds in dynamic industry and organizational conditions.

Rapid change especially characterizes high-tech organizations: A new technologically sophisticated product of today becomes a commodity within months. As a result, the window of opportunity for client receptivity to the students' story is very narrow.

The discussion that follows underscores the disparity between the storytelling framework and my observations of what students actually did in the high-tech project. Students either resisted telling a story or told a story that was unresponsive to shifts in rhetorical situation.

THE HIGH-TECH PROJECT

My observations of, participation in, and assessment of students' strategic communications for the high-tech study depended directly on my role and biases in the study. I make these explicit below before offering a detailed discussion of their work and the part that story played in it.

My Role and Biases

Since the "method" of participant-observation is deeply subjective—"who speaks? who writes? when and where? with or to whom? under what institutional and historical constraints?" (Clifford, 1986, p. 13)—I outline here my responses to these questions as best I can.

I was assigned to be the students' communications specialist but was also informed by the director of the project that the student groups should be as autonomous as possible. As the communications specialist, I had set duties, including a lecture at the study orientation about strategic communications, review of the midpoint presentations with individual speakers, review of several all-class rehearsals of the final presentation, and consultation with a student-appointed reports' committee on their writing processes and products. At orientation, I discussed my role in the project as a communications specialist, the importance of establishing credibility with the client and how this is achieved, tactical issues such as group-writing processes and presentation skills, and key points of the story framework that I had not as yet formulated as a whole—the need to establish a point of view that is clear but flexible, the students' multiple roles in the project, the importance of telling the client a compelling story, the destabilized audience who "participate" in the project and in the presentation from their own points of view.

Later in the study, I rehearsed students for the midpoint presentation and reviewed videotapes with each presenter afterwards. At that point, I introduced the notion of multiple versions of stories that need to be adapted to different audiences. My next intervention was as advisor to the student leader of the class in his efforts to prepare for the final reports and presentations; through our discussions, we determined that I would review all reports with the key writers and critique the students during two rehearsals. I also attended the two final presentations, one in the United States and the other in Germany, and, in both instances, discussed the speakers' performances with them privately.

In light of the value placed upon autonomy for the student groups by the faculty director, I explicitly told the student leader of the study that I "worked" for him as a consultant—that I had a set number of hours to contribute to the study and a point of view that I would offer, but that he and the class need not assume that point of view as their own. Even though I consistently presented myself as the students' consultant—"one member of a group possessing some degree of specialized knowledge and in that respect no different from any other member of the group" (Bion, 1961, pp. 37–38)—the students gave me more say than I wanted to have in certain aspects of the study (for example, in the selection of student presenters), an issue of leadership and authority that is common in groups (Bion, 1961). My point of view—the authority I took—involved ideas I expressed about strategic communications as storytelling, even though these did not take shape as a full-fledged framework until the study was completed. In sum, I took authority by offering students certain key points about strategic communications as story, and this was the point of view I consistently held to in working with them.

Students' Resistance to Story or Resistant Story

As a participant-observer in the study, I found that the recurrent themes in students' strategic communications were either their resistance to creating a story or their naive attitude toward and use of a story line that they did create. Neither stance was articulated by them, nor in either case did they articulate their assumptions about the audience: From the evidence of their reports and presentations, it was clear that they viewed the audience anachronistically as a kind of Lockean blank slate composed of spectators who willfully suspend their disbelief and absorb a fragmented discourse in the first instance, or a story in the second, without scrutinizing it.

Resistance to Story

Students' resistance to creating story was evident in both phases of the study. In the first phase, they expressed no point of view unless pressed by one of the faculty advisors to do so; instead of constructing working hypotheses, they focused on collecting enormous amounts of data.

In the second half of the study, students' resistance to story was most striking in the final rehearsal of their presentations, in which several key leaders of the study used a notion of story to frame the successful outcome of the session. The faculty director for the study introduced the rehearsal by saying that he was looking for story—that is, for the internal integration of each presentation so that the beginning and middle of the presentation lined up with the strategic recommendations, and that he was looking for a consistent, powerful story line across all six presentations. I concurred with this objective as did the student leader of the class, who reinforced the focus on story by asking each group to tell its story and for the others to critique each presentation for story line.

Despite this "call for story," each presentation at the final rehearsal appeared to be a procession of slides, each of which was internally coherent but lacked any clearcut linking to the ones that preceded or followed it. In other words, there was no story. For instance, a group discussing health care and high tech inserted discussion of a high-tech home care device, their major recommendation, into an unrelated overview of global markets for medical products. A group that studied manufacturing and technology focused exclusively on the purchasing link in the manufacturing chain but did not explain why. (Drafts of the reports also appeared to be fragments of information and analysis; two of them, telecommunications and health care, even inserted presentation graphics into the reports without integrating the graphics into an ongoing discussion.)

Taken as a whole, the presenters, rather than assuming the multiple roles that they might take (for example, as listeners or advocates for a set of recommendations), appeared to be exclusively interpreters of computer graphics. In fact, the well-illuminated and centrally positioned computer graphics tended to take over center stage, reducing the speaker to the shadowy sidelines, not unlike a video game player whose activity is simply to act and react to graphics.

Resistant Story

In most cases, students' resistance to story gave way under the pressure of the study's leadership, and the groups created stories for their final reports and presentations. By the final presentation, they articulated their points of view both in terms of the recommendations their discourse lead up to and the frameworks and positions from which they presented their claims. Thus, in every case, beginning with the master of ceremonies for the presentations, students identified themselves as consultants and colearners, and also—based upon my urging that they consider their multiple roles—as potential customers for the company's high-tech products, since the students represented management from a large range of industries to which the client organization wanted to sell. By explicitly acknowledging their potential customer role, they were, then, able to identify how the needs of their industry might be met by the client.

In addition to articulating their roles, they identified a key framework and terminology for their analysis drawn from high-tech marketing theory and used by the client organization. (Three of the six reports—on manufacturing, telecommunications, and finance—also used this framework extensively.)

Despite the emergence of storylines, however, the stories in the final reports and presentations were naive in that the students held to the position that there was one absolutely truthful story and that the listener was a blank slate receptive to and unbiased about the students' stories and willing to take them in as a whole rather than breaking into them according to his or her own agenda. The naivete and rigidity of the students' storylines were especially evident in the groups' unwillingness to adjust their final U.S. presentation to the needs of a European audience (addressed in Germany a week after the U.S. presentations) and in the groups' management of the question-and-answer sessions that followed the presentations. This lack of flexibility occurred despite my explicit instruction to the speakers who gave the midpoint presentations that they would need to make several adjustments of language and focus when they presented in Germany at the end of the study.

With the exception of one final report and presentation, none of the groups considered the unique issues of a Eurocentric focus on high-tech marketing. (The one exception, the purchasing group, showed the advantages of introducing the Internet in Europe because of its capacities for language translation and for rates of currency conversion.) The health care group persisted in referring to U.S. government regulations about health care; the finance group assumed that the European situation was merely six months behind the U.S. scenario and looked at banking and investment from a U.S. perspective. And, despite the upheaval in the German office—a restructuring announced three days before our visit that affected everyone's job status in Europe—the student presenters did not reshape their storylines to take into account the reasons for the restructuring and the substantial concerns about job security experienced by members of the audience. A similar kind of inflexibility was demonstrated at the question-and-answer sessions at the final presentations in the United States and in Germany. For instance, following the manufacturing group's presentation, the group was asked to consider whether the company should sell to technology managers as well as to general managers. The students didn't see how their recommendations might be adjusted to this shift.

In sum, as late as the final rehearsals, most students did not get beyond presenting data and acting in the presentation as interpreters of slides. At the final presentations, they had progressed in that they had a story to tell, although they did not regard it flexibly, nor did they want it to be questioned.

CONCLUSION

The two approaches the MBAs took to the opportunities for storytelling in their strategic communications—to resist story altogether or to hold tenaciously and naively to one storyline—occurred sequentially. First the MBAs presented chunks of information in their reports and presentations, and, then through the instruction of the class's leadership, the groups put together storylines for their data and analysis that were impervious to the client's questions and agendas. In this section, I speculate further about the two approaches and suggest further research in order to test these notions.

Not until the final presentation in the United States could one discern a story line in the individual presentations and across them. Until then, they were characterized by chunks of information, one chunk per slide, that appeared to be arbitrarily sequenced, and by the dominance of image—multicolored computer graphics—over story. The absence of story and the sense of fragmentation, so characteristic of a postmodern sensibility (see, for example, Jameson, 1981, and Lyotard, 1973), left the listener or reader with the impression of the "fragmentation of time into a series of present moments" (Jameson, 1988, p. 28). As a spectator and coach at these practice sessions, I felt as though I were witnessing the activity of *bricoleurs* (the "handyman" sort of researcher that Levi-Strauss [1962/1970] describes as working with available odds and ends to put together a new object) or—more frequently—as though I had been invited to observe a Nintendo game, with the speaker clicking on one computer graphic after another, focusing on the kinetic activity of the multicolored graphics display. The students' unarticulated assumption seemed to be that the graphics should be the protagonist; the potential storyteller was off in the wings. The rapid display of computer image eclipsed the possibility for story, the visual supplanted the verbal, and sensation replaced meaning. (See Baudrillard, 1968/1983, and Lyotard, 1971.)

The students' approach to human communication does not seem strange to me once the technologies that the MBAs are immersed in are taken into account. Fragmented pieces of information—bits and pieces of data and analysis—characterize their professional environments. Many of these executives work in organizations in which much of the communication is conducted by e-mail, their research is conducted over the Internet, and their presentations are organized in the form of "decks"—presentation slides, each one of which may be shuffled like cards in a deck. These decks often take the place of a traditional report, although they lack the logical coherence of written discourse (Worley, 1997).

The technology is not neutral, then, but in fact contributes to the MBAs' unfamiliarity with story line. Not surprisingly, the advocates of strategic communication as persuasive and constitutive story were the faculty advisors who are less steeped in the technology or were educated in an earlier era less dominated by it. Are we, then, entering professional environments in which story will be less and less familiar—and therefore less powerful? Does the students' resistance to story and the faculty's insistence upon it mark a generational or occupational split—postmodern MBAs who resist narrative versus "modern" faculty leadership that wants to restore story? (See Jameson, 1981, on the need for narrative.)

From another perspective, the students' resistance to story may be attributed to their reluctance to assume narrative authority—to take up discursive space as the storyteller who advocates new strategic realities that may be contested by the client who is perceived by the students to have greater institutional power. (See Foucault, 1971/1976, on the hierarchical division of discursive authority.)

Once they got past their first drafts and rehearsals, the MBAs were able to create stories, but their rigidity about story raises other issues. Did they assume that the client would uncritically accept their version of the strategic situation and the direction that the company should take? Did they find that preparing multiple versions of strategic stories was just too difficult a cognitive and rhetorical challenge for them? In the latter case, did they then suffer from what psychologist Gergen (1991) calls the "saturated self," one aspect of which is the idea that "as we absorb multiple voices [or play multiple roles] we find that each 'truth' is relativized by our simultaneous consciousness of compelling alternatives" (p. 16). (Rather than discuss the burden of the "saturated self," Gergen describes it as our postmodern psychological condition, but the difficulty of this condition is embedded in the notion of saturation.)

Finally—and perhaps most important—the voices of the students themselves are significantly absent from my investigation of their strategic communications. The limitations upon my participation in their strategic studies did not permit that kind of data collection; however, further research calls for a multivoiced approach, for the students to assume narrative authority, too, and in doing so, to become coauthors with the researcher rather than objects of the researcher's investigation. (On the collaborative production of texts, see Blyler, 1996; Clifford, 1986.) Such an approach would most likely provide stories that compete with or corroborate the researcher's about the nature of strategic communications and the reasons for the forms that it takes.

REFERENCES

Applebee, A. N. (1978). *The child's concept of story: Ages two to seventeen.* Chicago: University of Chicago Press.

Bakhtin, M. M. (1986). *Speech genres and other late essays* (V. W. McGree, Trans.). Austin, TX: University of Texas Press. (Original work published 1979)

Barthes. R. (1974). *S/Z* (R. Miller, Trans.). New York: Hill and Wang. (Original work published 1970)

Baudrillard. J. (1983). The ecstasy of communication (J. Johnston, Trans.). In H. Foster (Ed.). *The anti-aesthetic: Essays on postmodern culture* (pp. 126–133). Seattle, WA: Bay Press. (Original work published 1968)

Best, S., & Kellner, D. (1991). *Postmodern theory: Critical interrogations.* New York: Guilford Press.

Bion, W. R. (1961). *Experience in groups and other papers.* New York: Basic Books.

Blyler, N. R. (1996). Narrative and research in professional communication. *Journal of Business and Professional Communication,* 10, 330–351.

Clifford, J. (1986). Introduction: Partial truths. In J. Clifford & G. E. Marcus (Eds.), *Writing culture: The poetics and politics of ethnography* (pp. 1–26). Berkeley, CA: University of California Press.

Coover, R. (1996). *Briar Rose.* New York: Grove Press.

Fischer, F., & Forester, J. (1993). *The argumentative turn in policy analysis and planning.* Durham, NC: Duke University Press.

Fisher, W. R. (1984). Narration as a human communication paradigm: The case of public moral argument. *Communications Monographs, 51,* 1–22.

Fisher, W. R. (1987). *Human communication as narration: Toward a philosophy of reason, value, and action.* Columbia, SC: University of South Carolina Press.

Foucault, M. (1976). The discourse on language. In A. M.S. Smith (Trans.), *The archaeology of knowledge and the discourse on language* (pp. 215–237). New York: Pantheon. (Original work published 1971)

Gergen, K. J. (1991). *The saturated self: Dilemmas of identity in contemporary life.* New York: Basic Books.

Hermans, H. J. M., & Kempen, H. J. G. (1993). The dialogical self: Meaning as movement. San Diego, CA: Academic Press.

Jameson, F. (1981). The political unconscious: Narrative as a socially symbolic act. Ithaca, NY: Cornell University Press.

Jameson, F. (1988). Postmodernism and consumer society. In E. A. Kaplan (Ed.), *Postmodernism and its discontents* (pp. 13–29). London: Verso.

Langellier, K. M., & Peterson, E. E. (1993). Family storytelling as a strategy of social control. In D. K. Mumby (Ed.), *Narrative and social control: Critical perspectives* (pp. 49–76). Newbury Park, CA: Sage.

Levi-Strauss, C. (1970). *The savage mind* (G. Weidenfeld & Nicolson, Ltd., Trans.). Chicago: University of Chicago Press. (Original work published 1962)

Lyotard, J. (1971). *Discours, figure.* Paris: Editions Klincksieck.

Lyotard, J. (1973). *Derive a partir de Marx et Freud.* Paris: Union generale d'editions.

Lyotard, J. (1984). *The postmodern condition: A report on knowledge* (G. Bennington & B. Massumi, Trans.). Minneapolis, MN: University of Minnesota Press. (Original work published 1979)

Rentz, K. C. (1992). The value of narrative in business writing. *Journal of Business and Technical Communication, 6,* 292–315.

Throgmorton, J. A. (1996). *Planning as persuasive storytelling: The rhetorical construction of Chicago's electric future.* Chicago: University of Chicago Press.

White, H. (1987). *The content of the form: Narrative discourse and historical representation.* Baltimore, MD: Johns Hopkins Press.

Worley, R. (1997, November). *The written report: On the road to obsolence?* Paper presented at the 62nd Annual Convention of the Association of Business Communication, Washington, D.C.

part IV
Narrative and Health Care Professions

7

Midwives' Birth Stories: Narratives that Expand the Boundaries of Professional Discourse

Mary M. Lay
University of Minnesota

Recently, scholars have described how narrative, "typically devalued" in professional communication, reflects, reproduces, or alters cultural values and ideologies of discourse communities and therefore has much to teach us about these communities (Blyler, 1996, p. 330; see also Barton & Barton, 1988; Journet, 1991; Killingsworth & Palmer, 1996; Mumby, 1987). As scholars of professional communication, we have often focused on the genres that organize the knowledge created and disseminated within organizations and how apprentices within those organizations learn the forms of discourse or the genres so "essential to professional success" (Berkenkotter & Huckin, 1995, p. 1; see also MacKinnon, 1993; Winsor, 1996). A study of narrative can extend that focus, if, for example, we ask how narrative might appear in or frame the genres that organizations and professions have created to respond to recurring situations (for additional definitions of genre, see Bazerman, 1988; Miller, 1984; Swales, 1990). In this essay, I explore a genre that takes the form of narrative and that was developed by traditional midwives—the birth story. Birth stories have many features of traditional narratives, as I will explain in the first section of this essay, and teach us much about the ideology of the midwifery profession. However, I believe that an exploration of birth stories extends what we know about professional discourse in a unique way.

Although birth stories were developed by traditional midwives to accomplish what we might term the usual functions of professional discourse—such as problem solving and extending knowledge—birth stories were also developed to help midwives resist dominant cultural messages about birth.[1] The stories reaffirm the ideology of midwifery in the face of opposition and stress, they unify the home birth community's resistance to the dominant belief about birth, and they allow emotional release for practitioners who often function underground or outside more widely recognized or understood professional systems. Therefore, in this essay on birth stories, not only do I describe a form of narrative or a genre that may be new to the majority of scholars of professional communication, but I also explore how birth stories specifically support traditional midwives in their resistance. And I hope that in future studies of narrative as professional discourse, we ask to what extent we might see these two functions of narrative in other settings.

Traditional midwives, also called lay or direct-entry midwives, generally serve home birth communities; they practice legally in 18 states, illegally in 9, and alegally elsewhere, as they are not prohibited from practicing but also have no means of becoming licensed or registered with state or governmental agencies.[2] Unlike their nurse-midwife sisters, who obtain a degree in nursing before taking a specialized course in midwifery and are certified by the America College of Nurse Midwives, traditional midwives often learn and update their practices through birth stories. Although undoubtedly shared for centuries within the midwifery community, birth stories were defined as an essential form of professional discourse during the home birth or natural birth movements in the 1970s, particularly at the Santa Cruz Birth Center in California and at the Farm, a commune in Summertown, Tennessee (see, for example, Gaskin, 1990; Lang, 1972).

Birth stories were celebrated in the 1970s and remain essential in the 1990s because they build unity among the midwives, convey advice to practitioners who may be without formal training, create knowledge about birth based on actual experiences in the home birth community, and provide an emotional outlet for those who must handle life and death situations. Birth stories originate within the personal experiences of midwives and the women whom they serve and resist medicalized abstractions about birth that may deny individual choice and silence individual voices.

Feminist theorists discuss the importance of women's personal experiences as a source of knowledge—the critical and methodological stance of standpoint theory. For example, Smith (1990) suggests that the "direct embodied experience of the everyday world" serves as the "primary ground" (pp. 21–22) of knowledge:

> The standpoint of women situates the inquirer in the site of her bodily existence and in the local actualities of her working world. It is a standpoint that positions inquiry but has no specific content. Those who undertake inquiry from this standpoint begin always from women's experience as it is for women. We are the authoritative speakers of our experience…. From this standpoint, we know the everyday world through the particularities of our local practices and activities, in the actual places of our work and the actual time it takes. (p. 28)

Harding (1987) also proposes that women's experiences be used as "a significant indicator of the 'reality' against which hypotheses are tested" (p. 30). For feminist theorists, this (re)discovery of women's experiences often leads to activism or empowerment of women to "correct both the *invisibility* and *distortion* of female experience in ways relevant to ending women's unequal social position" (original emphasis, Lather, 1991, p. 71).

Feminist theorists also recognize that not only are women's experiences devalued within dominant cultural discourse, but also gender itself is socially constructed. As Scott (1991) says, "[W]e need to attend to the historical process that, through discourse, positions subjects and produces their experience. It is not individuals who have experience, but subjects who are constituted through experience" (p. 779). Scott's comment raises issues of agency and resistance—to what extent is the individual's sense of experience tempered by cultural definitions of womanhood or femininity? To what extent can she draw upon her experiences to resist dominant cultural discourse about her abilities, roles, and potential? I suggest that birth stories, developed within the gendered community of traditional midwifery, demonstrate how discourse may be used to support the specific community and counter dominant cultural discourse, to recover women's experiences and to resist cultural assumptions about women and birth.

DESCRIPTION OF BIRTH STORIES

Luce (1996), a Vermont traditional midwife, summarizes the epistemological basis of birth stories as follows:

> As midwives, we honor where the most essential wisdom and knowledge of birth lie—not in science and technology and medical definitions, but in women's bodies, in the flowering of the natural birth process, in the language—the poetry and the metaphor and the stories—that grow from experience, and in the natural world of which human birth is a part.... Midwifery is a calling, not only to assist women in childbirth, but to help to preserve the culture of natural and women-centered birth. We do this by our witness and the retelling of birth stories that embody in their narrative what is being preserved and what is being lost in medicalized, technologized birth. (pp. 9–10)

Birth stories, then, reflect and maintain the ideology of natural and safe birth, trust in women's knowledge of their bodies, and empowerment of women through birth when they are allowed to choose where, with whom, and how they birth. Within the midwifery community, birth stories function much like those narratives described by Maines and Bridger (1992): They are "...collective acts. They are almost always cultural enactments in that they link private and public realms, they link events into temporal arrangements that give people a sense of continuity, and they provide versions of reality that contribute to the flow of meaning that rests at the heart of any society" (p. 366). However, the community that traditional midwives and their home birth clients create is often close, small, and underground, so that birth stories argue against the ideology of the greater society, one that has accepted "medicalized, technologized birth," to use Luce's terms. Therefore, birth stories reflect and reproduce the ideology of safe and natural birth, and they also share and celebrate individual experiences and emotions that confirm or define that ideology.

My primary source for birth stories was the computer listserv MIDWIFE, located at midwife@fensende.com. MIDWIFE is a public and unmoderated discussion group consisting of over 180 traditional midwives (the majority of participants), nurse-midwives, home birth clients, doulas, birth educators, and physicians. Birth stories are frequently published in national journals such as *Midwifery Today*, national newsletters such as *MANA News* (produced by the Midwives' Alliance of North America), regional newsletters such as *Heart Tones* (produced by the Minnesota Midwives' Guild), and books such as Gaskin's *Spiritual Midwifery* (1990). However, because I believe they represent the most spontaneous form of the narrative, I focus on birth stories disseminated over the listserv. The listserv reflects birth stories offered primarily to peers, who give immediate feedback; in essence, the narratives initiate professional conversation. I stayed in the role of "lurker on the listserv," not making my presence known, in order to avoid inadvertently encouraging censorship and self-editing of the birth stories. However, because the participants come and go to the listserv and may use pseudonyms because of their often legally vulnerable positions, traditional research practices such as follow-up interviews have been impossible. Although the guidelines on intellectual property in cyberspace allow me to use these postings without permission, to protect their anonymity I have assigned all listserv participants pseudonyms and removed all e-mail addresses (for intellectual property guidelines, see Gurak, 1997). I have corrected spelling errors within the messages but have not edited for grammatical or syntactical problems.

I pulled 115 birth stories from the listserv between June 6, 1996, and January 17, 1997. The listserv, as expressed by one participant, enables midwives in particular "to get together, unwind, share their clinical problems, ask for help in improving our practice, share the joys and sorrow of being a midwife, discuss our shoes and the kind of cars we drive, discuss the music we use at births, and how best to pick up the mess" (listserv communication, August 28, 1996). The "meaning" of the list, expressed by another participant, is "to learn, have a shoulder to cry on, a place to list our joys, and yes, even a place to vent our frustrations" (listserv communication, November 21, 1996).

The birth stories shared on the list also serve as a form of peer review, an important activity within the regional traditional midwives' guilds throughout the United States. For example, the Minnesota Midwives' Guild and the Oregon Midwives' Guild review annually all births that their members attend, give special attention to any problematic births, and ask members to justify any departure from normal protocols.[3] The Michigan Midwives' Guild offers peer review for "anyone who requests it and it is mandatory in any life/death, or legal situation" (listserv communication, November 5, 1996). "Grace," a listserv participant, explains the importance of peer review for her: "If I ever had a death that was preventable, I NEED TO KNOW that and either get out of my practice or figure out how to make sure that it never happens again. Sometimes it's only in reviewing the case with others that you can see those things. What I can't do is be a fearful midwife. As far as I'm concerned, that's an oxymoron. Midwifery is about faith in the process (though not blind faith)" (listserv communication, November 11, 1996). Although the peer review over the listserv is more informal and casual than review within guild meetings, the feedback is similar in balancing emotional support with constructive criticism.

In a discourse community spread across the country, if not the world, birth stories contain all the elements of dramatic narrative. The reader must understand as much as possible what it was like to "be there" for any particular birth. For example, "Nancy" shares complications in delivering the placenta by creating characters, plot, dialogue, and metaphor:

> The mom was a 7th day Adventist with a poorly balanced diet.... When the nice birth was over I thought I was on easy street with her.... Into the 2nd hour waiting I feel the uterus and it is too high and too hard...I put some fundal [body of uterus] pressure on just to see if I can see leakage or clots passing. Mom tell me she feels placenta coming, starts to push, and shoots out a clot the size of a cannonball and begins to bleed, no placenta yet, I recommend transport [to the hospital], parents refuse so I am doing controlled cord traction...and the cord just slithers into my hand.... I tell them I will have to remove manually if they won't go in.... I had been told "it's just like peeling a grapefruit" Ha! Her fundus kept going higher and higher and part of it was stuck tight. I finally had to take what I could get and then try to get my hand out.... What I was not prepared for was the way my emotions struggled against me as I took that placenta. It was the only time I had to do it, but it made me sick. I couldn't think with her yelling "don't let me die," it gave me the willies. I guess no one can ever really tell you how it feels to have your guts hit the floor and just lay there. (listserv communication, September 17, 1996)

To help the reader understand what it was like to be at a particular birth, a birth story may often fall into the "story-discourse mode" of narrative, in which the story progresses through dynamic instability, to use Phelan's (1989) terms. These instabilities range from those "between characters, created by situations, and complicated and resolved through actions," such as the life-threatening condition of Nancy's client, to those of "value, belief, opinion, knowledge, expectation—between authors and/or narrators, on the one hand, and the authorial audience on the other," such as Nancy's discovery that removing the placenta manually was not as easy as peeling a grapefruit (p. 15). Such instabilities both engage the reader in the dramatic action of the narrative and challenge or extend the accepted practices and beliefs of the discourse community. For example, Nancy's readers might now be convinced that such cases should be transported to the hospital regardless of the parents' wishes. Moreover, although the client's fears of dying are essential to the story, equally important in birth stories is what Chatman (1990) would call the "slant" of the narrator, "the psychological, sociological, and ideological ramifications of the narrator's attitudes" (p. 143), in Nancy's case, a struggle between her role as helper and her personal repulsion by the act she is called upon to perform. Finally, birth stories are driven by plot, "a structuring operation elicited by, and made necessary by, those meanings that develop through succession and time" (Brooks, 1984, p. 12). Nancy makes a story out of the events at this birth—a story enhanced by metaphor and mimesis. And, to support the midwifery community as it creates its own knowledge of birth and resists the knowledge potentially imposed upon it by the dominant discourse, birth stories contain both physical and emotional detail.

SUPPORTING THE IDEOLOGY OF TRADITIONAL MIDWIFERY

Mumby (1987) links ideology and narrative within organizations or professions:

> Ideology addresses and qualifies subjects by giving them an overall sense of the limits and possibilities of the social world—ideology provides a sense of what it *means* to be a social actor.... Narrative—as one mode of symbolic structuring—is a material instantiation of ideology. It is an everyday organizational practice that structures "lived experience" in a particular way for organizational members. (p. 118)

The ideology of traditional midwifery is conveyed through birth stories: a belief in the natural process of birth, an acceptance of the unpredictability of the process tempered by a suspicion of medical intervention, and an affirmation of clients' lifestyles and birthing choices. As one Maine midwife comments after delivering twins, "We were lucky as ever that Mother Nature knows how to do this complex thing" (listserv communication, June 6, 1996).

Despite this belief in the natural birth process, traditional midwives must accept that they cannot control each birth and therefore must prepare to face death. For example, "Bonnie" offers the story of her first baby death:

> Thursday night was the first time in approx. 250 births, that I have lost a baby in labor. We spent the next hour looking for heart tones. Never found any. And she couldn't remember when she last felt the baby move. We called her back-up doc, "Dr. Smith," who is very supportive of midwives and homebirth.... He came to her house with another doppler and a portable monitor.... I'm thinking the baby's dead and this is picking up the maternal pulse (and it turns out later, I was right), but Dr. S. is saying that it's the baby...they had to do a C/S [Caesarean section] right away, which they did. It was around midnight by the time the baby was born. When it was all over and after they put this poor couple through all this hell and kept giving them hope that everything might be okay, they said the placenta had completely abrupted and the baby had been dead for 6-8 hours. So what the hell was Dr. S. up to.... Here's my self assessment of the whole thing: the baby

died before I went to her house the second time, and nothing could have changed that, save for divine intervention. (listserv communication, June 24, 1996)

Bonnie's attitude is quite different from "Dr. Smith's." She asserts that birth technology and surgical intervention only contributed to the couple's emotional pain.[4]

In response to Bonnie's birth story, "Ellen," a traditional midwife serving the Amish in Indiana, comments, "All of us who do this will someday hold a dead baby, if we do it long enough. Some babies die. It is horrible, surrealistic, and nightmarish. But we who deal with life, are sometimes given death, instead. You can never prepare for it. Your mind and spirit always rail against it" (listserv communication, June 24, 1996). And Grace tries to comfort Bonnie by sharing her own story of death:

Baby deaths are very hard to cope with. You'll find yourself going back and chewing on the situation over and over again, wondering at what point you "could have" prevented it. In the case of my one baby death at a homebirth, the baby had sounded great through labor...according to my assistant, who had done most of the listening to FHT [fetal heart tones]. I fretted for a long time that maybe if I had only listened myself, maybe I could have heard something.... Probably not, but we seem to like to torture ourselves over these. If only, if only...I was devastated after my homebirth baby death—considered leaving midwifery—how could I have ever put myself out on such a limb when life and death are so uncontrollable??... It was really torturous for awhile, but I was finally able to realize that some babies die, that I really can't control all the outcomes, but I can also own the great amount of good that I can accomplish by doing what I'm doing, the births that would have been [Caesarean] sections if I had not have been there. (listserv communication, June 24, 1996)

However, although "David," a British physician, in turn comforts Grace, he also asserts his faith in medical intervention: "Reading between the lines, this baby was probably dead before your visit in early labor.... Dr. Smith was in a difficult position. He couldn't be sure. Any of us would sooner a CS [Cesarean section] than lose a baby...I did a CS three months ago on a woman who I'd scanned and seen no fetal heart movement.... Baby was very sick for a few weeks, she's now gone home and seems fine!" (listserv communication, June 25, 1996).

Thus, through birth stories, traditional midwives reaffirm acceptance of the natural process and, at times, share their suspicion of medical intervention. They also support their clients' decisions and lifestyles. For example, a Montana midwife narrates how she responded to one hurried birth:

Well, I finally became a road midwife. Had a client call from 140 mi away and really cooking so they asked if I would meet them on the road.... I drove about 90 mi when I passed them so I did a U-turn and pulled in front of them on this long hill where they had pulled over. I grabbed a glove and ran back to the pickup (crew cab) and she had 2 BIG tears running down her face.... I had her lie down and checked her real quick (water had broken about 20 mi back) and she was almost complete with just a teeny tiny lip, of course as soon as she relaxed that was gone so 3 min later we had a 6 lb baby girl!!! I jumped in and we headed for Great Falls, she kept the placenta until we got in front of the birth center and she had maybe 1/4 cup of blood—everybody was fine and we laughed all the way in relief.... That's life in Montana working with Hutterites, it took her an hour to get him off the combine. (listserv communication, August 21, 1996)

Thus, the ideology of midwifery supports individual choice. In another example, "Georgia" tells of helping one set of parents say good-bye in their own way to their infant:

As soon as I wiped the baby's face, Mom and Dad both picked up a towel and began to clean off the old blood. She was sitting leaning closely over him as was dad. Tears were coming in torrents, and they literally washed him with their tears.... These guys were very uninhibited in their approach to the body of the baby and were just so strong in their beliefs that they didn't need me. Very healthy and powerful for them. But what it left me with was the feeling of just having looked death in the face. (listserv communication, August 13, 1996)

The ideology of traditional midwifery, as expressed through birth stories, affirms the natural process and necessary unpredictability of birth. Midwives support their clients' values and beliefs and are suspicious about medical intervention in the birth process. A midwife practicing within a birth center reminds the listserv of the origins of the word *midwife*—"with woman":

Well, it just so happened that I did all the labor support for her, held her hands, brushed the hair out of her eyes, gave her "mas agua" [more water] and told her she was doing great. She ended up on her h&k [hands and knees], baby born in the caul [membranes covering the head] and I did not see one thing. Not only that, but I was sore for the next 3 days from the mom pulling on my arms with all her might. I believe I truly got a taste of what it means to be "with woman" and the two births back to back—first catch and no hands on—happened just the way it is supposed to. (personal communication, September 10, 1996)

RESISTING THE DOMINANT DISCOURSE ABOUT BIRTH

For traditional midwives, knowledge originates in women's direct and everyday experiences, not in the medical abstractions about women's bodies and reproductive functions that have been accepted into the dominant cultural discourse about birth. This dominant discourse often characterizes birth as a dangerous event best handled by physicians in a hospital setting. Even the most practiced midwives create and test birthing techniques in their everyday practice and offer the results of these experiences within birth stories. For example, in one birth story, "Ellen" shares a technique for turning a breech baby. Within the 17 states that license traditional midwives, attending breech births at home is usually contraindicated. Midwives must either be surprised by the breech position during labor or get permission from a physician to attend a suspected breech. However, by attending an obvious breech birth and by conveying her story, Ellen resists the dominant discourse about breech birth:

> That same week the other two midwives and I did the 37 week home visit for a mom having her second baby with us. She had been on a slant board for a couple of weeks with no luck. The baby was getting really large, but we put her on the floor, and I and one other midwife started slowly moving the baby. It is a technique of gently pushing the baby a little, and then waiting for the baby to settle into the new position. We hold the baby, keeping it from moving back. The third midwife was on heart tones the entire time. They stayed excellent, and after about 10 minutes, this baby swung down into a nice vertex [head first] position, and has also stayed there. (listserv communication, June 10, 1996)

Through the direct experience of helping her clients during birth, Ellen creates new techniques, new "truths" about birth conditions, which she conveys to her sister practitioners through birth stories. And her personal experience attests that she and her sister midwives can successfully turn breech babies without medical intervention.

One measure of the traditional midwives' success in resisting the dominant cultural discourse about birth might be found within the birth stories themselves. After telling a birth story, certified nurse-midwives and physicians on the listserv often request the advice of all participants, including traditional midwives. For example, "Anne," a certified nurse-midwife in Pittsburgh, tells of a compound presentation with abruption (head plus another body part appearing with the premature separation of placenta) in order to learn more about the condition:

> Now I have a question I'd like to pose about a birth I had a couple of days ago.... I checked her and she was complete with a bulging bag which ruptured during my exam for a huge amount of fluid. Then the only presenting part I could feel was a right hand.... Fearful of a cord prolapse, I transferred her to the hospital. At the hospital the hand was still there but I could just barely reach the head. She was contracting mildly about every 3-4 minutes. We tried pinching the baby's hand to have the baby withdraw it, but it didn't work.... So, two questions. 1. Is there another way we could have handled the initial compound presentation? Have people had successful vaginal births in such a case? What did you do? 2. Was the abruption related to the presentation, or the way we handled it? (listserv communication, July 27, 1996)

The listserv participants respond to Anne with additional questions and with suggestions, often conveyed through similar stories. But it is a traditional midwife who offers the following success story about a similar condition:

> Ten years ago I had a client with AROM [artificial rupture of membranes] no contractions. I checked her for some reason and went into either an ear or a mouth. So

surprised I didn't explore very long. My partner and I were serious into a discussion of whether we would deliver this one at home or not. A little while later checked her again after she was having contractions and found that the head was now in place but there were fingers in front of it. This baby birthed in about an hour. She also had two true knots in the cord. I still wonder if this child gives this mother trouble. (listserv communication, July 28, 1996)

The listserv participants reenact birth experiences through narrative to share or create knowledge about birth that seldom would be accepted by the dominant medical community. Connecting with each other through the specific physical and emotional details of birth stories enables them to resist that dominant discourse.

"EXORCISING" THE TROUBLES OF BIRTH

Finally, to resist successfully the dominant discourse about birth, the midwifery discourse community uses birth stories to solicit emotional support after difficult or tragic births. As one listserv participant responds to Anne, "Sometimes, as they say, meconium [the baby's first bowel movement] just happens" (listserv communication, July 29, 1996). Given that the ideology of traditional midwifery both relies on the natural process and accepts the unpredictability of birth, birth stories "exorcise" the trauma of birth, as one listserv participant calls it (listserv communication, August 2, 1996). Without this emotional outlet, traditional midwives would be more likely to feel uncertain about their practices.

For example, one midwife begins her birth story with "I had my first scary birth last night and I need to get it off my chest" and ends the story with "I still don't think mom and dad knew how high our adrenaline was pumping or the seriousness of the situation. Well, thanks for listening—this has been therapeutic" (listserv communication, August 2, 1996). And "Rebecca," a certified birth educator in Georgia, retells losing the baby of a mother with preeclampsia (a toxemia that induces convulsions). She begins with "First of all, let me say that I am so glad ya'll are here to talk to." And, after narrating the details of the case, she turns from plot to discourse: "OK, now to vent some. This is not what I signed up for! Birth is supposed to be fun and uplifting! Or at least not so terribly awful! I don't want this job, I don't want to do this! Why, why, why, why, why?" (listserv communication, August 5, 1996). The listserv participants respond to these questions in Rebecca's birth story by sharing their own experiences and responding to Rebecca's emotional trauma:

My thoughts are with you as you go through this. Because we are so passionate about childbirth, it does rip us apart when things go wrong. I sometimes wonder how do I let myself get so close to my students. Is it because their births are so much like our births, because we are women with the same dreams and wishes, because all we want to do is hold that sweet little baby in our arms and nurse it at our breast? Is it because in our minds we cannot bear the thought of our babies ever being ripped away from us since they are so very much a part of us? (listserv communication, August 6, 1996)

Because it's never real until you experience it.... It's OK to feel lost and helpless. Death is the great humbler—not a damn thing we can do, but keep walking through the grief.... It's life.... None of us signed up for what we might get, we just have to take it as it comes...sometimes good, and sometimes bad. The only way to avoid the sorrow is to avoid the joy too. If we want the joy we have to take the sorrow too—if we want to be fully human, that is.... Isn't that the point to it all? (listserv communication, August 6, 1996)

And Rebecca affirms that this sharing has helped her bear her emotional burden: "Ya'll just don't know how much you've all helped, even if it wasn't by replying personally, but just being here, being patient, and letting me ramble" (listserv communication, August 9, 1996).

The traditional midwives use birth stories to affirm that as women they both benefit and suffer from a close personal connection with their clients. And they ease this emotional burden as they tell and respond to birth stories. Without this release, the midwives might find it impossible to deal with life-and-death situations within a dominant culture that negates traditional midwifery.

CONCLUSION

As Journet (1991) says, "Nonfictional narratives are also constructed; they too impose significance and coherence on a mass of data by using plots to select and order events in ways that reflect the writer's ideological and theoretical orientations" (pp. 449–450). Birth stories are nonfictional narratives that reflect the ideology of traditional midwifery, a profession that shares uneasy boundaries with modern medical practice. For example, one traditional midwife on the listserv describes her interaction with the medical community:

When I transport to this hospital, I'm required to stay. I can't see or speak to my client, and I'm usually met at the door by security guards. The security guards are assigned to stay, one on either side of me, the whole time I'm there. So I have to stay until I am excused. Usually after delivery or when the problem is controlled. And meanwhile, no communication with medical personnel about the client's history or the situation. But one doctor will come out and harass me periodically.... "Well, you almost killed another one, huh." (listserv communication, August 24, 1996)

Thus, birth stories establish, affirm, and reinforce the ideology of home birth and traditional midwifery, an ideology that trusts the natural process but accepts its unpredictability. Also, through detailed retelling of both the physical and emotional details of birth, midwives create and share knowledge, receive careful feedback and advice, and establish a sense of community. Birth stories then become a form of professional discourse for traditional midwives and their sister nurse-midwives, doulas, and birth educators. But they also resist the dominant discourse that proposes birth is best handled within the hospital setting by formally trained medical personnel.

By understanding the importance and place of birth stories in this discourse community, as scholars of professional discourse we learn more about the ideology of this sometimes silent and underground practice and expand our own knowledge of the value of narrative within professional discourse. But we also begin to sense that narrative in general may provide an appropriate way to resist values and beliefs that narrators and their audiences consider questionable or alien. If narrators tell their stories in dramatic detail, engaging their audiences in reliving the experience with them, they create a concrete knowledge base that may resist more abstract or generalized constructions that might define their professions or organizations. These abstractions and generalizations may come from inside or outside the organization. And if audiences respond to narrators' depictions of the emotional trauma of operating contrary to the dominant beliefs, narrators might find further understanding and support for resisting these dominant beliefs. So far, our studies of apprenticeship into organizations, particularly as those apprentices learn the organization's genres, have neglected to ask about those who might resist the values and beliefs reflected within genres. Future studies of narrative as used in a variety of organizational and professional settings might reveal tensions between resistance and acceptance of dominant discourse similar to the ones I found in reading midwives' birth stories.

NOTES

[1] Although it is beyond the scope of this essay to describe in detail the beliefs about birth that persist within both the medical and general cultures of the United States, interested readers will find fuller descriptions of these beliefs in such sources as Arms, 1975; Donnison, 1977; Martin, 1992.

[2] As of 1999, the 18 states that license, register, or certify traditional midwives are Alaska, Arkansas, Arizona, California, Colorado, Delaware, Florida, Louisiana, Minnesota, Montana, New Hampshire, New Mexico, Oregon, Rhode Island, South Carolina, Texas, Washington, and Wyoming. Traditional midwives are illegal in Iowa, Kentucky, Maryland, Missouri, North Carolina, Ohio, Virginia, and West Virginia. However, in other states, such as New York, where licensing is available only to certified nurse-midwives, traditional midwives have recently been arrested and charged with the felony of practicing midwifery or nursing without a license (Schlinger, 1996, p. 25).

[3] I attended the January 18, 1997, peer review session of the Minnesota Midwives' Guild, in which the one traditional midwife went through her annual peer review of all cases and two midwives were sanctioned for going outside of the guild's protocols in attending an unplanned home birth. Information about the Oregon Guild came from a listserv message on November 1, 1996.

[4] Recently Pollock (1997) completed a study of birth stories offered by women who primarily delivered in the hospital. She found that most were comic and

> ...rose out of even the depths of terror and anger to embrace the emerging baby and the norms by which it was deemed healthy and whole. Whatever critique a story offered, it was more often than not tempered by expressions of gratitude to the institutions that protected the mother and/or child's health.... Several [stories] even seemed licensed by what medical discourses designate a "good outcome" to elaborate and to embellish the preceding dangers and conflicts, with the effect, whether intentional or incidental, of improving the climax, of ensuring relief in the final orderliness of all things. With all the flourish of a Shakespearean comedy, they delivered order from disorder and pleasure from abandon, transgression, and pain. (pp. 12–13)

With rare exceptions, Pollock found that her mothers' birth stories demonstrate confidence in "our own normality and, in turn, invite a sense of superiority to death, disaster, and deformity, as if all it takes to avoid such ends is the proper exercise of courage and technology, as if death were a moral failure and abnormality were the cost of betraying the social order" (p. 13). Most mothers had confidence in medical science and testing and considered ambiguity "the enemy and must be cut up and cut out first by abstract, rational, and then by surgical means" (p. 26; see, also, Carpenter, 1985, and Dwinell, 1992, for another source of mothers' birth stories). Again, the traditional midwifery community relies on the natural birth process, accepts ambiguity, and is suspicious of medical intervention.

REFERENCES

Arms, S. (1975). *Immaculate deception: A new look at women and childbirth in America.* Boston: Houghton Mifflin.

Barton, B. F., & Barton, M.S. (1988). Narrative in technical communication. *Journal of Business and Technical Communication, 2 (1)* , 36–48.

Bazerman, C. (1988). *Shaping written knowledge: The genre and activity of the experimental article in science.* Madison, WI: University of Wisconsin Press.

Berkenkotter, C., & Huckin, T. N. (1995). *Genre knowledge in disciplinary communication: Cognition/culture/power.* Hillsdale, NJ: Erlbaum.

Blyler, N. R. (1996). Narrative and research in professional communication. *Journal of Business and Technical Communication, 10,* 330–351.

Brooks, P. (1984). *Reading for the plot: Design and intention in narrative.* Oxford, England: Oxford University Press/Clarendon Press.

Carpenter, C. (1985). Tales women tell: The function of birth experience narratives. *Canadian Folklore, 47*(1-2), 21–34.

Chatman, S. (1990). *Coming to terms: The rhetoric of narrative in fiction and film.* Ithaca, NY: Cornell University Press.

Donnison, J. (1977). *Midwives and medical men: A history of inter-professional rivalries and women's rights.* New York: Schocken Books.

Dwinell, J. (1992). *Birth stories: Mystery, power, and creation.* Westport, CT: Bergin & Garvey.

Gaskin, I. M. (1990). *Spiritual midwifery* (3rd ed.). Summertown, TN: Book Publishing.

Gurak, L. (1997). *Persuasion and privacy in cyberspace: The online protests over lotus marketplace and the clipper chip*. New Haven, CT: Yale University Press.

Harding, S. (1987, Fall) The method question. *Hypatia, 2,* 19–35.

Journet, D. (1991). Ecological theories as cultural narratives. *Written Communication, 8,* 446–472.

Killingsworth, M. J., & Palmer, J. S. (1996). Millennial ecology: The apocalyptic narrative from silent spring to global warning. In C. G. Herndl & S. C. Brown (Eds.), *Green culture: Environmental rhetoric in contemporary America* (pp. 21–45). Madison, WI: University of Wisconsin Press.

Lang, R. (1972). *Birth book*. Felton, CA: Genesis Press.

Lather, P. (1991). *Getting smart: Feminist research and pedagogy with/in the postmodern*. New York: Routledge.

Luce, J. (1996, July). Keeping alive the vision. *MANA News, 14,* 1, 8–10.

MacKinnon, J. (1993). Becoming a rhetor: Developing writing ability in a mature, writing-intensive organization. In R. Spilka (Ed.), *Writing in the workplace: New research perspectives* (pp. 41–55). Carbondale, IL: Southern Illinois University Press.

Maines, D. R, & Bridger, J. C. (1992). Narratives, community, and land use decisions. *Social Science Journal, 29,* 363–380.

Martin, E. (1992). *The woman in the body: A cultural analysis of reproduction*. Boston: Beacon Press.

Miller, C. (1984). Genre as social action. *Quarterly Journal of Speech, 70,* 151–167.

Mumby, D. (1987). The political function of narrative in organizations. *Communication Monographs, 54,* 113–127.

Phelan, J. (1989). *Reading people, reading plots: Character, progression, and the interpretation of narrative*. Chicago: University of Chicago Press.

Pollock, D. (1997). Origins in absence: Performing birth stories. *The Drama Review, 41*(1), 11–42.

Schlinger, H. (1996, January). New York state: Witch-hunt or political strategy? *MANA News, 14,* 1, 24–25.

Scott, J. W. (1991). The evidence of experience. *Critical Inquiry, 17,* 773–797.

Smith, D. E. (1990). *The conceptual practices of power: A feminist sociology of knowledge*. Boston: Northeastern University Press.

Swales, J. M. (1990). *Genre analysis: English in academic and research settings*. Cambridge, England: Cambridge University Press.

Winsor, D. (1996). *Writing like an engineer: A rhetorical education*. Mahwah, NJ: Lawrence Erlbaum.

8

Prehospital Care Narratives: A Time for Reflection and Professional Growth

Roger Munger
James Madison University

> For future treatment and for future care? Yes, it would be a problem if you don't have a prehospital care report because then you can't look back.
> —anonymous emergency medical technician

Often the first of many medical reports written on patients suffering from life-threatening illnesses or injuries, run reports document the care and treatment given by prehospital care providers (for example, paramedics, emergency medical technicians, and first responders). Although formats vary, run reports usually feature a combination of fill-in-the-blanks, check boxes, short answer spaces, and lined white space. Typically, the lined white space on run reports is comprised of four sections: Chief Complaint, Subjective Assessment, Objective Physical Assessment, and Comments. Collectively, the text written in these four sections constitutes the prehospital care narrative. While some providers make a distinction between the different types of information documented in each section, in practice, many providers use the available white space to write a continuous narrative.

My purpose in this chapter is to explain how run narratives are important occasions for reflection on patient care practices and opportunities for growth for emergency medical service (EMS) professionals. The study described in this chapter suggests that narrative is especially suited for documenting events such as those occurring in the EMS profession. Also, narratives written by professionals in the workplace not only help them to accomplish their work, but also provide them with time to consider their practices. In my research, I used a variety of data collection techniques to examine providers' practices and to insure the confidentiality and safety of my study's participants and their patients. Data sources included field notes on over 150 hours of observing providers treat patients and write run reports, taped interviews with 10 providers from a volunteer ambulance squad and two officials from the New York Bureau of Emergency Medical Service, 227 run reports (written during the years 1965 to 1997), and over 200 articles related to run reports from EMS journals. I have included in this chapter extended excerpts from providers in the field. In this manner, I hope their own voices—the voices of highly trained and experienced EMS professionals—underscore the vital importance of narratives to this profession. I begin by discussing the important role narrative plays in EMS documentation practices. Specifically, I suggest that narrative—as opposed to check boxes alone—is more effective in helping providers account for their actions during complicated emergency situations. Next, I explain how narrative helps providers reflect on their patient care practices. Finally, I argue that such reflection enables providers to grow professionally.

IMPORTANCE OF NARRATIVE SPACE

While the lion's share of information written about run reports in the EMS literature focuses on medico-legal issues and this genre's capacity to communicate medical information to hospital personnel, providers first think of this workplace genre as a tool for patient care. As such a tool, the formal features (for example, check boxes, short blanks, lined white space, etc.) and layout of the run report serve as instructions to providers delivering patient care. For example, according to Coe (1987), forms direct attention and motivate us to seek information: "[Forms] move us to consider certain types of things, to search for particular information and, generally, to find something (if only 'N/A') to fill every slot" (p. 18). Instead of reading on the form, for example, "check vital signs three times before arriving at the hospital" or "ask the patient if he or she is allergic to anything and record response in space provided," providers see three sets of boxes for recording vital signs and a short blank space after "allergy to" in a section labeled "Past Medical History." These blank spots on the form prompt providers to gather and record the necessary information.

Although the run report's check boxes and short blanks certainly play a role in prompting providers to seek out additional information while caring for patients, it is the run narratives written in the lined white space that have the capacity to play a central role in immediate and future patient care. While many EMS agencies have opted for run report forms featuring only check boxes and short answer spaces, participants in my study feel, almost unanimously, that check boxes and short answer spaces cannot function in the same manner as the lined white space. While many providers, when asked whether they would prefer a run report form made up of only check boxes, quickly answered "yes," further discussions with them revealed that check boxes would be inadequate. Although a scannable form would certainly shorten their report writing work, they admit that the check boxes could not adequately capture the essence of patient care and that they, as professionals, need free response—meaning, narrative—space in which to write comments.

Representing Actions

Almost universally, providers believe the run narrative is a better representation of what they are doing. Providers argue that some of the patient care information they gather cannot be "quantified with a pencil." They explain that they were taught to do *interpretive thinking* in their training, and white space allows them to document it. The providers are trained to chart patient care (in a narrative format) and not to check boxes. One provider argues, "We can't do this [use check boxes]. You teach us to do it [charting]. You can't tell us to do all the things this list says to do on this form, unless you give us more [white space]" (personal communication, November 18, 1996).[1] It is not as if the providers think the information would be lost; they want to say, "Look, we did thoroughly what we were supposed to do" (personal communication, November 18, 1996). The narrative spaces on run reports help providers document their actions and, thereby, provide evidence of their life-saving skills.

A frequent comment by providers talking about the lined white space on run reports is that they all want space to write a narrative:

> I like the ability to write something down because then I can describe it in my own words and then I'm not held to the limitations of the check boxes themselves. (personal communication, February 3, 1997)

> I know no two ambulance calls are alike, there's no such thing as a routine ambulance call, you need a place to put a scenario. (personal communication, February 9, 1997)

Clearly, from the above examples, it seems providers do not feel they can adequately communicate all the relevant patient care information by check boxes alone. Narrative, it seems, is particularly well-suited to documenting unexpected actions such as those likely to occur during emergencies and unexplained illnesses.

Accounting for Complex and Unforeseen Situations

A run report form featuring only check boxes cannot adequately account for all the diverse situations providers face in the field. The narrative allows providers to further describe patients, treatments, and emergency scenes in ways impossible through check boxes alone. One provider, for instance, explains, "That's why the narrative is important...you put down everything because you may do something that seems logical on scene but not write it down and then...people will say why did you do that" (personal communication, February 9, 1997). When asked about check boxes, many providers feel that documenting an ambulance run using check boxes would not be possible due to the countless variables. For example, two providers comment on the impracticality of having a check box for every situation:

> I believe it would make me uneasy...because each situation is different and I can't agree that all situations will be able to fit into check boxes. (personal communication, February 10, 1997)

> You'd have to end up with multiple sheets full of check boxes if you couldn't write things. You'd spend more time looking for things and you can't account for all possibilities. Also, the narrative format gives you a flow to patient assessment, patient care, patient treatment. It's kind of difficult to achieve that [flow] with check boxes. (personal communication, February 3, 1997)

In fact, many providers believe that a form composed of almost all check boxes would be "tough to handle" (personal communication, February 23, 1997) and "not...worthwhile" (personal communication, February 20, 1997). Two experienced EMS personnel offer specific examples of how check boxes are inadequate for documenting all possible emergency situations and complex illnesses:

> I don't believe there's a check box where you can show...if the patient was inside the car, under the car, on top of the car, around the car, out of the car, there's so much that goes on at the scene that you have to put down or that I feel you have to put down that's important. (personal communication, February 3, 1997)

> I think it's going be very difficult to pick something up like a patient was fine, woke up, all of a sudden had chest pain, took pain medicine, went back to sleep. That's kind of hard to paint that history of what went on.... The objective stuff is pretty much gray, it's difficult...to write, to be definitive in a check box format. (personal communication, February 9, 1997)

Checking boxes may be adequate to record several discrete facts; however, providers feel they need narrative space to "paint that history of what went on." That is, narrative helps providers to show relationships between events and communicate the frequently "gray" areas of patient care. Since "at least two versions of the same set of events can be imagined" (White, 1987, p. 20), narrative is better suited than check boxes for documenting prehospital care practices.

IMPACT OF NARRATIVE ON PATIENT CARE PRACTICES

The value of prehospital care narratives to providers out in the field, specifically, and the EMS profession, in general, was readily apparent when I observed providers as they went about their duties during ambulance runs. Run reports guide providers during the various stages of patient care and in addition, the narratives they write help them make sense of what is going on during the ambulance run. Schön (1987) argues, "The problems of real-world practice do not present themselves to practitioners as well-formed structures" (p. 4). However, by using the narrative space as a diagnostic aid, providers are often able to sort emergencies into standard pigeon holes. Creating and recognizing standard narratives of, for instance, a diabetic coma or a myocardial infarction (a heart attack) help providers identify and treat life-threatening illnesses. Thus, for EMS practitioners, narratives are useful tools for treating patients.

Making Sense of Chaotic Events

Narratives help providers make connections between signs, symptoms, treatments, and outcomes. For example, one provider talks about a particular instance when writing the run narrative helped him better understand the events of the run, "Look what I wrote here.... This and this they coincide and that's probably what was going on" (personal communication, February 9, 1997). The hectic pace of emergency care frequently limits providers' ability to understand the larger overall situation while providing immediate patient care. On one ambulance run, for example, numbers are recorded: "BP 120/80, pulse 120 and regular, respirations 18 and labored." Providers administer oxygen and place the patient on a cardiac monitor. In the midst of patient care, providers are focused on providing life saving treatment. Writing the narratives, however, enables providers to step back from the situation and make sense of the jumbled flow of patient care data. For instance, instrument traces such as a strip from a cardiac monitor are also analyzed and included in the narrative. The physical reality of a 6-inch strip showing a line resembling an irregular picket fence is converted into writing: ventricular fibrillation. While writing the run narrative, for example, providers transform signs and symptoms into a coherent—often standard—narrative.

   This sort of reflection-in-action (Schön, 1983, 1987), which the narratives allow for, is crucial to patient care. Such reflection, according to Schön (1987), involves practitioners making "new sense of uncertain, unique or conflicted situations of practice" (p. 39). Caught up in the midst of an emergency, the lined white space provides an opportunity for providers to put what is happening on paper. The act of recording events on the preprinted form often results in providers gaining a better understanding of the entire event. For example, one provider explains how writing the narrative allows her to understand the bigger picture of a patient's illness:

> When you're...with the patient you're really...just geared towards figuring out what's wrong and trying to alleviate the problem.... But when you sit back and you write all these little symptoms the person presents to you and everything they say, you kind of get a bigger picture of what's going on and then you look, oh this person has, you know, this type of disease. (personal communication, February 20, 1997)

For this provider, writing a narrative of the ambulance run provides her with an occasion to sort out what is going on, make a tentative diagnosis, and then adjust her care accordingly. Similarly, another provider by virtue of documenting his findings is able to make sense of what was happening:

> We weren't sure if it was an overdose, an attempted suicide, or what and in going back through slowly what we saw at the scene and what we did and then in our treatments we noticed how they thought the man had tried to hang himself. He was actually just drunk and trying to change a light bulb is pretty much what we figured out...the fact that there was no mark on his neck or anything and he was found on the floor, semi-responsive with a rope above him and the lights out and going back through it we realized that the power was not on and it was not attempted suicide but just a bad light bulb changed by a drunk. (personal communication, February 9, 1997)

Initially, the provider is not able to decide on the cause of the patient's injuries. However, by transforming patient care data into a coherent narrative, this provider realizes that the patient's injuries resulted from alcohol intoxication and not a suicide attempt. This example illustrates how powerful a tool narrative is for providers trying to understand a series of events. The opportunity to write a narrative encourages providers to link events and speculate on their relationship.

Stimulating Memories

In addition to helping providers sort through collections of signs and symptoms, writing the narratives helps jog providers' memories and enable them to understand specific events in terms of standard emergencies. First, the run report's narrative spaces serve as a heuristic. That is, the process of writing the narrative enables providers to recall details about the emergency that they might not ordinarily be able to remember:

> During a traumatic situation...you focus on the life threatening injury. When I sit down to write this or as I'm going to the hospital and I'm jotting down some information on this, I'll go through my process...I might remember if I'm writing down, oh yeah, she was moving her leg very weirdly or like really holding her leg...but I may not think about that while I'm in the car, it'll come as I need it.... I'll remember something that I saw and record it. (personal communication, February 3, 1997)

Unlike competitive athletes who may have video recordings of their actions or student writers who have past papers with teachers' comments on them, providers have no record of their practices save their memories and their run reports.

Moreover, since similar emergencies occur over and over again, individual ambulance runs tend to blur together. The providers' opportunity, therefore, to work through the call on paper immediately after the fact is important. With the opportunity to reflect, many of the small details about an ambulance run are preserved. In the short term, for individual patients, these details may figure into the treatment they are given. In the long term, providers can build on past experiences and not have to "reinvent the wheel" for each new patient. In a more general sense, Schön (1987) argues for the value of this type of reflection to a profession:

> Each new experience of reflection-in-action enriches his repertoire.... Reflection-in-action in a unique case may be generalized to other cases, not by giving rise to general principles, but by contributing to the practitioner's repertoire of exemplary themes from which, in subsequent cases of his practice, he may compose new variations. (p. 68)

Schön's concept of building a "repertoire of exemplary themes" is crucial to understanding the value of narrative to providers. After responding to, treating, and documenting several heart attacks, for example, providers begin to develop a standard heart attack narrative—both as a mental schemata and on paper. Likewise, after treating a few intoxicated patients, providers create a standard narrative of a drunk. In this manner, they are able to build a repertoire of narratives concerning common emergencies and illnesses. Once they have created this repertoire, providers can call upon these standard narratives while treating patients and use such narratives as a diagnostic tool.

The connections providers make while writing the run narratives have the potential to affect the outcome of a patient's emergency. An experienced provider, for example, recalls one instance when his documentation enabled him to better care for a patient:

> I had a traffic accident patient that came in back boarded, looked to be minor injuries. He had an increasing blood pressure, increasing pain in his head, and basically got put in a hall. I stayed with him because I realized it was serious and they didn't take the time to look at my information and finally I had to call somebody over because he was going south very quickly. (personal communication, February 10, 1997)

Although the patient seemed stable and not in danger, the series of increasing blood pressure readings documented in the narrative led this provider to stay with the patient and eventually get necessary help. The provider mentally matched the narrative he had written with a standard narrative for a much more serious and life-threatening emergency. As an opportunity to reflect, providers use the run narratives to guide their actions as they care for patients, to prompt their asking of important questions, and to sort out the events of ambulance runs. In addition, as I will discuss in the next section, the narrative enables reflective activities that shape future practice as well as providing a time for professional growth.

A TIME FOR PROFESSIONAL GROWTH

My observations of providers on ambulance runs and analysis of their reports suggest that the value of these prehospital care narratives extends well beyond an opportunity to record and make sense of complex and chaotic events. Surprisingly, many providers acknowledge that their run narratives are seldom read. One provider who has written over 3,000 run reports for both volunteer and commercial ambulance squads comments, "To tell you the truth, I don't think I've ever seen a doctor pick it [a run report] up" (personal communication, February 10, 1997). Another provider comments, "I don't recall a time when the nurses actually picked up and looked other than to find out the name and the address and, you know, like vitals" (personal communication, February 23, 1997). Judging from the responses of the providers I interviewed, it seems providers *know* that much of the information they write in a run narrative is, most likely, never going to be read in a patient care setting.

However, when asked whether they would be willing to omit certain items from their narratives, they respond as if their reports are frequently read: "Because that [a portion of a narrative] gives an idea of how severe his pain is and where its going and can help lead to the diagnosis that he was probably having a heart attack" (personal communication, February 10, 1997). This provider's response seems to assume that someone—someone who can diagnose—will read this report. Yet, observational data and interviews with providers reveals that this information will not likely be read at the hospital. If not for other personnel providing immediate patient care, then for whom are these reports written?

My study's findings suggest that the run reports *are read* and that they *are useful*. Granted, run narratives are useful to guard against legal claims. However, saying that these narratives are written primarily for legal audiences seems inadequate in explaining the workplace practices I observed.

The value of prehospital care narratives is as a retrievable record of past events that enables providers to reflect on their own and others' professional practices. Sometimes, it is only after the patient has been transferred to the next level of care that providers have a chance sit down and write the run narrative and review the emergency from start to finish. While many providers acknowledge that when they write run reports they learn things "all the time" (personal communication, February 20, 1997), my study suggests that composing and reading run reports, especially run narratives, helps providers make sense of their professional practices in two specific ways. First, providers examine their own past actions, evaluate them, and change future actions based on their evaluations. Second, and in a similar fashion, providers learn from other providers' experiences. The end result is improved patient care and, thus, a better EMS profession.

Using Run Narratives to Reflect on Past Actions

The value of run narratives to the EMS profession was apparent when I asked providers if they ever reread their past run reports. The report is the only record besides the providers' memories of what occurs during a call. As such, the report provides EMS personnel with opportunities to reflect on their past actions. When rereading the reports, providers review what they did in the past, evaluate their actions (often, in light of newly learned skills and techniques), and make changes in their patient care and documentation practices.

As part of the interviews for this study, I had providers reread two to four prior reports, and I then asked them questions about what they had read. The providers, especially those who did not have frequent access to past run reports, benefited from having a chance to look back. One provider, for instance, remarks, "Yeah, just looking at these three [run reports] was kind of neat because I can see things already like [omitting] that *15 minute* or *that O2 with 15 liters*.... Geesh, I would have written that down these days and it's kind of interesting to see what I did" (personal communication, February 1997).

My study's participants, almost universally, recognized the value of having a chance to reread their past run reports. Providers benefit by spotting patterns in the way they write their narratives. As one provider explains, these patterns sometimes represent bad habits, "Let people at the agency see if there any patterns developing. Myself, I've seen some patterns that I really shouldn't be going that way, I should go back to be more thorough in certain sections. I noticed that I've dropped certain abbreviations and things" (personal communication, February 3, 1997).

Some of the providers were able to further elaborate on what they gained as a result of reading their past reports. One provider notices a bad habit developing in his documentation because he uses boiler plate phrases for almost all patients. As a result, he took steps to be more descriptive in his documentation:

> I got into a habit of writing *lungs, cap refill, neuros, motors* on every [run report] exactly the same way and I realized that I was just getting that into a habit of form rather than trying to be more descriptive in some sense. Almost becoming a check box myself that I write out." (personal communication, February 10, 1997)

Likewise, another provider noticed inaccuracies in his patient assessments after rereading his narratives. Once this bad habit was noticed, the provider explains how he learned a better method of documenting a patient's neurologic ability:

> I used to put down the patient had full motor or full movement with their arms and their legs. Well, in order to actually test that, you have to do all sorts of things that you didn't do so that wasn't a proper explanation of what I was testing for.... So now I write positive motor that the patient can actually move not that they can do it in all fashions. So that taught me something. (personal communication, February 23, 1997)

In the above examples, the opportunity to reread narratives enables providers to notice trends in their practices and make adjustments. The ability to make adjustments in their patient care practices helps providers grow as EMS professionals.

As windows to the past, run narratives are invaluable to providers. Providers are able to examine how their skills have progressed over the years as they gain experience and new training. Without the narratives, these providers would have to rely only upon their memories. They may not be able to notice the progress and growth they have made as professionals in the EMS community. The run report narrative, therefore, enables providers to think back on what they did in the field and to change their future practices based on their reflections.

USING RUN NARRATIVES TO LEARN FROM OTHER'S EXPERIENCES

Although the provider with the highest level of training and, thus, responsibility for patient care, physically writes the prehospital care narrative, composing the narrative is a collaborative act. Writing the narrative generates much talk about the emergency and the providers' actions. While writing the narrative, the in-charge provider (or crew chief), for example, asks other crew members to share their recollection of events, evaluate possible phrasing, and proofread the report. The crew chief may also comment on events and evaluate his or her crew members' actions. Consequently, reading and writing run narratives gives providers an opportunity to learn from other more experienced and skilled providers. As Schön (1987) writes, "Students...are helped...by senior practitioners who...initiate them into the traditions of practice" (p. 16–17). Thus, while filling out run reports, more highly trained crew chiefs use this time to teach important aspects of patient care. For example, one veteran provider sometimes uses his run narrative as an opportunity to discuss with his ambulance crew different treatment options allowed for by various medications. Here, he explains how effective the narrative is for this type of activity: "I'm doing medications that can really alter the course of treatment with a patient. I mean there's different options.... So, going back through with the crew it's like why do you think we did this to combat effectively?... They [run narratives] work really well" (personal communication, February 9, 1997).

In this case, the provider is able to educate other crew members immediately after the patient is transferred to the next level of care. In this manner, the less experienced providers "also learn the forms of inquiry by which competent practitioners reason their way, in problematic instances, to clear connections between general knowledge and particular cases" (Schön, 1987, p. 39). Mediating this type of talk and reflection is the run report narrative.

Narratives also help providers learn from others long after patients have been transferred to the next level of care and the ambulances have returned to the station. As a retrievable record, the narrative makes the events of the ambulance run available to more providers than just those on the run. Consequently, past run reports represent a vast resource of patient care case studies and documentation styles that providers can use to grow professionally.

By reading other providers' run reports, some providers comment that they gain new methods of writing their own narratives: "I have learned also just the writing and the documentation itself…how to better document things as far as how to put the same thought in the small amount of words is a good example" (personal communication, February 17, 1997).

Similarly, one provider, who has been writing run reports for over 30 years, still learns better ways to describe specific illnesses and symptoms from reading other providers' reports: "I can say that I think…reviewing other people's [run reports] helps me write better [reports]. Some people have a real good knack about really describing what they see, so I think it can be used as a real good learning tool…. You really learn a lot I think" (personal communication, February 10, 1997).

In the above accounts, both providers learn better ways of documenting ambulance runs from reading other providers' narratives. Without such an opportunity, providers would have no way of comparing their practices to other EMS professionals' practices.

Finally, many providers feel that reading run reports is a good way to learn about prehospital care:

> Just learning the process of what you go through at the scene when it's written out neatly in a report, you can see how it's supposed to go rather than when you're at a scene and someone is telling you to get vitals and hook up the O2 and you don't get to see everything else going on. It's a training tool for new people. They can look and see how a whole scene goes. (personal communication, February 20, 1997)

As this quote illustrates, the narrative is not only a tool for patient care but also a tool for training new EMS professionals. The narrative helps new providers step back from the seeming chaos of an ambulance run in a low-stress, safe environment and look at the big picture of how all the small elements fit together to form competent patient care. In this manner, senior practitioners "remake a part of their practice world and thereby reveal the usually tacit processes of worldmaking that underlie all of their practice" (Schön, 1987, p. 36).

Opportunities to look back at past ambulance runs—both their own and others'— seems to lead providers to improving their patient care techniques. The narrative stimulates providers' critical evaluation of past actions in a less stressful environment: "When you put it all out before you in the written report, you go, 'Ahh I should have done this.'… You know that should have been first because you're looking at it now not caught up in the situation" (personal communication, February 3, 1997).

Providers comment frequently on the chaotic pace of patient care in the field and on more quiet times when they are able to sit back and analyze their performance in a critical manner. The above quote illustrates how the run narratives provide EMS professionals with a chance to gain some perspective on their actions—how to better care for patients, what questions to ask, and what approaches to take. Without such opportunities, these insights would be lost, perhaps, in the rush back to the station or to the next call.

IMPLICATIONS OF STUDY

This study illustrates the importance of the reflective activities providers engage in while composing and reading run narratives. In the specific case of the prehospital care providers I studied, the opportunity to write narratives affected how they delivered patient care and grew as professionals. To understand the vital importance of narratives to EMS professionals, consider a world in which providers merely checked off boxes on a scannable form, or, worse, completed no ambulance trip reports at all. In such a world, patients would most likely still receive competent care, medical professionals would possibly still get the information they need to care for patients, and providers would not spend the majority of their time filling out paperwork.

However, providers would have to rely upon their memories to guide them in the *flow* of patient assessment and care. The vast numbers of check boxes would not likely provide the same sort of guide. In addition, providers would go from one emergency call to the next, responding to the immediacy of ill or injured patients. Reacting to events as they occur, they would not likely have a chance to think through events and be proactive in their care. They would have few opportunities to make sense of the jumbled and chaotic events comprising, say, a trauma victim in full cardiac arrest. Finally, knowledge-making in the EMS profession, perhaps, would be largely based on lore, personal accounts from memory: "I once had a patient...." They would not be able see how their skills have progressed; nor would they be able to catch deficiencies in their patient assessment techniques as easily. New providers would have no way of learning about workplace practices except from personal accounts of other providers or actually going out on ambulance runs. In short, patient care would decline, development of life-saving skills would slow, and the profession as a whole would suffer.

Opportunities for reflective practices seem crucial and, consequently, so do formats provided for documenting their actions. Numerous health care professionals (see, for example, Dautermann, 1993; Hunter, 1991; Pettinari, 1988; Reynolds, Mair, & Fischer, 1995) and professionals in law enforcement and social work (see, for example, Paré, 1993) regularly write narratives as part of their daily work. Unfortunately, increased workloads and advances in technology have pushed some professions toward easily scanned check box forms. However, my study suggests that opportunities to write narratives are crucial to some professions' ability to serve society and to the professionals' growth.

More generally, this study argues that narrative is especially well suited for reflection on experience and for documenting that experience. Narrative encourages writers to create order out of chaos, see relationships, and seek closure for a sequence of events. The act of ordering events, as this study illustrates, helps writers understand and learn from the experience. Moreover, as White (1987) argues, narrative may be particularly suited for the discourse of the professions since narrativity "signals at once its objectivity, its seriousness, and its realism" (p. 24). Through narrative, professionals are able to present their workplace practices as objective and, consequently, establish their professional authority. For example, EMS personnel in the field, like physicians in hospitals, derive their power through "their ability to create 'objective representations' of the patient's condition" (Cicourel, 1985, p. 170).

Narratives such as the ones written by EMS professionals are valuable tools that enable professionals to accomplish numerous actions, reflect on their practices, and adapt these practices to better serve the community. As researchers, teachers, and practitioners of professional communication, we would do well to understand and support these efforts. As researchers we can continue studying workplace narratives in the midst of the contexts in which they are created and used. That is, in order to adequately understand workplace narratives, we should study narratives in action, as parts of larger systems (see, for example, Cole & Engeström, 1993; Engeström, 1996). As teachers of professional communication, we should value workplace narratives such as those written by EMS personnel. Students preparing for their chosen profession would benefit from activities allowing them to practice the types of reflection and growth made possible by narrative. We can, thus, prepare them to continue these practices once they enter the workplace. Finally, when designing workplace documents, we should—in many cases— resist the trend toward predetermined check boxes. Instead, we should create documents that feature spaces for narrative and, thus, encourage the type of reflection and professional growth practiced by EMS professionals in this study.

NOTE

[1] All participants in this study remain anonymous, as does their ambulance squad. I have omitted participants' names and changed certain identifying features in an effort to protect their identity.

REFERENCES

Cicourel, A. (1985). Text and discourse. *Annual Review of Anthropology, 14*, 159–185.
Coe, R. (1987). An apology for form; or who took form out of the process? *College English*, 49, 13–28.

Cole, M., & Engeström, Y. (1993). A cultural-historical approach to distributed cognition. In G. Salomon (Ed.), *Distributed cognitions: Psychological and educational considerations* (pp. 1–46). Cambridge, England: Cambridge University Press.

Dautermann, J. (1993). Negotiating meaning in a hospital discourse community. In R. Spilka (Ed.), *Writing in the workplace: New research perspectives* (pp. 98–110). Carbondale, IL: Southern Illinois University Press.

Engeström, Y. (1996). Developmental studies of work as a testbench of activity theory: The case of primary care medical practice. In S. Chaiklin & J. Lave (Eds.), *Understanding practice: Perspectives on activity and context* (pp. 64–103). Cambridge, England: Cambridge University Press.

Hunter, K. M. (1991). *Doctors' stories: The narrative structure of medical knowledge.* Princeton, NJ: Princeton University Press.

Paré, A. (1993). Discourse regulations and the production of knowledge. In R. Spilka (Ed.), *Writing in the workplace: New research perspectives* (pp. 111–123). Carbondale, IL: Southern Illinois University Press.

Pettinari, C. J. (1988). *Task, talk and text in the operating room: A study in medical discourse.* Norwood, NJ: Ablex.

Reynolds, J., Mair, D., & Fischer, P. (1995). *Writing and reading mental health records: Issues and analysis in professional writing and scientific rhetoric.* Mahwah, NJ: Lawrence Erlbaum.

Schön, D. (1983). *The reflective practitioner: How professionals think in action.* New York: Basic Books.

Schön, D. (1987). *Educating the reflective practitioner.* San Francisco: Jossey-Bass.

White, H. (1987). *The content of the form: Narrative discourse and historical representation.* Baltimore, MD: Johns Hopkins University Press.

part V
Narrative and Electronic Sites

9

The Rhetorical Construction of Environmental Risk Narratives in Government and Activist Websites: A Critique

M. Jimmie Killingsworth
Texas A&M University

Martin Jacobsen
West Texas A&M University

Narrative modeling provides a useful tool in the rhetorical criticism of online communication, another arrow for a quiver that already contains analysis modeled on oral conversation (Gray, 1993) and argument, both oral and written (Gurak, 1997). Like these other approaches, narrative modeling, or narrative imagination, is especially helpful not only in the critique but also in the design of communication that aims toward action outcomes, whether instrumental or activist. Our contention in this essay is that the first step toward designing effective sites for the World Wide Web is to develop a narrational sense of what users may do with the information, to construct possible users' stories, and then use these stories to approach the task of web design critically.

As Schriver (1997) argues, "in the rush to design home pages and databases of information, not many have spent time thinking about how people will actually experience their Web designs—that is, how people will understand and make use of the prose and graphics they find" (p. 390). The phrase "experience their Web designs" hints at the importance of narrative imagination in the creation and critique of Web designs. Experience has a narrative structure. If Websites are to capture and/or conform to that experience, designers must cultivate a narrative imagination. While Schriver rightly advocates usability testing as the primary means of gauging the demands of experience, she grants some credence to the famous assertion of Ong (1975) that "the writer's audience is always a fiction" (p. 6). The need for rhetorical insight and rhetorical criticism does not go away with vigilance in usability testing. Testing itself requires some insight into rhetoric, and of course, one must have something to test—a prototype or model built upon the designer's sense of a fictional or ideal audience. Moreover, the designer must be able to critique the results of user testing by imagining possible users with needs that differ somewhat from the test subjects, especially in designing websites with a maximum reach and range of possible users. The rhetoric that works best for websites providing information for action on issues like environmental protection requires that the producer recognize the narrative habits of mind that users of instrumental and activist discourse typically apply.

To accommodate information or technology to users, the frequently cited goal of technical communication, as conceived by Dobrin (1989), the first step in design must be to answer the question, "Who is supposed to do what with this information?"—a question that Killingsworth and Palmer (1999) recommend as a routine exercise for students learning to design professional documents of all kinds. The best answer takes the form of a possible narrative, the user's story, or a story with the user as the agent, and ideally, the hero.

What kind of story would this be? Killingsworth and Gilbertson (1992) advance the idea that genres of technical discourse might be understood and compared to one another by creating "kernel sentences" for the different genres. The kernel sentence for a basic technical report, for example, might be "We did this," while the kernel sentence for an instructional manual would be simply "Do this." From the grammatical structure of the kernels, we learn that the producers of the report ("We") assume the subject position, whereas the user of the instructional manual, the implied "you," occupies the subject position of the kernel "Do this." The subject is, of course, the primary actor represented in this simple grammar.

Each genre has its own peculiar type of action and agent of that action. Beyond these basic genres, action relations get more complex. The kernel sentences of websites that provide information for human action ought to be, like that of the basic report, narratively structured, but these kernel sentences must also represent an exchange of information that shifts the position of possible action from the producer to the user, creating something like a combination of the basic kernels for the report and the manual, with an added shift toward future action: "We give you this information so that you can do that." Instrumental and activist documents share this basic structure—they want to get people working (see Killingsworth, 1992)—though scholars in professional communication have been wary of aligning business and technical writing with activist discourse, possibly because most students in the field are headed for jobs in business, not for work in political activism.

In the study on which this essay is based, we compared a government website and an activist website in the hope of showing differences in the ways that two groups with different purposes attempted to put people to work. To our surprise (and frustration), however, the websites we chose—those of the U.S. Environmental Protection Agency and Greenpeace International—appear to be quite similar. They seem designed for promotion of the sponsoring agency rather than for cultivating user action. The kernel sentence that dominates these sites is indeed narratively structured—like the basic report kernel, "We did this"—but the subject position is not shifted toward the user; the sponsoring agency remains dominant. In taking this position, these agencies confirm the worst fears of many scholars about the World Wide Web: that the leading motive in Web design is marketing and public relations. Users seeking a strong foundation for political or community action may quickly grow frustrated in this environment. The Web has a powerful potential for serving public action needs, but much work must be done and many already dominant conventions challenged before that work can go forward. Narrative-based rhetorical criticism can help in advancing toward these goals.

In the next section, we develop more fully our rhetorical critique of the environmental websites in light of the early promise of hypertext theory. From that foundation, we offer in following sections an extended analysis using narrative modeling or "possible user narratives" as the point of entry.

RHETORICAL CRITIQUE OF ENVIRONMENTAL
PROTECTION WEBSITES

When examined through the lens of rhetorical criticism, the sites of government agencies and activist organizations most directly connected with environmental policy formation actually increase the distance between site users, decision making, and action. A number of strategies contribute to this effect, including the limitation and fragmentation of perspectives on political action into traditional subject positions such as "concerned citizens" and "scientists and researchers" (as opposed to, for example, "grassroots organizers" or "victims of environmental racism"); the positioning of agencies as expert educators (as opposed to, for example, public servants or facilitators in an information clearinghouse); and the modeling of information to be received passively (in the manner of news, entertainment, and class notes as opposed to issues in need of action and research). The simultaneous appearance of "information resources" and interactive links, however, suggests that the designers of the sites may not consciously intend to treat users as passive. The designers may simply be following convention and may be further limited by the medium of the Web, where fragmentation and intensive specialization of topic, for example, may be needed to help users navigate the site.

Our observations tend to reinforce the findings and critical attitudes of second-generation scholars on the rhetoric of computer-mediated communication (CMC),

such as Gurak (1997) and the other feminist critics she cites. After a first generation of scholarship marked by an almost promotional enthusiasm for CMC (see
Bolter, 1991; Landow, 1994a, 1994b), more recent research has revealed that the
mere existence of interactive technology and the possibility of consensual communication hardly guarantee increased participation, whether in the classroom or
at the site of government decisions. Of course, rhetorical potential is never automatically actualized; that much is obvious. The more edifying point is that existing rhetorical conventions and attitudes toward users often override the will of
designers in agencies to achieve full functionality in the available electronic media.
If the designers are marketeers with the aim of promoting the agency—perhaps
"Webmasters" hired from the business community—then the possibility of putting
users to work may recede in importance as the subject position of the agency takes
precedence in the presentation.

The form of analysis that best reveals the inadequacies of the websites in question is rooted in an understanding of narrative. Because of an interest in putting
readers to work—indeed transforming the notion of "reader" to a more active figure, that of the "user"—professional communication shares with the discourse of
political activism an interest in narrative. Narrative embodies, or in-forms, action.
It should be empowering. The active sentence in English "I do this" is the grammatical foundation, the kernel sentence for narrative. If users of a website are to be
placed in the active position, they must emerge from their reading experience with
the ability to say, "I (should) do this." The producers of the website ultimately dis-
appear from the representative kernel as surely as the manual writer disappears
from the kernel "Do this" and recedes in importance as the responsibility for action
shifts to the user.

To achieve sensitivity to narrative, to gain insights into the instrumental or
activist potential of a given text, and to dramatize the possibilities for critique, we
recommend generating imaginative narratives, or possible narratives, of users with
varying perspectives. Since both instrumental and activist rhetorics are concerned
with potential action to be undertaken by the reader or user of the text ("After reading, I will do this") rather than self-reflexive accounts of the writer's action that
excludes the possibility of an active response from the reader ("Sit still while I tell
you about what I did"), the rhetorical analyst needs to isolate possible perspectives
on action or "subject positions" (see Killingsworth & Palmer, 1992; Laclau &
Mouffe, 1985). Who is the "I" in an imaginary narrative, or possible narrative, that
sketches the trajectory of action resulting from the act of reading the text? Asking
the simple question "Who is supposed to do what with this information?" effectively reveals the contours of this kind of imaginary narrative and hints strongly at
the effectiveness of the text under analysis in creating active subject positions or
accounting for possible perspectives on action.

Our contention is that the websites we analyze tend to stifle action and reduce
readers to relatively passive roles. The sites do not accommodate activist subject
positions other than self-reflexive positions, a deficiency revealed by the reduction

of possible narratives. To demonstrate the deficiency, we offer one possible narrative, or activist perspective, then return to the question of accommodating user agency in the hypertextual medium of the Web. We present the narrative as a first-person story—not so much for dramatic effect (in truth, such stories seem a bit forced even to us), but rather to model the kind of narrative imagination that we think is absent in much of the design we see evidenced in print and online today.

A POSSIBLE NARRATIVE: THE SCIENTIST AS BUDDING ACTIVIST

Join us, then, in imagining one of many possible user narratives, a subject position that is clearly overlooked by the designers of the sites, but that hardly requires a great mental stretch to imagine:

Call me Anna George—Dr. Anna George. I'm a professor of geology at a state university in a small Texas town. I feel that I have become a citizen at risk. I'm worried about toxic poisoning in my town. The pond beside the house where my son's Cub Scout troop meets has been declared a toxic hazard because of arsenic poisoning resulting from years of illegal dumping by a local industry. The tap water stinks of chlorine and causes intestinal discomfort if you drink too much or too frequently. We drink bottled water at my house. The town's water has been declared unfit to drink, though the sources of the condemnation range from somewhat reliable to less than reliable.

As a citizen, I want to reduce the risk of walking along the edge of a pond or drinking a glass of tap water, but how? I'm not an ecologist, but neither do I feel part of what the people in the media call "the general public." John Q. Citizen, as he appears in the news, strikes me as undereducated and self-serving, someone who only wants to be protected so that he can consume as much as possible with the minimum of damage to his health and peace of mind. Of course, the news machine is just another business, an outgrowth of the entertainment industry, so I should probably expect this image of the public to emerge. I know I may seem cynical, but just watch and see if you don't agree.

I'm at the point where I can't sit by and be entertained by the news anymore. I feel my family and I are at risk and I want to do something about it. I've never been an environmental activist but have appreciated the efforts some groups have made to raise the public consciousness. Once that is done, I always figured the law would take over and protect us. But something is not happening right in my town. My own consciousness has been raised high enough to take me over the threshold of action. Being a scientist myself, though, I don't want to join in unprepared. I've gone to the library and read a bit about alternatives to chlorine treatment in water. I've also read stories about concerned citizens taking action, the environmental justice movement, Love Canal, on and on. I resist taking on the victim role that seems to wear so well with the American public. And why is that? My friend the sociology professor tells me that when people feel powerless, the only way to take the step over into action is to behave first like a wronged victim. That way, you bring over sympathizers and build coalitions. But I usually don't feel particularly powerless. I'm a senior tenured professor. I live in a big house with a nice yard. I make a good salary. But now, my family and I *are* at risk, and as we drift into greater risk without doing anything about it, we find ourselves in a position of decreasing power. It is time to find out who's responsible for making this chemical mess in my backyard and make them clean it up.

So what do I do? I go to the World Wide Web, which is touted as the most direct route to empowerment that a well-placed person with a strong computer can take these days. I go right to the heart of government regulation, the website of the Environmental Protection Agency. On the home page, I find a list of categories with buttons to click that will send me to different pages or sites. I am confronted with the need to define my role, and the problems begin. The choices the buttons give include "kids," "students and teachers," "concerned citizens," "scientists and researchers," and "business." The placement of the "kids" and the "students and teachers" buttons at the top of the list worries me right away. I guess there's going to be a problem finding the right level of information.

I opt for "concerned citizens." Once into the site, I face more choices. Now I must select among topics that don't conform especially well to my interest. I find some newsy reports on toxic threats at the national level—much less information than what I found by scanning magazines in the library and no more timely—give up, and decide to see what EPA has to say about my region. Under the option "Surf Your Watershed," I enter my zip code and get an array of possible choices again. I can read reports on EPA-monitored sites, mainly dry-cleaning operations (the toxic threat of which, and the scale of that threat, is suggested by the amount of attention the EPA gives them), or I can order a map showing activities in my region. I order the map. It arrives in easily downloadable form in 24 hours and is a good map. I can use it in class. But I'm no closer to doing something about protecting my town's water supply than I was before I entered EPA cyberspace.

Since there's no way to search for specific information and no way to enter reports of possible problems, I decide the EPA is glad to tell me about anything it has already done but is not particularly interested in giving me the information I might want or the directions I might need for action.

To heck with the government, then. I'll try the activist groups. I get to the Greenpeace International home page. Again, topics on buttons. But this time the buttons are done up in cute little icons, colors worthy of the Teenage Mutant Ninja Turtles adorning relatively meaningless little pictures—a whale, a boat, a skull and cross bones, an envelope, a group of people, a coffee cup (of all things!). I select the skull and cross bones and arrive at what ought to be the right place: the toxins site. Here I find a dumping ground of news releases about what Greenpeace is doing in specific places around the world, decidedly not my home town. If I want to go beyond the news, I can read the full texts of a dozen or so technical reports compiled by Greenpeace scientists without benefit of peer review—amateur science, or pseudo-science by my standards. No thanks.

What about the acclaimed interactivity of the Web? In my frustration, I press the icon with a picture of people milling around (an image of THE PUBLIC?) only to find out the one way I can participate in Greenpeace activities: give money. I go to the site under the envelope icon—a symbol for e-mail, it turns out—only to find the opportunity for queries guarded by a disclaimer that Greenpeace gets more mail than it can answer. My cynicism grows, but I take one more shot. I select the coffee cup icon out of simple curiosity. I get to a place where I'm invited to join a chat room and exchange messages with other people like me. (Warning: Greenpeace is too busy saving the world to monitor this site.) Just for meanness, I feel like joining the chat and asking if I'm the only one there who feels she's not being taken seriously.

Just like the EPA site, the Greenpeace site seems intended to entertain and possibly inform me of what is going on with the organization, give me the illusion of interaction, then reduce me to a participation factor of zero.

A CRITIQUE OF THE EXPERIENCE FROM THE PERSPECTIVE OF HYPERTEXT THEORY

The experience of our imagined user—the frustration and the cynicism that comes from arriving at one dead end after another and from getting the impression that no one is taking you seriously—cannot be fully comprehended by current hypertext theory, though it offers a starting point. We will show that we need an overlay of rhetorical theory, and more specifically narrative analysis, to understand the problem with the websites.

Criticism of hypertext and websites has focused mainly on problems of navigation, such as "disorientation: the tendency to lose one's sense of location and direction in a nonlinear document; and cognitive overhead: the additional effort and concentration necessary to maintain several tasks or trails at one time" (Conklin, 1987, p. 17). In the sites we are investigating, navigational angst is only the beginning of the trouble. The EPA page, after centering a statement of "Our Mission:...to protect human health and to safeguard the natural environment" (EPA), offers buttons that seem to be clearly labeled but never really lead to anything but tables and lists of EPA offices, articles, and projects. The user never has a chance to get lost because there isn't anywhere to go. The Greenpeace page offers buttons that generate menus, which is much worse because the user is overwhelmed by the need for so much initial processing. The menus themselves become texts and divert users from their purpose—finding information they can use to solve a problem immediately threatening to them.

Where is all the power the World Wide Web is supposed to afford? The dream of the early hypertext (or "cybertext" or "cyberspace") theorists was of a medium that offered a site for participation, thoroughly democratized with many possibly openings and links (see Bolter, 1991). The power supposedly resides in, or is distributed among, multiple users who create a text that takes on something like a life of its own: "[a] cybertext is a self-changing text...controlled by an immanent cybernetic agent, either mechanical or human" (Aarseth, 1994, pp. 71–72). In the case of both the Greenpeace and EPA sites, the cybernetic agent is not particularly "immanent." Both sites claim for themselves and exert agentive control in two ways. First, every page at both sites is clearly labeled as either Greenpeace or EPA (similar to a running head in a print text), and everything contained on any individual page is placed below a header. Even articles or pieces not originally generated by these organizations are placed on a page with an organizational header and an organizationally controlled URL. Whatever the topics addressed may be, the real topic, in both design and location, is the organization in control of the sites. This self-promotional approach soon becomes an advertisement, complete with a link to the statistics for the site itself: Any hope of actually locating information that may apply to a local threat wanes under the shadow of the header at the top of the screen.

Greenpeace and EPA allow no room for wandering. In fact, while the Greenpeace site offers an "Other Sites" option, these other sites are offered in a frames format—that is, a web page with an index that guides the user. This index is, of course, controlled by Greenpeace. The default site for this frames page is the following disclaimer:

> Please note that listing any of the following linked sites is for directory purposes only and does not, in any way, imply endorsement of any of the sites, their views or policies or the accuracy of information that they contain. We have no control over the content of these sites. The lists of links are regularly updated but are by no means exhaustive. (Greenpeace International)

This disclaimer appears in full as the first chunk of text on the frames page. Immediately below it is a hyperlink back to the Greenpeace main site. This arrangement hardly seems accidental. The moment an actual hypertextual possibility emerges, the Greenpeace site seeks to distance itself from sites it does not control.

As Gray (1993) explains in her study of "conversational" problems with hypertext, "In a similar way, social actors may not share with hypertext the meanings of various words and categories that are not literally equivalent. This may not become visible until the interaction becomes troubled" (p. 48). The subject of our imaginary narrative is plenty troubled. She has trouble getting anywhere. She doesn't really have the option of reading through and finding something by accident, which we would call "browsing" in a print source. The EPA site has a link titled "Browse," but this link ultimately leads only to a list of all the links we already have on the main screen. Again, Gray's analysis of hypertexts is pertinent: "When category confusion results from lack of shared literal meanings for categories and mistaken inferences about the categories that are specified in the hypertext"—as in our geologist's foiled expectations for what lay beyond the sites' buttons—"actors need alternate strategies to obtain sought-after information. Relevancy... is subject to negotiation. Relevancy is negotiated when actors go way off a subject, beyond the paths that result from category confusion, but still expect and hope that they can find useful information in this fashion" (p. 64). Our imaginary users can't "go way off a subject." They are circumscribed by the design of the site and can hardly get started, let alone look around. The only subjects of these sites are the organizations they represent, and not any action they may support.

The challenge is to get beyond the author-centeredness of sites like the ones we have analyzed and create sites that encourage and support multiple subject positions—the kind of site that hypertext ought to be able to support, if there is any validity to early hypertext theory. The literature on Web design is not much help. As Schriver (1997) says, "there are now dozens of cookbooks on everything from designing home pages to managing your GIFs and JPEGs [graphic file formats]" but "almost no books that present empirical evidence about how people read and interpret what they encounter on the Web" (p. 390). Our rhetorical analysis of the EPA and Greenpeace sites bears out Schriver's contention that "too many companies are rushing to get their information on the Web without giving much thought to whether the information is worth reading or whether it is presented in a way that makes the experience—of searching, reading, and using—enjoyable" (p. 407).

A CRITIQUE OF THE EXPERIENCE FROM A NARRATIVE PERSPECTIVE

To overlay the perspective of narrative analysis, we begin with the question, Who is supposed to do what with this information? The question allows us to grasp the narrative elements of the information. If the "who" becomes the citizen at risk, the most frequent answer suggested by the EPA and Greenpeace websites is the following: The citizen at risk is supposed to become informed about the nature of the risks. Or, the citizen at risk is supposed to become informed about the risks that the EPA chooses to reveal and claims to monitor or that Greenpeace has had some experience with.

If the purpose of professional communication is to design information for users who are going to make decisions or take action, the verb *inform* as used in these statements of purpose becomes problematic. With the adjectival *informed*, as in "informed action" or "informed decision," we have no problem, but when *inform* becomes an end in itself, when it does not lead to actions or decisions, when it is the operative term in the kernel sentence of the narrative "we inform you," it strikes us as a weak embodiment of the news-as-entertainment model. Our colleagues in journalism tell us that the verb means something like "educate" or "teach"—hence, we suppose, the nod toward education in EPA user categories like "kids" and "teachers and students."

But the literature on professional communication, even the textbook literature, teaches us to look toward outcomes beyond the act of communication. One of the unfortunate—and probably accidental—results of this outcome-awareness is a tendency to reduce education to vocational training, a direction that many professional communication teachers seem willing to take. That's not what we're arguing for—an uncritical demand that all information be reduced to that which is relevant to specific jobs or needs. One of the reasons for including activist discourse in our study is to avoid this unwelcome trend. We're suggesting that another possible direction for professional communication is toward community service and activism. If we can teach people to craft information for users to do fancy operations on computers, there's no reason why we can't teach Web design that accommodates users who need other kinds of action-oriented information, who want to find out what's happening in their communities and then change it or participate in decisions about it as environmental activists.

If Greenpeace and the EPA want to accommodate users who will put information into action, who will become active agents in narratives of their own devising, there are plenty of directions the agencies could take in designing their websites. They could build search engines into their sites, for instance, so that users are not limited to the roles and issues that the agency can dream up or that they've previously addressed. They could link to local organizations beyond their own regional offices, such as state and local agencies. They could be a bit more critical about Web conventions that have become standard operating procedure thanks to the many code-stealing, copy-catting, self-styled Webmasters in business now—conventions such as starting with a table of options, buttons whose titles may or may not correspond to what users think they're looking for, or the idea that scrolling should mostly be avoided in favor of screen-fitted chunking. Not every user on the Web enjoys surfing. Some may enjoy strolling or even contemplative resting. But hypertext is too often designed for hyperactive users. Other kinds of users may find the number of shifts required to get simple information frustrating and tiresome. Our imaginary geologist quickly tires of blind alleys. We suspect most users do. Where's the reference librarian in these sites? Shouldn't groups that offer websites ostensibly as a public service take full responsibility for performing interactive services, at least answering e-mail? But the drive to put up a website—to be a "presence on the Web"—apparently outruns everyone's thinking about interactive potential, the consequences of information, the nature of mediated access, the producer's responsibility to users, and the costs of that responsibility.

Narrative modeling, as we have described it briefly in this essay, points the way toward greater sensitivity to users' needs in Web design. Unlike the Greenpeace site, which seems devoted to limiting the user to the role of passive observer of the organization's heroic actions, we see evidence that the designers of the EPA site have expended some effort toward imagining who their users might be—students, teachers, researchers, etc.—and accommodating the interests of those users. But even there, the user does not appear in an active role but is imagined primarily as a passive vehicle for information. The narrative model we have in mind places users in active subject positions. "Accommodate" in this view means giving the user a plot for action, a story to live out. Such is the purpose of instrumentalist writing, as professional communication scholars have learned from decades of studying instructional manuals, and such is also the purpose of activist writing. The narrative imagination holds the key to a kind of "technology transfer" in the field of technical communication. It becomes a means by which we can take what we know about instrumentalist discourse and activate that know-how in fields of social practice that require technical understanding, such as risk communication and environmental protection. By asking "Who will do what with this information?," we can initiate designs that look beyond the act of communication to acts of community involvement and that understand users not as passive recipients of information (the rhetorical counterpart of the victim at risk) but as agents of informed actions.

REFERENCES

Aarseth, E. J. (1994). Nonlinearity and literary theory. In G. P. Landow (Ed.), *Hyper/text/theory* (pp. 51–86). Baltimore, MD: Johns Hopkins University Press.

Bolter, J. D. (1991). *Writing space: The computer, hypertext, and the history of writing.* Hillsdale, NJ: Lawrence Erlbaum.

Conklin, J. (1987). Hypertext: An introduction and survey. *IEEE Computer, 20*(9). Available: http://www.studio-e.com/E-MEDIA/R.Conklin.87.htm

Dobrin, D. N. (1989). *Writing and technique.* Urbana, IL: National Council of Teachers of English.

Environmental Protection Agency (EPA). *EPA home page.* Available: http://www.epa.gov/

Gray, S. H. (1993). *Hypertext and the technology of conversation: Orderly situational choice.* Westport, CT: Greenwood.

Greenpeace International. *Greenpeace International home page.* Available: http://www.greenpeace.org/index.html

Gurak, L. J. (1997). *Persuasion and privacy in cyberspace: The online protests over Lotus Marketplace and the Clipper Chip.* New Haven, CT: Yale University Press.

Killingsworth, M. J. (1992). Realism, human action, and instrumentalist discourse. *Journal of Advanced Composition 12,* 171–200.

Killingsworth, M. J., & Gilbertson, M. K. (1992). *Signs, genres, and communities in technical communication.* Amityville, NY: Baywood.

Killingsworth, M. J., & Palmer, J. S. (1992). *Ecospeak: Rhetoric and environmental politics in America.* Carbondale, IL: Southern Illinois University Press.

Killingsworth, M. J., & Palmer, J. S. (1999). *Information in action: A guide to technical communication* (2nd ed.). Boston: Allyn & Bacon.

Laclau, E., & Mouffe, C. (1985). *Hegemony and socialist strategy: Toward a radical democratic politics.* London: Verso.

Landow, G. P. (1994a). *Hypertext: The convergence of contemporary theory and technology.* Baltimore, MD: Johns Hopkins University Press.

Landow, G. P. (Ed.). (1994b). *Hyper/text/theory.* Baltimore, MD: Johns Hopkins University Press.

Ong, W. J. (1975). The writer's audience is always a fiction. *PMLA, 90,* 6–21.

Schriver, K. A. (1997). *Dynamics in document design.* New York: Wiley.

part VI
Narrative and Society

10

The Business of Living: Letters from a 19th-Century Landlady

Margaret Baker Graham
Iowa State University

The notion that society is divided into public and private spheres has profoundly shaped the work traditionally undertaken in the academy. "Private" refers to the domestic life—activities that occur within the home and involve the family, particularly women and children. "Public," on the other hand, refers to traditionally male-dominated activities that occur in sites such as the government, military, and industry. The assumption that the public but not the private warrants attention has been tacit in academic research generally. Millman and Kanter (1987), for example, have noted that sociology "has focused on public, official, visible, and/or dramatic role players and definitions of the situation; yet unofficial, supportive, less dramatic, private, and invisible spheres of social life and organization may be equally important" (p. 32). Although sociology has moved to a consideration of the private as well as the public, the move is less apparent in professional communication. The name itself, "professional communication," brackets the public from the private, rendering the private sphere invisible. Durack (1997) has noted that researchers in technical communication typically assume that the site of inquiry should be the workplace, which is defined as located apart from home. Researchers in business communication (e.g., Smeltzer, 1996) have argued that the appropriate purpose of research is to further the goals of business and industry, which, again, are assumed to be separate from the private sphere.

This essay uses narrative studies to define and explore connections between the public and private spheres. Narrative is an effort to interpret or create meaning out of events. That is, narrators take events that do not have inherent meaning and display those events to create meaning. In 19th-century Germany, from which much of the Western tradition of history is taken, meaning was displayed to produce a grand narrative that reinforced nationalism. This tradition, Iggers (1997) states, operated from the premise "that in fact there was such a thing as *history* in contrast to a multiplicity of histories" (p. 4). Postmodern historians, however, have moved the focus of history from "the 'center' of power to the 'margins'" (p. 102) in order to create meaning from the stories of those whose lives have been rendered invisible by the concept of the grand narrative. Although narratives about professional communication have traditionally excluded connections to the private sphere, a postmodern imperative is to examine not only what is visible but what has been rendered invisible, to note what has been legitimized in a discipline and what has not.

By examining public stories of the Civil War and the private stories of one 19th century landlady, I am bringing to academic research what Finke (1992) calls "the 'noise' of history" (p. 11). From a feminist perspective, I contest traditional archival research by showing the interplay between private documents (family letters and records) and public documents (government and military letters and records as well as newspapers articles and advertisements). This interplay demonstrates that the distinction drawn between public and private spheres is a fiction that nevertheless has very real consequences in people's discourse and their perception of reality.

My investigation focuses on the letters and documents of Margaret Bruin Machette, a white woman born in 1817. Her father was literate but her mother was not, and Margaret may have been in the first generation of women in her family to read and write. Shortly after her 17th birthday, she married Charles Chambers Machette, a 37-year-old widower from St. Charles, Missouri. Her husband was a successful merchant, but when he died in 1851, Margaret Machette suffered economic reverses and had to support herself and her five children. She left St. Charles, eventually settling in Fulton, Missouri, where she ran a boardinghouse for young men attending Westminster College.

In Margaret Machette's time, a married woman or widow who had to work could retain her middle class status only by working within her home, and being a landlady was an obvious possibility. As the family letters suggest, being a landlady to college men also allowed Margaret Machette to trade room and board for lessons in algebra, grammar, astronomy, and Latin for her daughters, who as females, could not attend Westminster College. By finding a way to both support and educate her children, she practiced the entrepreneurship increasingly associated with women who have created their own businesses when male-dominated businesses have not welcomed women or have practiced values women have rejected (Buttner & Moore, 1997). Unfortunately, being a landlady was a precarious occupation during the Civil War, when economic hardships brought many Missourians to bankruptcy and when the armies depleted most of the student population of Westminster College. She was forced to cease her business by 1870.

Margaret Machette's extant letters to her daughters begin in October 1860, after she was already working as a landlady. While the letters by themselves create a private story of one family in the 19th century, I juxtapose them to public stories told in newspapers and in government and military documents to make three arguments. First, rather than being separate as capitalistic and Western thought maintains, the private and public spheres are permeable. Second, moving public events to the margins to focus on a landlady invites a critique of traditionally held beliefs about narrative. Third, the widely held belief in the separateness of spheres produced gendered differences in people's perceptions of reality and the discourses they used. The resulting tension between separateness and permeability leads to a necessary tension and balance between two approaches to feminist research, cultural feminism and nonessentialism. This analysis, I hope, invites reconsideration of the boundaries that have been placed on public and private narrative and professional communication research. Although ignoring the home has most notably rendered women's work invisible, it can also marginalize men's work that occurs in the home. Professional communication may be richer if we extend the boundaries of our research to sites we have traditionally ignored.

THE PRIVATE AND PUBLIC: SEPARATION AND PERMEABILITY

"Public" is a shorthand for an array of sites—for example, the office, battlefield, courtroom, factory—that men have traditionally dominated. "Private," on the other hand, is narrowly conceived as the home, the one site where women have traditionally been located. To a large extent, the public is about the production or protection of capital, while the private is about the consumption of capital. In a society where families or small communities provide for their own needs, a distinction between public and private does not exist as it does in a capitalistic society, where wage earners are set apart physically and socially from nonwage earners.

Besides being a manifestation of capitalism, the distinction between private and public is also a manifestation of patriarchy. Hartmann (1987) comments, "In a Marxist-feminist view, the organization of production both within and outside the family is shaped by patriarchy and capitalism" (p. 111). That is, patriarchy and capitalism conspire to reinforce the belief that the public and the private are separate spheres and that women belong in the private and men belong in the public sphere. However, as feminist materialism has shown, the notions of "private" and "public" represent a simplified and often false dichotomy about the home and business, consumption and production, women and men.

Baron (1994) observes that "the hegemony of capitalist discourse lay, at least in part, in its ability to label public and private spheres as if they were distinct and independent realms of activity" (p. 151). Shapiro (1994) similarly argues,

"'Permeability' and 'overlap' describe more accurately than does 'separation' the complex and ambiguous relations between the world prescribed for men and the designated realm of women" (p. 6). When she was a landlady who made her house both her home and her business, Margaret Machette, the subject of this essay, merged the private and public spheres of life. However, the two spheres were not otherwise separate. To the contrary, the two worlds already and always intersected. Even if Margaret Machette had not been a landlady, as a homemaker she participated in the economy of her community. The products and produce she described buying in her letters were, after all, purchased at the stores of local businesspeople. As the sole provider for her family and a woman who participated in the production of capital by working as a landlady within the home, Margaret Machette was positioned to both contest and participate in this notion of public and private spheres. Two stories that demonstrate Margaret Machette's relationship to the public are about a man who worked for her and a tax she owed.

A Story of Andrew

As an employer, Margaret Machette hired a man named Andrew to work around her property. In October 1863, she wrote a letter to her daughter Susan describing his efforts to make molasses for her. (The letters have been edited to standardize spelling, punctuation, and capitalization.)

> Andrew commenced making the molasses on the 21st which was Wednesday and on the next day the ground was covered with snow which continued to fall till in the night. They had [a] very cold time working with the cane. It turned out very poor. We have only 30 gallons of molasses.

Andrew's labors connect to Margaret Machette's narrative of a landlady and also become part of a brief narrative of Andrew himself, who is mentioned twice more by Margaret Machette's daughters. On April 18, 1864, Abigail wrote her sister Susan: "Uncle Andrew starts to California next Monday. Are you not sorry to hear it? Poor fellow, he does not want to go at all. But prefers doing so to joining the army. Ma is busy making him some calico shirts to take with him. Ma feels that she will be almost broken up when Andrew leaves." Then in January 1865, Cornelia, another sister, wrote Susan: "I got a letter from Andrew the other day. He wrote so badly I could not make it out, except something about you being such a *pretty lady* &c."

These letters, when combined with other documents, create a narrative that connects Andrew's story to the public narrative of war and slavery. "Uncle" Andrew, to judge by Cornelia's comment, was nearly illiterate; that he could write at all, though, is somewhat unexpected because he was undoubtedly black, and blacks in that time period often did not receive formal education. The daughters similarly refer to a black worker in their home as "Aunt Lucinda." There were no men in the

Machette family named Andrew, and white children of that time referred to an uncle by his last name (e.g., "Uncle Machette"). It is also likely that Andrew was a slave whom Margaret Machette hired from Andrew's owner. She saved the following receipt from Henry Wright, a neighbor:

Andrew has worked since the first of January, 28 whole days and 4 half days making 30 days in all. I have charged you 70 cents per day making *$21.00.*

Missouri was a slave state, and Margaret Machette's husband had owned slaves in St. Charles, so it is not unexpected that the family would be complicit in the slave system. Occasionally in the 1860s, the local paper, the *Missouri Telegraph*, advertised both the selling and the hiring of slaves. For example, in 1860, the paper advertised that "one likely negro girl, aged 7 years" would "be sold to the highest bidder for cash." The following year, the practice of hiring slaves was documented in another announcement in the *Missouri Telegraph*:

SLAVE HIRING
Below will be found a list of the prices
paid for the hiring of slaves belonging to
the Brooks' estate, F. G. Nichols administrator,
at New Bloomfield:
      John, man..$ 156
      Charles, man...141
      Chetsey, man...150
      Cupit, boy, 15 years old........................120
      Bill, boy, 12 years old 40

Andrew's story is connected not only to the practice of slavery but also to efforts to build Union troops. His decision to leave for California in April 1864 to avoid fighting in the Civil War was undoubtedly a response to General Order No. 135, issued on November 14, 1863. The order reads in part:

Whereas the exigencies of the war require that colored troops should be recruited in the State of Missouri, the following regulations, having been approved and ordered by the President, will govern the recruiting service for colored troops in Missouri, viz:
    I. All able-bodied colored men, whether free or slaves, will be received into the service, the loyal owners of slaves enlisted being entitled to receive compensation as hereinafter provided.
    II. All persons enlisted into the service shall forever thereafter be free. (Department of War, 1900, p. 1034)

By the end of February 1864, Fulton had enlisted 70 black men, and the number of black recruits for all of Missouri was 3,706 (*Missouri Telegraph*, February 26, 1864). In August 1864, four months after Andrew had left Missouri, Joseph Holt of the Bureau of Military Justice wrote to Edwin M. Stanton, secretary of war:

The recruiting of colored troops in Missouri may be regarded as virtually closed. Between four and a half and five regiments have already been enlisted. When to these is added the large number of able-bodied men who have escaped to Kansas, or have been carried by their masters into the disloyal States, it is not estimated that more than the material for a single regiment capable of military duty remains. (Department of War, 1900, p. 577)

Andrew was probably one of those black men who left the state rather than serve in the military, and Margaret Machette, by helping him to leave, contested the war effort.

A Story of the Military Tax

Another story that Margaret Machette recounted to her daughter Susan intersects with the more public record of the Civil War. On December 29, 1864, Margaret Machette, after she mentions mortgaging her property, wrote to her daughter Susan: "I paid my taxes. There is a military tax of three dollars levied on your head. What do you think of that—every man and woman over eighteen and under forty-five have to pay. I will pay it this week for you." A few days later, on January 1, 1865, Margaret Machette wrote to correct her earlier statement: "I told you in my other letter that you was taxed three dollars. It is a mistake. Your brother misunderstood Mr. Brooks. It is I that is taxed the three dollars military." Extant is the receipt for the tax, which shows that she paid 10 dollars, presumably 3 dollars of which went for the military tax she owed:

> Received from Margret Machett [sic] Ten dollars in full for her state county & military Tax for the year 1865 on her personal property and the following real estate in Callaway County Mo 50 89/100 Acres part E[ast] 1/2 18.47.9
> W King Collector

This tax that Margaret Machette paid is a response to military and governmental action documented in correspondence from federal and state officials. Abraham Lincoln issued General Order No. 232, dated July 19, 1864, which, in part, proclaimed:

> Now, therefore I, Abraham Lincoln, President of the United States, do issue this my call for five hundred thousand volunteers for the military service....
>   Volunteers will be accepted under this call for one, two, or three years, as they may elect, and will be entitled to the bounty provided by the law for the period of service for which they enlist. (Department of War, 1900, p. 515)

Missouri's quota was 26,678 men, and Callaway County's district owed 2,876 men (*Missouri Telegraph*, July 29, 1864). Although Missouri's quota was reduced because of previously earned credits, including credits earned from the earlier call for black troops, they still owed over 25,000 men (Department of War, 1900, p. 515). Payment of troops was set forth in Circular No. 27, issued by the War Department, also on July 19. It stated that recruits would be paid $100 for each year of service for up to three years and that "No premiums whatever for the procuration of recruits will hereafter be paid for by the United States" (Department of War, 1900, p. 518). Thus, by default, states were responsible for paying recruits. In accordance with Missouri law, the state's monetary obligation was paid by counties and cites. If men in Callaway County's district signed up for the minimum of one year, the district's debt for nearly 3,000 troops would be over a quarter of a million dollars.

After receiving Lincoln's order and Missouri's quota, Willard P. Hall, governor of Missouri, wrote two letters with decidedly different tones, yet each suggesting the difficulty of asking citizens, many of whom were loyal southerners, to provide both men and money for the federal effort. The first letter, appearing in the August 12, 1864, issue of the *Missouri Telegraph*, threatened enforced draft in the state militia if the call was not heeded. Addressed "To the People of the State of Missouri" and signed without a complimentary closing, it reads in part:

> I appeal to the people of Missouri to respond to the call promptly and with alacrity....
>
> If the troops asked for by General Rosecrans [commander of the Federal forces in Missouri] are not promptly provided, it will be my duty to furnish him such a militia force as he may require. That militia force cannot be paid, for the reason that the State has not sufficient means for the purpose.
>
> The question is, therefore, presented, whether you will do your duty as paid soldiers of the United States, or whether you will do your duty as detailed militia of the State without pay. The choice should be readily made.

However, neither the call to arms nor the taxation process moved speedily, and the War Department promised to institute a draft if the deadline of September 5 was not met. On August 28, Governor Hall sent a letter to Stanton, secretary of war, pleading—this time with the salutation of "Sir" and an obsequious closing—for more time:

> Volunteering for the U.S. service is progressing very well in this State at present—so much so that I have strong hopes of filling up the eleven new regiments of twelve-months' men called for by General Rosecrans by the 8th of next month. I believe that the entire quota of Missouri under the last call of the President can be filled by volunteers by the middle of October next.
>
> Under our statutes counties and cities are authorized to give bounties, and for this purpose may levy taxes to pay any amount. Many counties have already levied taxes for that purpose; but as it takes time to collect the taxes, or even to borrow money, the means to pay the bounties is in many cases not yet provided.
>
> As Missouri has always promptly filled her quotas with volunteers and has in addition furnished a large militia force not yet credited to her, I trust you will not think it unreasonable in me to ask a postponement of the draft in this State for one month from and after the 5th proximo. We do not seek to avoid furnishing our quota; on the con-

trary, we are most anxious to furnish all the troops called for from the State. All we ask is a little more time.

   With great respect, your obedient servant.... (Department of War, 1900, pp. 644–645)

Contrary to Governor Hall's statement, volunteering was not "progressing well." Hall's request was turned down, and Missouri, along with several other states, was told to begin drafting soldiers on September 19. Missouri officials continued to ask for extensions and exemptions and never fully met the quota before the war's end in April 1865. In her part of the story, Margaret Machette this time complied with the war effort, and almost one third of her year's taxes went to pay troops.

NEW NARRATIVES FOR NEW PURPOSES

Traditional archival research on the military tax would no doubt focus on government and military action and correspondence; to make a landlady the focus of an investigation of the military tax displaces public action and communication from the center and forces an unresolved competition between the voices of public officials, on one hand, and the voices of private people, on the other hand. The result of such juxtaposition is different and less contained than narrative traditionally privileged in Western society. White (1981), for example, assumes that meaning-making requires a narrator to "display the coherence, integrity, fullness, and closure of an image of life that is and can only be imaginary" (p. 23). But unity of coherence and closure may not be necessary to narrative. The story of Andrew is an example of how narrative can achieve meaning without attaining closure. The last mention of Andrew is by Margaret Machette's daughter Cornelia, but to end the story there focuses the narrative on the Machette family rather than on Andrew. To suspend closure of this story forces the reader to consider Andrew as the focus: Was he still a slave when he left? If he was, did he leave with his owner's blessing? Or did Margaret Machette abet in his escape not only from the federal army but also from slavery? What happened to him after Cornelia's last reference? And to return to Margaret Machette, rather than trying to achieve narrative unity by resolving her complicity in slavery with her action to help Andrew escape, perhaps it is better to admit to unresolved tension, the same unresolved tension that existed for many whites of her era.

   The story of the military tax seems to reach closure better than the story of Andrew; however, it too can be problematized: For Margaret Machette, the ending of the story appears to be the day she paid the tax. For the secretary of war, the ending might be the surrender of Lee, after which armies would be disbanded and troops would no longer need economic support. For the governor of Missouri, the story might go on long after the war ended as the debts that the state was forced to incur continued to depress the state's economy.

To fight against the inclination to provide the unity that closure and coherence produce is, according to Finke (1992), a feminist approach to history. Rather than reconciling or ignoring contested meanings or events that have not been privileged traditionally, the feminist historian constructs a narrative where tension remains unresolved: "History, conceived of as an unresolvable tension between 'what really happened' and the multiple and dialogic narratives about it, provides a means by which feminists might destabilize oppressive representations of gender and locate on the margins of discourse—in the 'noise' of history—possibilities for more egalitarian cultural formations not yet even recognizable as representations" (p. 11). The life and discourse of a landlady can be seen as the "noise" that has been ignored by historians who are generally interested in constructing grand narratives of war and politics, and by professional communication researchers who are generally interested in industry and corporations. One result of such "noise" is a more egalitarian narrative of professional communication than is traditionally offered because it brings to light the lives of women and other groups of people who have been ignored.

CULTURAL FEMINISM AND NONESSENTIALISM

Although Margaret Machette's life demonstrates the permeability of the private and public, that is not to say that the two spheres were the same. Her stories are conceived of as "noise" because they compete with the male-dominated grand narratives of war and government. The separateness of the public and private spheres may be a fiction, but the concept of separateness produced very real consequences for women and men. These consequences have been a focus of cultural feminism, which examines gendered differences as social constructs. Proponents of cultural feminism have been severely criticized for dichotomizing gender. Although cultural feminism has oversimplified gender differences and implied that all women, regardless of race or social class, are similar, it would be a mistake to assume that the concept of private and public spheres, as conceived by patriarchy and capitalism, did not produce a tendency for gendered differences in discourses and lifestyles. Nonessentialism, while it attempts to refute cultural feminism by calling into question generalizations about groups of people, is vulnerable to perpetuating the status quo of academic research. That is, if women cannot be discussed as a group, then the condition of women cannot be researched or redressed (Flynn, 1995). Trying to balance and retain the tension between cultural feminism and nonessentialism, feminist historians must not collapse "the noise of history" and the grand narratives into one narrative. As Finke (1992) states, it is important that the works of women and people of color "are not simply assimilated into 'ideas and ideals' of the canon" (p. 158). Finke is interested in contested meanings in literature, but her ideas can also be applied to professional communication.

One aspect of cultural feminism that is useful to retain is the notion that the concept of public and private spheres might produce a tendency for women and men in the same station of life to use language differently and to perceive the world differently. Iggers (1997) states that historians today analyze "language as a tool for approaching social and cultural reality" (p. 123). Traditional Western autobiography, almost by definition, centers on the individuality of the writer, yet women have been taught to be self-effacing. Smith (1987) writes, "Since the ideology of gender makes of woman's life script a nonstory, a silent space, a gap in patriarchal culture, the ideal woman is self-effacing rather than self-promoting, and her 'natural' story shapes itself not around the public, heroic life but around the fluid, circumstantial, contingent responsiveness to others" (p. 50). Even in letters to friends and families, women often subordinate their own stories to those of others. Spacks (1988), discussing the letters of women in 18th century Great Britain, demonstrates how "the ideology of self-subordination" leads to "suppression of narrative about the self" (p. 181).

Hartsock (1983) notes that gendered experience evolving from capitalism and patriarchy "forms an important ground for the female sense of self as connected to the world and male sense of self as separate, distinct, and even disconnected" (p. 295). She continues, "The female construction of self in relation to others leads…toward opposition to dualisms of any sort, valuation of concrete, everyday life, sense of a variety of connectedness and continuities both with other persons and with the natural world" (p. 298). Because domestic labors are repetitive, continuous, and localized, women whose lives are focused in the private sphere are more likely to focus their narratives on the local and specific and less on the global and abstract.

Constructed by the notion of the private sphere, Margaret Machette practiced the gendered impulse to value the concrete and everyday experience. Focusing on the private—the local and familial—she did not take commonality between experiences for granted. Repeatedly she told her daughters "you can't imagine" and "you have not the most distant idea" as a way of cautioning them not to presume beyond their own experiences. Margaret Machette made few generalizations and carefully qualified those she did with "perhaps," "I think," and "I believe." Once, on April 22, 1889, she tentatively offered an opinion about church leadership: "I begin to think people are much alike in one respect—that is, a few in every church want to rule"; however, she immediately backed away from generalizing: "I mean the Presbyterians—other churches I don't know any thing about." Margaret Machette recognized the foibles of people, but she appeared unwilling to extend the most obvious of conclusions to actions she had not witnessed.

While the narratives of Margaret Machette demonstrate the circumscription of the domestic sphere, they also reveal the possibilities that occur for women when their labor is legitimized. Margaret Machette apparently focused on the local and concrete all her adult life, but her profession of landlady granted her temporarily the power of agency. Her letters while she was acting as wage earner are full of stories about her labor and economy in running a business and a home. She describes, in a letter written on January 22, 1864, for example, spending 11 dollars for ice for her ice house and paying 12-1/2 cents per pound for 50 pounds of butter that she salted. One of her longest stories, written on January 13, 1864, about her labors concerns a cold snap:

> It is thought to have been the coldest weather we have had for thirty years. At any rate it came near freezing us to death here. Lizzie and your brother had to come down to my room and stay till it moderated. We lost all our plants. I brought everything into my room to keep [them] from freezing but it froze as hard in there as anywhere else. I had all the work to do that week as the negroes had holiday. We had but two boarders that week. It was fortunate for me—I tell you I made very little cooking do. I froze ice cream in the dining room by simply sitting the freezer on the floor and stirring the cream occasionally.

By writing about her own activity when she was a landlady, Margaret Machette moved toward, to paraphrase Smith (1987), making her life a story rather than "a nonstory." Her letters suggest, then, the potential that earning one's own livelihood has for allowing women to become the heroes of their own stories. After she stopped being a landlady, Margaret Machette continued to lead an industrious life, but this activity is revealed through her daughters' letters about their mother. By 1870, when she ceased to be a landlady and became a homemaker only, Margaret Machette wrote stories about people around her and no longer focused on herself.

The loss of agency in Margaret Machette's later letters seemed to occur not because she ceased participating in the economy of her community but because she practiced her society's values, which legitimized labor that produced capital for the laborer and treated as invisible labor that did not. That her language appears to be gendered yet changeable demonstrates the permeability of the public and private spheres as well as the balance and tension between cultural feminism and nonessentialism.

CONCLUSION

The juxtaposition of the life and letters of a landlady with the public events and documents of her times shows the interplay and tension in the notion of public and private spheres and offers an idea of inclusive narratives that decenter public narrative. Drawing from presidential proclamations and gubernatorial correspondence as well as the letters and documents of private citizens also expands the scope of archival research in professional communication. The texts that professional communication researchers choose points to the political nature of academic research and historical narrative. As feminists and neo-Marxists have pointed out, women, people of color, and people of low status are less likely to record their stories or to have those stories preserved. However, if one ranges among the array of texts that have survived—private letters, newspaper ads and articles, public letters, and government documents—then new subjects and approaches for professional communication research emerge.

Because of their departure from traditional research, feminist approaches may remain on the margins of academic research, just as the narratives of women like Margaret Machette have remained on the margins of her society. I hope, though, that the "noise" of this kind of research will suggest to some how historical narratives could be rewritten. Feminism, as well as multiculturalism and materialism, can offer new topics for research and can, consequently, expand our understanding of that thing we call "professional communication."

REFERENCES

Baron, A. (1994). On looking at men: Masculinity and the making of a gendered working-class history. In A. Shapiro (Ed.), *Feminists revision history* (pp. 146–171). New Brunswick, NJ: Rutgers University Press.

Buttner, E. H., & Moore, D. P. (1997). Women's organizational exodus to entrepreneurship: Self-reported motivations and correlates with success. *Journal of Small Business Management, 35*(1), 34–46.

Colored recruits in Missouri. (1864, February 26). *Missouri Telegraph*, p. 1.

Department of War (1900). *The war of the rebellion: A compilation of the official records of the union and confederate armies* (Series 3, Vols. 3-4). Washington, DC: Government Printing Office.

Durack, K. T. (1997). Gender, technology, and the history of technical communication. *Technical Communication Quarterly, 6*, 249–260.

Finke, L. A. (1992). *Feminist writing, women's writing*. Ithaca, NY: Cornell University Press.

Flynn, E. A. (1995). Review: Feminist theories/feminist composition. *College English, 57*, 201–212,

Hartsock, N. C. M. (1983). The feminist standpoint: Developing the ground for a specifically feminist historical materialism. In S. Harding & M. B. Hintikka (Eds.), *Discovering reality: Feminist perspectives on epistemology, metaphysics, methodology, and philosophy of science* (pp. 283–310). Dordrecht, Holland: D. Reidel.

Hartmann, H. I. (1987). The family as the locus of gender, class, and political struggle: The example of housework. In S. Harding (Ed.), *Feminism and methodology: Social science issues* (pp. 109–134). Bloomington, IN: Indiana University Press.

Iggers, G. C. (1997). *Historiography in the twentieth century: From scientific objectivity to the postmodern challenge*. Hanover, NH: Wesleyan University Press.

Important from the war department. (1864, July 29). *Missouri Telegraph*, p. 2.

Millman, M., & Kanter, R. M. (1987). Introduction to *Another voice: Feminist perspectives on social life and social science*. In S. Harding (Ed.), *Feminism and methodology: Social science issues* (pp. 29–36). Bloomington, IN: Indiana University Press.

Proclamation. (1864, August 12). *Missouri Telegraph*, p. 1.

Negro girl for slave. (1860, March 23). *Missouri Telegraph*, p. 2.

Shapiro, A. (1994). History and feminist theory: or, talking back to the beadle. In *Feminists revision history* (pp. 1–23). New Brunswick, NJ: Rutgers University Press.

Slave hiring. (1861, January 4). *Missouri Telegraph*, p. 2.

Smeltzer, L. R. (1996). Communication within the manager's context. *Management Communication Quarterly, 10* (1), 5–26.

Smith, S. (1987). *A poetics of women's autobiography: Marginality and the fictions of self-representation.* Bloomington, IN: Indiana University Press

Spacks, P. M. (1988). Female rhetorics. In S. Benstock (Ed.), *The private self: Theory and practice of women's autobiography* (pp. 177–191). Chapel Hill, NC: University of North Carolina Press.

White, H. (1981). The value of narrativity in the representation of reality. In W. J. T. Mitchell (Ed.), *On narrative* (pp. 1–23). Chicago: University of Chicago Press.

11

Story Telling, Story Living: Sustainability, Habermas, and Narrative Models in the Rot Belt

Nancy Blyler
Iowa State University

> The [land within the drainage area of the Missouri River] has
> become the agricultural equivalent of the declining manufacturing centers of the Great Lakes
> in the 1970s and '80s. Move over, Rust Belt. Here comes the Rot Belt.
>
> Strange, 1996, p. 1C

The connection between stories and the lives we live is important in contemporary discussions of narrative (see Perkins & Blyler in this collection). As Allison (1994) claims, "we exist narratively and are better understood as story*livers* rather than as storytellers" (original emphasis, pp. 108–109). And as Bruner (1987) asserts, the "cognitive and linguistic processes that guide the self-telling of life narratives achieve the power to structure perceptual experience, to organize memory, to segment and purpose-build the very 'events' of a life" (p. 15). In a real sense, then, we are the self-stories we narrate.

Because, however, our self-stories are drawn from and reflect the narratives of our social groups, we are also, says Bruner (1987), "variants of the culture's canonical forms"—variants, that is, of "narrative models" (p. 15) that reveal, through the possible lives they suggest, what a given culture is like. As Bruner summarizes, "the tool kit of any culture is replete not only with a stock of canonical life narratives

195

(heroes, Marthas, tricksters, etc.), but with combinable formal constituents from which its members can construct their own life narratives" (p. 15).

Bruner's concept of canonical narrative models is illustrated in a compelling way by the Rot Belt of my epigraph. The Rot Belt is a region where two radically opposed narrative models struggle for ascendency: the models of the family and the factory farm.[1] As Strange's (1996) analogy to a familiar manufacturing region—the Rust Belt of the Great Lakes area—suggests, this struggle involves social decay: in the Rot Belt, the decline of the family farm as a viable narrative model. Despite this decline, however, a third narrative model—related to but not the same as that of the family farm—is possible: the story of the Rot Belt "transform[ed]" through a resurgent interest in what Stange calls sustainability (pp. 1–2C).

Strange (1996), who draws on biology and ecology to discuss sustainability, claims that entities "cannot survive in isolation." Rather, they are "ecologically sustainable," that is, can continue undepleted, only "in the context of community."[2] Says Strange: "In the natural world, the principles of community sustainability are well-defined. A 'community' is a mixture of different species that share a place, interdependently, through symbiotic [mutually beneficial] relationships." (p. 2C). Though individuals in a community may cease to exist, the community itself does not. "Life goes on," Strange asserts, as these symbiotic relationships link entities "in the context of continously changing community." (p. 2C).

Because I believe sustainability in Strange's ecological and communal sense is a worthy social goal, I argue in this chapter that society's canonical narratives must model a world built on such symbiotic relationships and people's self-narratives must reflect it. To make this argument, I turn to Habermas's views of science and technology and his theory of purposive-rational and communicative action.

Although a German social critic such as Habermas may seem far removed from the Rot Belt and Strange's notion of sustainability, I find Habermas's dark vision of the growing power accruing to science and technology and the warning he sounds about the effects of this power reflected in the narrative struggle I describe. Further, I believe that Habermas's theory of purposive-rational and communicative action can illuminate Strange's concept of sustainability and show us how it might be achieved.

In this discussion of sustainability, Habermas, and narrative models in the Rot Belt, I have two purposes: I want to illustrate why the narrative models to which society gives allegiance matter and point to the urgency of transforming many places—including the Rot Belt—through an interest in sustainability, understood in the context of community.

I begin with the two narrative models struggling for ascendency in the Rot Belt.

NARRATIVE MODELS IN THE ROT BELT: THE FAMILY VERSUS THE FACTORY FARM

In the Rot Belt, the narrative model of the family farm—with its echoes of the farm in "Old MacDonald," the children's nursery rhyme—is fast being displaced by the narrative model of the factory farm.

Old MacDonald Had a Pig, and Other Farm Animals Too

"Going to Dad's farm," says my native Iowan husband, "is like stepping back into the 1950s, or before."

Looking at the root cellar, the old brooder house, and—off across the pasture— the foundation of the one-room country school where my husband attended first grade, I agree with his assessment. This "century" farm on the eastern edge of the Rot Belt—this place that has been in my husband's family for over 100 years and where my husband, his father, his father's father, and his grandfather's father were all born and raised—seems part of a bygone era. My father-in-law's tractors—fondly nicknamed the M and the Johnny Popper—are not the monsters I've seen at the Iowa State Fair. And farm animals, which in late years have dwindled to nine cats and a renter's herd of cattle, still have the run of the old barn, the pastures, and the fields of harvested corn.

"When I was young," says my husband, "everyone kept chickens, a few cows for milk, and cattle and hogs. Dad still made his hay with horses, and I remember how excited I was when I finally got to drive Dick and Topsie. When farmers started to plant a lot of soybeans, Dad never would grow them. He always said the soil might wash because the farm was too hilly for beans."

Catching the evening breeze, we walk down to the large garden that still stretches from east to west in front of the farmhouse. "We didn't have much money," my husband says, "but we always had food. I helped Mom with the gardening, and she made jelly, canned, and baked bread, cakes, and pies. We had plenty of eggs from the chickens, and in the fall Dad would have a steer or a hog butchered.

"On Saturdays, we took our milk and eggs to town to sell. For a kid, town was wonderful. With all the neighbors there, you couldn't find a place to park on Main Street. We'd finish our business, pick up a few groceries and butter brickle ice cream cones for my sister and me, then head back to home."

My husband's story of the family farm he knew as a boy—where people, animals, and the land shared a place interdependently, existing in symbiotic relationships—may seem part and parcel of an agrarian myth: As Berry (1996), a Kentucky farmer, activist, and writer, ironically comments, in our day and age "millions of country people have been liberated from land ownership, self-employment, and other idiocies of rural life" (p. 76). Indeed, in connection with this liberation, Old MacDonald farms like my father-in-law's are fast disappearing, having decreased by two thirds since the 1940s (Satchell, 1996; Strange, 1996). What is replacing this narrative of the family farm as what Bruner (1987) would term a canonical narrative model?—the model of the factory farm.

The Factory Farm Has Lots of Pigs—and Not Much Else

"Just say NO to hog factories," reads my friend's t-shirt, referring to the rapid growth of corporate hog farms in the populous, central Iowa county where we both live. Although this county is not within drainage area of the Missouri River, the Rot Belt's narrative could be ours as well. Factory farming has arrived.

Dominated by enclosed confinement buildings holding thousands of hogs and enormous manure lagoons (Satchell, 1996), the factory farm is a seemingly inevitable outgrowth of the technological revolution that since the 1950s has rapidly and radically transformed agriculture. Whereas the family farm is integral to— and can be likened to—an interdependent, sustainable community, the factory farm is but one distinct stage in a sophisticated system of production, where what are often large corporations contract with farmers either to house sows in farrowing units or to feed the sows' offspring until they reach market weight (Anthan, 1996; Satchell, 1996). In these contract operations, the farmers may concentrate on little other than raising hogs, hauling in rather than growing what the hogs eat.

Indeed, at times, the scene of the factory farm is even more desolate than this description suggests, as the land where the confinement buildings sit has no farmer or farm family living on it and no animals in hog yards or fields. Warrick and Stith (1996) describe a setting reminiscent of a futuristic prison, where all that can be seen are acres of seemingly empty land dotted with enclosed, computer-regulated complexes of buildings (p. 1C). Little life is visible on farms such as these.

With this trend toward a sophisticated production system and reliance on confinement technology, the corporations seek to control the entire process, from producing feed through breeding, raising, and slaughtering the hogs (Satchell, 1996). Land ownership is consolidated, as smaller, independent farmers—who may have raised some hogs as part of their operations—find they cannot compete (Satchell, 1996) and sell out, thus allowing fewer and fewer entities to oversee more and more land (Berry, 1990; Strange, 1996). Berry (1996) quotes statistics from the *New York Times*, saying that "between 1910 and 1920 we had 32 million farmers living on farms—about a third of our population.... By 1991, the number was only 4.6 million, less than 2 percent of the national population" (p. 76). Among hog farmers the trend is similar (Satchell, 1996). The small, sustainable family farm is out; the large factory farm is in.

As land ownership is consolidated, the towns in rural areas such as the Rot Belt also suffer (Satchell, 1996; Strange, 1996). Gone is the busy Main Street of my husband's boyhood. This Main Street has been "transformed," says Strange, "from a thriving outdoor minimall" to a place where the fastest growing jobs are those that many other regions of the country do not want: service positions (such as nursing home aides and telemarketers) and positions in correctional institutions and hog factories (p. 2C). Indeed, as my husband and I drive the 90 miles to my father-in-law's farm, we note with sadness the vacant buildings and boarded-up storefronts that make up so many Main Streets, where perhaps only a QuikTrip is now open. Factory farms do not bring business to the small shops in rural towns, and as a result, local economies are dealt a killing blow (Satchell, 1996).

The residents of rural areas who remain—if they live downwind of a hog confinement operation and are subjected to its odor—may soon be among those millions Berry mentions who have left their farms. Often unable to open their windows or go outside in warm weather, and suffering from numerous medical complaints, these residents testify to the impact such operations have had on their lives, their livelihoods, and their relations with the natural world (Carpenter, 1996; Satchell, 1996; Solberg, 1996). My friend, for example—who lives just a quarter of a mile from a new factory farm, the first in our county—worries that her spinning and weaving business will be affected. The odor of manure, she fears, may saturate the wool she spins in her small, wood-heated studio and the beautiful knitted and woven products she makes and stores there.

Though clearly serious, odor is not the only problem associated with factory farms. What to do with hog waste and how to keep it from contaminating the soil and groundwater are, if anything, more pressing. Currently, manure is held in huge settlement and evaporation lagoons and/or injected, spread, or sprayed on land where, for a price, farmers have agreed to allow the waste to be deposited. These options all have serious drawbacks. Lagoons, for example, can only hold so much manure, after which they must be emptied, and they can and do break or leak, polluting streams, killing fish, and endangering groundwater. Indeed, the mayor of my small city spoke recently of being awakened in the night by a telephone call alerting him to the fact that a manure spill had occurred, and manure was moving down the creek toward Ames (personal communication, February 15, 1998). Manure leaks even more disastrous than this have now become all too routine in Iowa.

Further, manure that has been overapplied pollutes the water and poisons the soil. "Why," my husband says, "some fields in turkey-raising states in the South are so toxic that nothing will grow—and no one knows when or if those fields will recover." The same is true of fields where hog manure is overdeposited (Lehmer, 1994).

So why do farmers choose to operate these factory farms?[3] One reason, of course, is that operating a factory farm is one way—though not the only way—to make a living from the land in a time when the economic return on farmland and the commodities produced there is down (Anthan, 1998). Another powerful impetus, however, may be the concept of progress (Lehmer, 1994).

The attraction of this word *progress* may help explain why the narrative of the factory farm is fast displacing the narrative of the family farm as the canonical model in the Rot Belt.[4] In the next section, I use Habermas's views on science and technology—including his belief about scientific, technological progress—and his theory of purposive-rational and communicative action to discuss this displacement of one narrative model by another.

HABERMAS AND NARRATIVE MODELS IN THE ROT BELT

Habermas is useful for this discussion of the narrative models because he (1968/1970a) theorizes about the growing power accruing to science and technology in our society, focusing not on scientific and technological developments per se, but on the value society accords to science and technology and on the effects of this valuing on social life. In his insightful analysis, Habermas contrasts what he calls purposive-rational action and the technocratic consciousness with an approach to the world based on communicative action.

In the next two sections, I suggest ways this contrast can help us understand the narrative models of the factory and the family farm, beginning with purposive-rational action, the technocratic consciousness, and the narrative model of the factory farm.

Purposive-Rational Action, the Technocratic Consciousness, and the Narrative Model of the Factory Farm

Purposive-rational action, according to Habermas (1968/1970a), is action that, in the manifestation most useful here, aims at the controlling reality (the second type of purposive-rational action is strategic action, which aims at "influencing the decisions" of an entity seen as an "opponent" [1981/1984, p. 285]). Those engaging in purposive-rational action are "egocentric" because they focus on advancing their own interests rather than on "harmoniz[ing]" the interests of all concerned (1981/1984, p. 286). With purposive-rational action, therefore, both the natural world and other people are seen as entities to be dominated—as "the object[s] of possible technical control" (1968/1970a, p. 88).

Habermas (1968/1970a) is clear about the effects of an orientation toward purposive-rational action on our relations with nature. Agreeing with Marcuse, he discusses our propensities for "seek[ing] out...an exploited nature" where it is viewed as an "object" (p. 88). When we regard nature in this way, Habermas claims, we are thoroughly under the sway of the technocratic consciousness.

The Technocratic Consciousness

According to Habermas (1968/1970a), the technocratic consciousness is alluring because it suppresses our desire for what Habermas terms a different type of action: a way of relating to people and nature that does not involve domination. He attributes this alluring quality—this power accruing to the technocratic consciousness—to a lengthy process whereby science, technology, and economic growth have become intertwined, emerging finally as driving forces in social life. Because of these links among science, technology, and economic growth, their mutual advancement appears to us to be absolutely necessary if society is to develop.

Indeed, to Habermas (1968/1970a), the lure of scientific, technological progress and economic growth is so great that, both as individuals and as a society, we may no longer even want to envision a different way of relating to the world. After all, Habermas asserts, scientific, technological progress has made us increasingly more comfortable, which appears to legitimize the need to dominate and control.

Habermas (1968/1970a) believes, however, that this egocentric focus on domination and control has had a disasterous effect on social life. Specifically, the technocratic consciousness is so powerful that the only questions we ask pertain to purposive-rational action: questions concerning "technical rules based on empirical knowledge" (p. 92), which can be answered by "large-scale industrial research" (p. 104). Indeed, under the sway of the ideology of science and technology, society no longer even recognizes that other questions based on a different form of action exist—within Habermas's vision, a frightening situation indeed. To him, "the concealment of this difference [between forms of action]" proves how powerful the technocratic consciousness is (p. 107).

Habermas's theory of purposive-rational action and the technocratic consciousness can help us reflect on the model provided by the narrative of the factory farm.

Narrative Model: The Factory Farm

The narrative model of the factory farm, I contend, illustrates Habermas's worst fears concerning purposive-rational action and the power of the technocratic consciousness. Note, for example, the strongly progressive nature of this narrative, which is undergirded by large-scale industrial research and linked directly to economic growth. Factory farms, after all, are only possible because of scientific research and technological developments that facilitate control of the hog-raising process. Further, factory farms are often justified in terms of their economic efficiency (Anthan, 1998), their contribution to economic development (Solberg, 1996), and the number of jobs they create (Miller, 1996; Satchell, 1996).

As in Habermas's (1968/1970a) vision, then, scientific and technological progress and economic growth are intertwined in the narrative model of the factory farm. According to Habermas, however, society need not be oriented in this way toward purposive-rational action and the technocratic consciousness. Rather, another type of action is available: communicative action, which is linked ultimately to what Habermas calls emancipation. Below I discuss this type of action in relation to the narrative model of the family farm.

Communicative Action, Emancipation, and the Narrative Model of the Family Farm

Communicative action, which Habermas (1968/1970a) suggests is the "alternative to existing technology" (p. 88), does not involve scientific and technological domination and control. Instead, communicative action is based on a consensus reached between coequals, which "define[s] reciprocal expectations about behavior." Rather than drawing validity from "empirically true or analytically correct propositions"— as is the case with scientific and technical rules—this consensus is moral in nature, "grounded only in the intersubjectivity of the mutual understanding of intentions and secured by the general recognition of obligations" (p. 92).

Since, in communicative action, "participants are not primarily oriented to their own individual successes," this type of action is not egocentric. Rather, those engaging in communicative action, says Habermas, are "oriented to reaching an understanding" (1981/1984, p. 286), where their concern is the "creation of communication without domination" (1968/1970a, p. 113).

As with purposive-rational action, Habermas (1968/1970a) is clear about the effects of an orientation toward communicative action on our relations with nature. With this orientation, we "seek out a fraternal rather than an exploited nature." Hence, we "recognize nature as another subject," and we "try to communicate" (p. 88). In doing so, we focus, not on "technical problems" of domination and control, but instead on interaction (p. 103). We have, then, an interest in emancipation.

Emancipation

According to Habermas (1968/1971), emancipation is a state of awareness where we understand the differences between purposive-rational and communicative action and where communication approaches as closely as possible to an ideal state of "non-authoritarian and universally practiced dialogue" (p. 314). Though not fully realizable, emancipation is a norm on which our very concept of communication is based: Through the "pursuit of reflection" (p. 310)—which Habermas says (1970b) "knows itself as a movement of emancipation" (p. 198)—we reach a state of understanding, where we are no longer under the sway of the technocratic consciousness.

Habermas (1968/1970a) suggests, however, that our current orientation toward purposive-rational action and the technocratic consciousness have caused us to forget our interest in emancipation, in favor of our interest in expanding "our power of technical control" (p. 113). Moral and ethical issues, then, are displaced by issues pertaining to purposive-rational action, and an emancipated state slips further from our grasp.

Habermas's (1968/1970a) theory of communicative action and his views on emancipation—as well as his concern for the growing power of the technocratic consciousness—help us understand the model offered by the narrative of the family farm.

Narrative Model: The Family Farm

The narrative model of the family farm, I contend, illustrates Habermas's concept of communicative action. Recall that in this narrative model, a farm family has communal, symbiotic ties to other people, animals, and the land in an interdependent relationship where—I believe Habermas would say—nature is viewed as a co-equal, and the goal is to harmonize the actions of all concerned, including the actions of the natural world.

Despite, however, the orientation of the narrative model of the family farm toward communicative action, the displacement of this model by that of the factory farm is an example of Habermas's assertion that, in our society, an orientation toward communicative action has steadily been eroded as an orientation toward purposive-rational action—along with the technocratic consciousness—have gained strength. We must ask, therefore, whether, in terms of these narrative models, the potential for emancipation exists.

Germane to this question is Habermas's (1968/1970a) notion of a "conflict zone." In this zone, the ever-increasing comfort of our technological lives does not "seem convincing" (p. 120) because those who inhabit a conflict zone hold values that make them "immune to the technocratic consciousness" (p. 121). These people are instead guided by—and through self-reflection know themselves to be oriented toward—communicative action.

Habermas's (1968/1970a) discussion of the conflict zone allows us to posit that although a fully emancipated society may be an ideal that cannot be attained, we can still choose a different narrative model than one focused on purposive-rational action and the technocratic consciousness. Put in terms of the family and the factory farm—though the narrative model of the family farm is fast being displaced by that of the factory farm—an alternate model based on communicative action and emancipation is still available. In the next section, I turn to this alternate model.

AN ALTERNATE NARRATIVE MODEL

I contend that the story of a couple—the Thompsons, the *Des Moines Register*'s Farm Leaders of the Year for 1996—provides one example of a narrative model that can serve as a viable alternative to the narrative model of the factory farm. In 30 years of farming, the Thompsons have taken a different path than the one leading to the factory farm (Perkins, 1996). They have not, in other words, increased the size of their 300-acre family farm or relied on the technologies of control (for example, confinement buildings, manure lagoons) common to the factory farm. Instead, they have turned their science and technology to sustainable ends, welcoming nature as their coequal in an interdependent, communal relationship. As a result, I believe this couple's narrative offers a model that—because it is based on Habermas's communicative action and emancipation—transforms through sustainability.

I first met the Thompsons about eight years ago, when my husband and I went on one of the farm tours the couple hosts. On this tour, Dick Thompson talked enthusiastically about his low-input farming practices and his on-farm research. He showed us his farm equipment, which he had adapted to plant on permanent ridges so that he would disturb the soil as little as possible, minimize weed growth, and reduce his reliance on herbicides. He took us to his manure bunker—much smaller than the factory farm's manure lagoons—where he "brews" the "manure tea" he uses instead of chemical fertilizers, and to his fields, which—because of his practices—he has been able to farm chemical free and yet profitably for more than 10 years.

He walked us around his hog-raising operation, where sows are housed with their piglets in small, separate shelters, to reduce the possibility of disease and hence reliance on antibiotics. While we were there, he explained the reasoning behind an experimental house he and his son had designed—a roomy, A-frame shelter, where they could stand up and where, Thompson said, they could have a "better relationship" with the sow inside. And finally, he pointed to his corn crib—built tall, long, and narrow in the old style, for optimal drying of corn picked while still on the ear. "No need for me to be first at the elevator," he said, as a way of indicating the drying costs and energy he is able to save.

What I noticed at the time was Thompson's intuitive approach to science and technology through his farming practices and his research. "You just see what succeeds and what doesn't," I remember him saying, "and you go from there" (personal communication, July 16, 1990). This intuitive approach seems to me to require an interdependent, communal, and thus sustainable relationship with the land that I believe is rare in these times of conventional, high-input, chemical-intensive farming and "large-scale industrial research" (Habermas, 1970a, p. 104)—and virtually impossible with the factory farm. There could be, I believe, no better illustration of Habermas's concept of communicative action and self-reflective emancipation in relation to the natural world.

The story the Thompsons have chosen to tell and live suggests that an alternative to the narrative model of the factory farm, with its orientation toward purposive-rational action and the technocratic consciousness, is available. Put another way, though the narrative model of the family farm may be in decline and though a fully emancipated society is perhaps only an ideal, those who inhabit the Rot Belt and other agricultural places can still choose an alternate narrative model that is oriented toward communicative action and thus toward sustainability.

We must ask, however, why we in professional communication, who may exist far from this rural place, ought to care about narrative models in the Rot Belt. In my concluding section, I answer this important question.

NARRATIVE MODELS IN THE ROT BELT: WHY WE OUGHT TO CARE

We ought to care about narrative models in the Rot Belt for two reasons—one personal, the other professional. Concerning the personal, I argue that the narratives I describe represent, in slightly different guises, typical models available to us all in our lives, wherever we might be, and among which we all can choose. Concerning the professional, I contend that examining narrative models in the Rot Belt, exotic as these may seem, in fact furthers scholarly and pedagogic initiatives already underway in our discipline.

The Personal: Choosing Narrative Models

Habermas's vision of science and technology as they currently function in our society clearly warns us about a powerful and, in his view, destructive trend—one where what I have called interdependence or symbiotic relationships and community are supplanted by dominance and control. Furthermore, Habermas's theories of purposive-rational and communicative action suggest that, rather than being isolated instances, the narrative models I describe exemplify broad and commonly adhered to stances, or what Habermas (1971) terms "action orientations" (p. 3), governing society's approach to science and technology and to social life. Hence, purposive-rational and communicative action may drive many more narrative models than simply those of the factory and the family farm.

As one example, consider Ritzer's (1993) intriguing investigation of what he terms the "McDonaldization of society." Focusing on four factors—technological control, efficiency, predictability, and calculability (p. 24)—that have made the "McDonald's model" or the fast-food industry model truly "irresistible" (p. 9), Ritzer points to the many areas of our lives—for example, having our cars lubricated, using our credit cards, doing our banking at ATMs, microwaving our prepackaged meals—that have been McDonaldized. In each case, just as on the factory farm, control through standardization has been made possible by technology, and interdependence and community have been reduced.

On an even more serious note, Ritzer also describes the increasing trend toward McDonaldization—or what I believe Habermas would call purposive-rational action and technological control—in institutions such as universities and in vital service professions such as medicine. And finally, as a counterpoint, he discusses alternatives to McDonaldization, such as the movement toward the more personal bed and breakfast establishments instead of those—for example, budget motel chains—offering "McBed, McBreakfast" (p. 177).

Certainly, the many *petits recits* that make up Ritzer's narrative model of McDonaldization support my claim that the narrative models present in the Rot Belt represent common possibilities. I contend, therefore, that, if sustainability is a worthy social goal, in our personal lives we ought to carefully consider such narrative models and opt for those oriented toward communicative action and emancipation.

To this personal reason for caring about narrative models in the Rot Belt we ought to add a professional one: furthering our scholarly and pedagogic initiatives.

The Professional: Furthering Scholarly and Pedagogic Initiatives

My examination of narrative models in the Rot Belt furthers scholarly and pedagogic initiatives already underway in professional communication—initiatives that involve a political or what Thralls and Blyler (1993) term an "ideologic approach" (p. 14). In this approach, "social inquiry" is extended "to include the ideologic frameworks that shape language practices and thus thought and identities within professional communities" (p. 14).

My examination furthers this scholarly move toward the political in two ways. First, I draw on narrative theory to suggest that the stories we tell are one social mechanism for influencing thought and identities and thus for positioning us within our daily lives. With Bruner (1986), then, I claim that these stories model roles and worlds that are "permissible" for a given society (p. 66; see also Mumby, 1993, on narrative as a form of social control).

Second, my examination also supports the effort to empower that undergirds the ideologic approach, where, rather than being "passively shaped by the discourse" of social groups, people have the power to shape discourse themselves (Thralls & Blyler, 1993, p. 15). Drawing on Habermas's theories of purposive-rational and communicative action and his views of science and technology, I suggest that technological imperatives are becoming increasingly dominant in our lives. I also suggest, however, that although narrative models based on these technological imperatives and on purposive-rational action are powerful, they cannot be viewed as fully determining the lives we live. Rather, given Habermas's concepts of emancipation and the conflict zone, other narrative models—other permissible worlds—are viable alternatives. Finally, I argue that if sustainability is a worthy social goal, this trend toward purposive-rational action and the technocratic consciousness must be reversed, and I indicate the kinds of narrative models that deserve our commitment.

Given this discussion of narrative models in the Rot Belt, I want to close by reiterating that the stories we tell matter. I firmly believe that by telling and living stories oriented toward sustainability—oriented, that is, toward communal interdependence where people, animals, and the land share a place—we can, as Strange (1996) says, "make good places to live" (p. 2C).

NOTES

[1] I am not, of course, suggesting that only one narrative—or, following Lyotard (1979/1993), one metanarrative—of the family or the factory farm exists. Obviously, each family or factory farmer would tell his or her own story, or *petit recit*, differently.

Nonetheless, social groups can share what Bennett and Edelman (1985) call "stock stories" and Bormann (1985) calls "fantasies": simplified narratives presenting a "general story line" (Bormann, p. 7) that many people in a particular social group hold in common. Say Bennett and Edelman, "While the associations and their attendant stories that pass through a person's mind will not be identical with those that intrigue another,...they are not likely to be idiosyncratic either" (p. 165). The nonidiosyncratic nature of the narratives that family and factory farmers would tell is what I mean to suggest in this discussion.

[2] The word *ecology* comes from the Greek word *oikos,* and the German word *okologie,* according to Dennee, Peduzzi, & Hand (1995). Both of these roots mean "home," which seems appropriate for a community-based understanding of ecology.

[3] I would of course not want to suggest that every family farmer is noble while every factory farmer is not. I do firmly believe, however, that, as technology has advanced—for example, the technology that has allowed factory farms to exist as we know them—the capacity for doing harm to our natural and social worlds has increased.

[4] I do not mean to minimize the economic forces at play in the decline of the small-scale family farm. Consumers, it seems, are quite attached to the low food prices available in the

United States and thus give tacit—or at least monetary—support to bigness in agriculture, which in very complex ways has played a role in keeping prices low. Nonetheless, I argue here that economic forces cannot explain all of the power given to the narrative model of the factory farm. Rather, I believe that progressivist ideals—important in American culture since its beginnings—also play a role, and hence the attraction of a rhetoric of progress and of the word *progress*.

REFERENCES

Allison, J. M. Jr. (1994). Narrative and time: A phenomenological reconsideration. *Text and Performance Quarterly*, 14, 109–125.

Anthan, G. (1996, March 17). Farming still a family affair. *Des Moines Sunday Register,* p. 1J.

Anthan, G. (1998, February 22). Saving small farms not so simple. *Des Moines Sunday Register*, pp. 1–2J.

Bennett, W. L., & Edelman, M. (1985). Toward a new political narrative. *Journal of Communication*, *35*, 156–171.

Berry, W. (1990). What are people for? In *What are people for?* (pp. 123–125). San Francisco: North Point.

Berry, W. (1996). Conserving communities. In W. Vitek & W. Jackson (Eds.), *Rooted in the land: Essays on community and place* (pp. 76–84). New Haven, CT: Yale University Press.

Bormann, E. G. (1985). The critical analysis of seminal American fantasies. In *The force of fantasy: Restoring the American dream* (pp. 1–25). Carbondale, IL: Southern Illinois University Press.

Bruner, J. (1986). *Actual minds, possible worlds*. Cambridge, MA: Harvard University Press.

Bruner, J. (1987). Life as narrative. *Social Research, 54* (1), 11–32.

Carpenter, C. (1996, April 26). The bee yard and the hog confinement. *Des Moines Register*, p. 17A.

Dennee, J., Peduzzi, J., & Hand, J. (1995). *In the three sisters garden*. Montpelier, VT: Food Works.

Habermas, J. (1970a). Technology and science as "ideology." In *Toward a rational society: Student protest, science, and politics* (pp. 81–122) (J. L. Shapiro, Trans.). Boston: Beacon Press. (Original work published 1968)

Habermas, J. (1970b). Towards a theory of communicative competence. *Inquiry, 13*, 360–375.

Habermas, J. (1971). *Knowledge and human interests* (J. L. Shapiro, Trans.). Boston: Beacon Press. (Original work published 1968)

Habermas, J. (1984). *Theory of communicative action* (Vols. 1-2) (T. McCarthy, Trans.). Boston: Beacon Press.

Kerby, A. P. (1991). Introduction. In *Narrative and the self* (pp. 1–14). Bloomington, IN: Indiana University Press.

Lehmer, A. G. (1994, October). The people vs. hog confinement. *The Drummer*, pp. 1, 8.

Lyotard, J.-F. (1993). *The postmodern condition: A report on knowledge* (G. Bennington & B. Massumi, Trans.). Minneapolis, MN: University of Minnesota Press. (Original work published 1979)

Miller, A. (1996, January 26). Benefits from the large hog operations. *Des Moines Register*, p. 13A.

Mumby, D. K. (Ed.). (1993). *Narrative and social control: Critical perspectives.* Newbury Park, CA: Sage.

Perkins, J. (1996, February 11). Thompsons lead farm movement. *Des Moines Register*, pp. 1V, 10–11V.

Ritzer, G. (1993). *The McDonaldization of society: An investigation into the changing character of social life.* Thousand Oaks, CA: Pine Forge Press.

Satchell, M. (1996, January 22). Hog heaven—and hell. *US News & World Report*, 55, 57–59.

Solberg, L. J. (1996, January 26). All is not well for independent pork producers. *Des Moines Register*, p. 13A.

Strange, M. (1996, February 25). Transforming the rot belt. *Des Moines Register*, pp. 1–2C.

Thralls, C., & Blyler, N. R. (1993). The social perspective and professional communication: Diversity and directions in research. In N. R. Blyler & C. Thralls (Eds.), *Professional communication: The social perspective* (pp. 3–34). Newbury Park, CA: Sage.

Warrick, J., & Stith, P. (1996, May 5). Opposition is turning Iowa farmers into activists. *Des Moines Register*, pp. 1–2C.

Author Index

Subject Index

About the Editors

Nancy Blyler teaches in the rhetoric and professional communication program at Iowa State University. With Charlotte Thralls, she coedited *Professional Communication: The Social Perspective*, which won the 1993 NCTE award for best collection of essays in scientific or technical communication. She has won two other NCTE awards and has published in such journals as *Journal of Technical Writing and Communication, Technical Communication Quarterly* and *Journal of Business and Technical Communication.*

Jane Perkins is a communication specialist with A. T. Kearney, Inc., a global management consulting firm. She earned a Ph.D. in rhetoric and professional communication, has experience as an ethnographer, and taught in the professional communication graduate program at Clemson University. Her research and publications are primarily in narrative, global communication, and ethnographic learnings of corporate change communication. She is currently researching and implementing narrative approaches in nonacademic workplaces.

About the Contributors

Cheryl Forbes spent 17 years in magazine and book publishing as an executive editor and has written six books for a general audience, including one with her husband, mathematician Allen Emerson, on artificial intelligence. Since becoming a professor of writing and rhetoric, her research has included studies on the narrative strategies of such science writers as Stephen Jay Gould and Lewis Thomas.

Janis Forman, the director of management communication at the Anderson School at UCLA, received the Association for Business Communication's Researcher of the Year award in 1995. She has published extensively on collaborative writing and on translation. Her recent work includes a study of the genre of the case write-up (with Jone Rymer) and a project on organizational strategy and communication practices and strategies (with Paul Argenti). Her chapter in this collection is based on a presentation she gave in 1997 at Dartmouth's Amos Tuck School of Business.

Margaret Baker Graham teaches in the Department of English at Iowa State University. She has published articles on gender in *Management Communication Quarterly*, *Journal of Business and Technical Communication*, *Journal of Advanced Composition*, and *The Journal of Business Communication*. She is currently editing a collection of the Machette family letters, dating from 1822 to 1936.

Martin Jacobsen is completing doctoral work in English at West Texas A&M University. He serves as associate editor/Webmaster for the LINGUIST List and is writing a dissertation on literacy and hypertext. He has also designed a website for Romantic Circles (with Terence Hoagwood and Kathryn Ledbetter).

Debra Journet is a professor and chair of English at the University of Louisville, where she teaches in the doctoral program in rhetoric and composition. Her research on rhetoric and narrative in the biological sciences has appeared in such journals as *Written Communication*, *Social Epistemology*, *Technical Communication Quarterly*, and *Mosaic*.

M. Jimmie Killingsworth is a professor and director of graduate studies in English at Texas A&M University. He is the author of numerous works on technical communication, rhetoric, and American literature, including *Ecospeak: Rhetoric and Environmental Politics in America* (with Jacqueline S. Palmer, 1992) and *Signs, Genres, and Communities in Technical Communication* (with Michael Gilbertson, 1992), and the textbook *Information in Action: A Guide to Technical Communication* (second edition with Jacqueline S. Palmer, 1999).

Mary M. Lay is a professor of rhetoric in the Scientific and Technical Communication Program and the former director of the Center for Advanced Feminist Studies at the University of Minnesota. Her publications on traditional midwifery include "The Rhetoric of Midwifery: Conflicts and Conversations in the Minnesota Home Birth Community in the 1990s" (*Quarterly Journal of Speech*, November 1996). She is also coeditor of *Technical Communication Quarterly* and *Collaborative Writing in Industry: Investigations in Theory and Practice*.

Roger Munger is an assistant professor of technical communication at James Madison University. His current research interests involve the role of medical record genres in the health care professions. He has published in *Emergency: The Journal of Emergency Medical Services, Intercom*, and the *Writing Lab Newsletter*.

Kathryn Rentz is an associate professor in the Professional Writing Program of the English Department at the University of Cincinnati. She has published research on the relation between professional communication and ethics, genre theory, and narrative in such journals as *The Journal of Business Communication, Technical Communication Quarterly*, and the *Journal of Business and Technical Communication*.

Mark Zachry is an assistant professor of English at Utah State University, where he teaches courses in rhetoric and technical communication. His research interests include narrative, genre theory, and histories of professional communication. His 1998 doctoral dissertation, *Workplace Genres: A Sociohistorical Study of Communicative Practices in a Production Company*, is an historical study of the development of professional communication in a national company from 1920 until 1985. He is currently revising this study for publication.